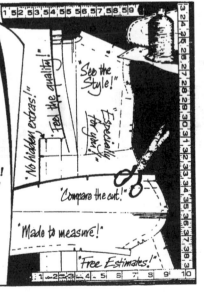

THE ENGLISH

CLERGY ASSOCIATION

**Patron: The Worshipful Chancellor June Rodgers
Chancellor of the Diocese of Gloucester.
Parliamentary Vice-President: Sir Patrick Cormack, F.S.A., M.P.**

Vice-Presidents: Sir William Dugdale, Bt., C.B.E., M.C., J.P., D.L.;
The Rt. Hon. Sir Robin Dunn, M.C., P.C.;
The Very Revd. Derek Hole, Provost of Leicester;
The Very Revd. Dr. Peter Moore, O.B.E., M.A., D.Phil., F.S.A.;
The Most Hon. The Marquess of Salisbury;
Dr. D. M. Tyrrell, B.D., M.A., Ph.D., A.C.I.S., A.C.A.;
The Venerable Tom Walker, M.A.;
The Rt. Hon. The Lady Willoughby de Eresby.

THE ASSOCIATION supports the integrity of traditional parish and
cathedral ministry alongside modern developments, particularly asserting in
broad terms the value of the *patronage system and the parson's
freehold* within the abiding worth of the Ministry of the Church of England as
by Law Established.

PARSON & PARISH, free to Members of the Association, is presently published
twice a year: Membership is £10p.a., £5 to the retired and to ordinands.

HOLIDAY GRANTS of a discretionary kind are made to Church of England
Clergy upon written application by the form in use to the Hon. Almoner.

LEGACIES & DONATIONS are especially welcome at a time of low
interest-rates.   P.C.C.s can become Corporate Members.

**Chairman: The Revd. J.W. Masding, M.A., LL.M.
E.C.A. Office: The Old School, Norton Hawkfield
Pensford, BRISTOL BS18 4HB**
Telephone: (+44) Chew Magna (01275) 83 0017

Deputy Chairman: Colonel John Hall; Vice-Chairman: The Revd. A.E. Harvey, M.Sc.
Treasurer: J.M. Hanks, Esq., LL.M., A.C.A.
Honorary Almoner: The Revd. J.D. Thompstone, M.A.
Editor of *Parson & Parish*: The Revd. M.G. Smith, M.A., B.D. (Oxon.)
Clerk to the Trustees & Hon. Secretary to the Council: J.H. Wearing, Esq., LL.B.

Benefit Fund Registered Charity No.: 258559.
Bankers: Coutts & Co., St. Martin's Office, Strand, London; Bank of Scotland, Birmingham.

My, how you've grown.

Thanks to a group of churchmen, Ecclesiastical was born back in 1887. At the end of 1996 our Group's assets exceeded £817 million. (You could say we've shot up). We still insure 93% of the Anglican churches in the UK and donate all available profits to the Church and charities. Our Parish Voucher Scheme is an innovative vehicle for boosting the funds of churches at the local level. We make regular charitable grants to dioceses too, in fact over the last 5 years, we contributed a total of £11.2 million making us the 24th largest corporate giver to charity in the UK and we're still an ethical organisation, run on Christian principles.

Looking after the Church and its members.

But there's another side to Ecclesiastical. We also offer a wide range of personal insurances and investment products. These include:
• Competitive, household and motor insurance that combines excellent cover with friendly service.
• A wide range of investment products including bonds, PEPs, endowments, unit trusts and ethical investments.
• Protection insurance such as critical illness cover and life assurance.
Our friendly knowledgeable staff will be delighted to discuss any of these services with you.

Call **01452 528533** to find out more, or email on: **gbeigmkg@ibmmail**

ECCLESIASTICAL

Beaufort House, Brunswick Road, Gloucester GL1 1JZ

CHURCH PULPIT

YEAR BOOK

A Complete set of Expository Outlines for the Sundays of the Year, also for Holy Days, Saints' Days & Special Occasions

1998

CHANSITOR PUBLICATIONS

*Published 1997 by Chansitor Publications,
a wholly owned imprint of Hymns
Ancient and Modern Limited, St Mary's
Works, St Mary's Plain, Norwich,
Norfolk, NR3 3BH*

ISBN 1-85175-142-4

*Typeset by Rowland Phototypesetting Limited,
Bury St Edmunds, Suffolk
Printed in Great Britain by
St Edmundsbury Press Limited, Bury St Edmunds, Suffolk*

Preface

The New Lectionary

Our readings have the immense advantage of following the scheme now in use almost universally throughout the Churches of the West. A three-year plan has been adopted, with each year centred on one of the Synoptic Gospels – thus, Year A is the year of St Matthew; Year B that of St Mark; Year C that of St Luke – which is the Gospel for this year of 1998. The Gospel of John is read each year, especially around Christmas, Lent and Easter.

This new Lectionary is the Church of England's version of *The Revised Common Lectionary* published in 1992 for the CCT by The Canterbury Press Norwich, which gives important and interesting information on many aspects of the Gospels and on lectionaries, plus a brief history of The Consultation on Common Texts.

The Church of England's new Lectionary (RCL) is authorised by General Synod (GS 1161A & B of July 1997) for use from Advent Sunday 1997. A large number of new or revised Collects and Post Communion Prayers for Sundays and Festivals have also been authorised, to go with the Readings.

The *Church Pulpit Year Book* is dedicated, as ever, to parish clergy, to NSMs and Readers, trusting that the material offered will be of help on Sundays, Festivals and weekday occasions. If using the book for the first time you are welcomed with pleasure.

Francis Stephens
CHANSITOR PUBLICATIONS *Editor*

Preliminary Note

For each Sunday of the year, *two* sermons are provided. The *first* is suggested for the 'Principal Service', assumed to be the main Eucharist, at which the readings will be from the New Lectionary (RCL, as authorised by the General Synod for use from Advent Sunday 1997 under GS 1161A) with the sermon probably based upon the Gospel reading appointed.

The *second* sermon is in most cases based upon the readings set out in the 'Second Service' – probably in many churches still Evensong. For Saints' Days and special occasions, *one* outline is provided, which can suit the Eucharist, or other service as may be desired.

Please feel free to adapt or alter, to suit the needs of your particular church or congregation; or to use the book as a quarry for themes and ideas. In any case the Indexes of *Subjects* and of *Texts* at the back of the book can be consulted to find an outline that suits or can be adapted.

Comments and suggestions are always welcome, also material for possible use in future editions. Please address your correspondence to the Editor, Church Pulpit Year Book, Chansitor Publications, St Mary's Works, St Mary's Plain, Norwich, Norfolk NR3 3BH.

Acknowledgements. The Editor gratefully acknowledges permission from the Central Board of Finance of the Church of England, to reproduce material from *The Alternative Service Book 1980*; *Lent, Holy Week and Easter*; *The Promise of His Glory*; *Patterns for Worship*.

Thanks are also due to many other sources, individuals and schools of thought, for help and material. The Editor trusts that the use of such material will be forgivingly regarded as a small aid to the advancement of the Kingdom. Thanks are due to Roberta Berke, the Revd Tom Devonshire Jones, the Revd Canon Phillip Roberts, the Revd Dr John Thewlis, the Revd Joanna Yates; and to Kenneth Baker of Chansitor Publications. Special thanks to my wife Roma for proof-reading and immense help in so many directions.

CONTENTS

For Indexes of Texts and Subjects, please see end of book. The readings are those approved in the General Synod of the Church of England, Report GS 1161A, and are those for Year C, the year of Luke in the 3-year cycles of the Revised Common Lectionary, except where otherwise stated.

SERMONS FOR HOLY DAYS, SAINTS' DAYS & SPECIAL OCCASIONS

When Richard died Janet not only lost her husband, she lost her job, her position in the community, his income and their home.

We have been trying to help her put her life together again.

The Corporation of the Sons of the Clergy was established 300 years ago, in Cromwell's time, to give support to clergy and their families in times of crisis.

We give cash grants to clergy and their dependants for a variety of reasons – to elderly retired clergymen or widows, for instance, who find heating or repair bills more than they can manage, for school uniforms, to provide books for ordinands in training, to help divorced clergy and their wives at the painful period of separation.

It isn't enough, of course. No cash grant can take the place of a loving husband, a father to see the children through the difficult years of adolescence, a leader in the parish, a breadwinner, a priest. But it is something; among other things it is a reminder that people care.

With your help we could do more. Please help us – in whatever way you can – with a legacy, a covenant or a donation.

Corporation of the Sons of the Clergy

1 Dean Trench Street, London SW1P 3HB.   Tel: 0171-799 3696.

Charity 207736

First Sunday of Advent *Fourth Sunday before Christmas* 30 November 1997 **'Look Up!'**

'May the Lord make your hearts firm, so that you may stand before our God and Father holy and faultless, when our Lord Jesus comes with all his saints.' 1 Thess. 3.9–13 (RCL) or 'Look up and raise your heads, because your redemption is drawing near!' Luke 21.28 (RCL & ASB)

Hope and Confidence
St Paul is looking ahead into the future, filled with hope and with confidence. Of course, like every believing Christian, his faith is rooted in the past, and in particular in the life and teachings of the Lord Jesus. In the mighty events of that life – on Calvary's Hill, in the Garden of the Resurrection, by the Lakeside and upon the Mount of the Ascension – and that vision of the Living Lord that transformed Paul's own life, on the road to Damascus – from all this comes the note of triumph in the Apostle's voice, when he calls to believers then and to us now: 'The Day is near!'

For Paul, the past is no dead thing, but instead a living experience; he sees the life of Christ as stemming from eternity, coming through time, and then again returning to eternity – all as one great and wonderful happening. So it is that we Christians, unlike the believers in the ancient faiths of the past, put our hope and trust, our Golden Age, in the future. Our religion is in no way built on fatalism nor on pessimism, but it is a faith of hope and love and trust. We Christians have always set our hopes on the future; the Advent call is certainly one of repentance, yet the thought of the kingdom – of the Lord's great Return, the Second Advent – is a thought full of joy.

Joy
Just as the season of Lent looks forward to a joyful Easter, so Advent looks forward to the gladness of Christmas. 'Hark the glad sound! the Saviour comes' (NEH 6) and 'O come, O come, Emmanuel!' (NEH 11) – these are typical Advent hymns, and express our joy and hope.

Much of the New Testament expectation of the end of the age, is couched in the pictorial language of its time, and is not always easy for us to understand in our practical and less spiritually-minded age. The all-important point to grasp, however, is the certainty of the great Event. The Millennium, of which we hear so much, is certainly the marking of two thousands years from the Birth of Christ; yet such a period is a mere momentary flash in the vast life of 'our' constellation, the 'Milky Way', and far less when we consider the tremendous ages of the distant stars, constellations of almost incalculable age. Yet, we look forward nevertheless, to that Coming, the completion of the mighty works of God in Creation and Redemption, will be a wondrous occasion of hope and of joy, of glorious expectation and of triumphant consummation.

Questions which have for so long remained mysterious and beyond our human grasp or ken, of mind, brain or spirit, will be resolved in the brightness of God's new Light; we will be able to see and understand something of the purpose God has, and has had, for us his creatures and for the world in which he has set us. Maranatha – Come Lord Jesus! (1 Cor. 16.22).

PRAYER FOR THE COMING OF CHRIST

Come, Lord, to your Church as Lord and Judge:
Help us to live in the light of your Coming
and give us a longing for your rule.
Maranatha –
Come, Lord Jesus.

Come to your people with your message of victory and peace;
give us the victory over death, temptation and evil.
Maranatha –
Come, Lord Jesus.

Come to us with power and great glory,
to lift us up to meet you, and to live with you for ever.
Maranatha –
Come, Lord Jesus.

(Patterns for Worship: 5.1)

Advent Sunday   *Second Sermon*   **Prepare!**

'The Lord shall endure for ever: he hath also prepared his seat for judgement. For he shall judge the world in righteousness.' Ps 9.7,8 (RCL) or 'Since we belong to the day, let us be sober, and put on the breastplate of faith and love, and for a helmet the hope of salvation.' 1 Thessalonians 5.8 (ASB & EP)

Signs of the Times

To many of us, we seem to be looking out upon a world full of distress and disturbance. There are troubles and violence in so many countries; there are 'wars and rumours of wars' between nation and nation; between one group and another there seems so easily to be distrust and hatred; class strife is constantly being stirred up, it seems. Our wonderful advances in telecommunication, in travel made easy, in international knowledge and scientific discoveries – all seem threatened. The world of nature is distressingly unbalanced due to our human exploitation and lack of thought for the future. Indeed, we may well say, 'What is the future? Will this over-crowded, over-burdened, over-used planet survive?'

The Kingdom of God

Through the centuries the prophets looked at the state of the world in their own times, and looked over and above the degeneration for the coming of the perfect Kingdom of God. The Psalmist looks for the judgement of the Lord (v. 16 in our Psalm) and he wants it now, right away – 'Up, Lord, and let not man have the upper hand' (v. 19) Paul tells his converts 'You know well that the day of the Lord will come like a thief in the night' (I Thess. 5.2). We are to keep awake and be sober (v. 6), build one another up (v. 11) and above all to be at peace among ourselves (v. 12).

St John in the Book of Revelation gives us his picture of the final days, and a wonderful and mysterious vision it is; perhaps too oriental and symbolical for our Northern temperaments. In Hebrew thought, however, the final victory of God is foreshadowed by the song of Moses, celebrating the victory over Pharaoh (in Exodus 15.1 – 18) and therefore the victory of the Lamb.

3

Between the Times ...

We can remember our Lord's own words: 'I go away, and come again unto you' (John 14.3). Our Lord came back with the glory and splendour of the Resurrection. Christians lived the life of the resurrection, in the light of the perfect Kingdom. They were together; they were filled with joy; they fearlessly proclaimed the Gospel in their lives and their converse, and lived as though the Kingdom had come. The Holy Spirit was certainly poured out upon them.

We Christians live now as those who wait for their Lord. We must avoid delays and procrastination, since now is the time in which we should be working, and the Gospel must be preached. If we look for the end, the coming of the perfect Kingdom, we must be seeking to make our society, our world, more in accordance with that Kingdom – more just, more loving, more righteous – for one and all.

Of the final victory we have no doubt; we believe in the death and resurrection of Christ, and therefore know that the final victory will be with the good. The veil will be withdrawn, and the Lord will be apparent for what he truly is. He will reign for ever and ever.

We look with longing for that perfect day when God will be all in all, and we rejoice in that perfection, which will be the achievement of God's loving purpose.

O Lord Jesus Christ,
before whose judgement seat we must all appear:
grant that, when the books are opened on that day,
we may stand with confidence through your merits,
for you are our blessed Saviour.

(Promise of His Glory)

The Second Sunday of Advent *Third Sunday before Christmas* 7 December 1997 'Prepare the Way of the Lord!'

'The voice of one crying in the wilderness: Prepare the way of the Lord . . . and all flesh shall see the salvation of God!' Luke 3.4 (RCL) or 'Every high mountain and the everlasting hills be made low, so that Israel may walk safely in the glory of God.' Baruch 5.7 (RCL)

A Strange Man

The news spread quickly, all the Gospels tell us, of the appearance of a strange man who began a preaching campaign. All call him 'a voice crying in the wilderness', a phrase borrowed from Isaiah; and the Baptist described himself in the same way (John 1,23). The words are appropriate indeed, since John the Baptist preached in lonely country on the edge of the wilderness, the desert as we would say. It may also be a tribute to John's powerful voice. John was not the kind of orator who caught his audiences by strength of voice, nor by saying pleasant things; the message he had was of the utmost importance, and everything he said was about that message or led up to it. As for himself, he said nothing; his message was of another.

The Message

John's message was that the coming of the great Saviour and Deliverer – long expected by the Hebrew people – was now close at hand, and everyone must lose no time in preparing for his coming; and the way to prepare was by repentance and amendment of life. Indeed, choosing his words to please his listeners was the very thing which John the Baptist would on no account do. He had harsh words for each group in the crowds in front of him, from the poorest peasants right up to King Herod himself. John pointed his finger at their own special sins; all felt the lash of his tongue.

This made his message, on the other hand, all the more real to each and every man and woman, in the crowds that flocked to hear him. They did not feel that he was talking to them only about the coming of a Deliverer, a Saviour, for the nation as a whole; instead he was dealing with them as individuals, each to prepare for the Saviour, the Deliverer, by personal repentance.

'Prepare the Way!'

John's message would be of vivid reality to those who heard him. In those days, there would be no well-kept, well-made roads over which wagons and carts could be hauled, by horses or oxen, through the wildernesses of the world. There would only be rough paths, often steep, often dangerous – and these would be made simply for the passage of cattle. If some important person was to pass that way, a proper road would have to be made.

In the Baptist's time, those who heard his message might want the Christ indeed – but were they prepared for him when he came? We know how easily and rapidly the emotions and feelings of the crowds changed; and we know also that this is true of our times and of ourselves. When we look at the events in the world about us, we see all too clearly how quickly and rapidly the emotions of the crowds, of the people, can change and do change; and how those at the head of events can be thrown down, pushed aside, rejected, when the people think that our lives and futures may be at risk.

For us, Christ wants us, we need Christ; too often our own concerns, our own pride, keep us away. We want Christ on our own terms; we want to retain our self-pleasing, our self-confidence, hide our secret sins. If we are to prepare truly for Christ's second Coming, that he may find us an acceptable people, we must go to him in all humility and repentance. Only thus can we receive from him the grace that he gives for that life, which is life indeed.

Advent 2   *Second Sermon*   The Evangelist

'Many writers have undertaken to draw up an account of the events which have happened among us.' Luke 1.1 (RCL) or 'All scripture is inspired by God and profitable, for teaching, for reproof, for correction, and for training in righteousness.' 2 Timothy 3.16 (ASB & EP)

Luke's Preface

Luke was not a Jew but a Gentile, a medical man, who had been converted to Christianity; he probably came from Asia Minor or Greece, and had certainly met Paul, and it seems gave up his medical practice to accompany the Apostle and keep a check on his health. Part of his writings – the accounts of the travels of Paul and himself in Acts – seem to be transcripts of diaries which Luke kept day by day. The fascinating point of Luke's accounts is where he drops into the first person; *'We* at once sought to go on to Macedonia' (Acts 16.10). He leaves it again after a couple of paragraphs but resumes briefly later; that he has some personal knowledge of events goes well with the claim he makes in v. 3 of his Gospel – 'having followed all things closely' and makes us feel at once that we are listening to the account of a man who 'had been there' or who knew closely and personally the characters he writes about.

A Born Writer

Luke is the one evangelist whose personality shows through his account. The dedication to 'Theophilus' may well be to a rich and influential Roman whom Luke hoped to convert; on the other hand 'Theopilus' – 'God-lover' or 'God-seeker' may be inserted to follow the custom of classic literary convention, when writing a preface to a book of importance.

Not only is Luke a 'born writer' with a conscious literary style, which at once distinguishes him from the other Gospel writers, but his preface suggests that he is writing 'an orderly account' as an improvement on other evangelists, and is anxious to correct false information that might have come to the ears of such as Theophilus.

Zechariah and Elizabeth

In Zechariah and Elizabeth we have examples of those who truly wait upon God. They lived at a time when religion, as a spiritual force, was at a rather low ebb. Yet God had preserved for himself a faithful remnant. And these two, the parents of John the Baptist, were part of that faithful remnant, as were Mary and Joseph, Nicodemus and a few more who come before us in the Gospels.

In Zechariah we have an example of one who could say he waited upon God – one of the essentials of piety in the Old Testament: 'More than they that watch for the morning, my soul waiteth for the Lord' (Ps 130.6). Though he and his wife had dearly longed for a son, that had been denied them until the hope seemed quite beyond fulfilment. Yet they remained true to God: and as we look at them, we realize that it is easier to consent to God's will when the demand is to act, than to consent when the demand is simply to wait, to direct our prayer to God, and look up.

Doubt and Illumination

It is clear that the old priest doubted God's Word.

'How shall I know this?' is a question which surely many of us would ask. He had waited a long time, and as the proverb has it, 'Hope deferred makes the heart sick.' Had he not already bowed his head to what appeared to be God's will for himself and his wife? The trial came with the blessing, and his heart was surely sick. Yet, in time his soul was illumined, and the promise of God was fulfilled – what joy there was! And from that joy, came the great and powerful Herald of the Christ, he who was named by Jesus as 'none greater' (Luke 7.28) on earth at least.

The Third Sunday of Advent *Second Sunday before Christmas* 14 December 1997 **'What are we to do?'**

'The multitudes asked John, "What then shall we do?" And he answered them, "He who has two coats, let him share with him who has none; and he who has food, let him do likewise".' Luke 3,10–11 (RCL) or 'Here is my herald, whom I send on ahead of you, and he will prepare your way before you.' Matt. 11,10 (ASB)

John's Message

John told the crowds who came out into the wilderness to hear him, and then asked 'What shall we do?' a message blunt and harsh. Instead of trying to attract hearers, he ran them down, telling them first of all to repent – 'Change your hearts'; you must not rely on being 'God's Chosen', 'Children of Abraham', and therefore assured of heavenly favour. 'All that is finished' said John, 'Repent, and prove your repentance by the fruits you show, the good works of generosity, fair treatment, justice in dealing with each other. Prepare, for already the axe is laid to the roots of the trees.'

Strong Stuff

Strong stuff indeed. And stronger to come, when 'the Mighty One', the Messiah, long-awaited, would follow. Like a farmer, he would separate the good grain from the chaff upon his threshing-floor –

the grain will go into the granary but the chaff into the fire – a fire that will not be quenched.

Although a call to repent was what the men and women who crowded around John heard most often from him, repentance cannot be considered the true theme of his preaching. The real message which he had for the Hebrew nation was, the nearness of the coming of the Saviour and Deliverer, the Messiah to whom the Jewish people were perpetually looking forward. Indeed, if we had only one single sentence by which to summarize the teaching of John the Baptist, to those who had never heard him, we would do best to say, 'Christ is near!'

Joy and Glory
With what enormous joy the ancient prophets looked forward to the Coming of the Lord – as we hear today the words of the prophet Zephaniah. Although he speaks of the 'Day of the Lord', when his people will be crushed by enemies because of their sins. But after more threats against Jerusalem, he utters consolations in beautiful language –

> 'Sing aloud, O daughter of Zion; shout, O Israel!
> Rejoice and exult with all your heart,
> O daughter of Jerusalem!'
>
> (Zeph. 3.14)

and continue with a vision of the King of Israel, the Lord, being in the midst of the city, a warrior who gives victory; who will renew the nation in his love, and bring the people home, gathered together, renowned and praised amongst all the peoples of the earth.

The Message Repeated
There have been many times through the years when John's words could fairly be used to describe the situation of a nation, or even a large part of the world. We read in the pages of history of those brave and dedicated souls who have carried the Gospel for the first time, to nations and countries ignorant of Christ. It was a stage in the history of our own nation when we could truly say that Christ was near, as Augustine came to preach the gospel in the spring of AD 597 with his followers, and was greeted by Ethelbert, King of Kent, and his Christian queen, an event being

recognized by ourselves in the Church of England with great rejoicing this year.

Christ's Coming

Do we ever stop to think how wonderful it was, that our Lord should come into this world of ours at all, as he did at the first Christmas? How wonderful it is that, in a different sense, he continues to come near nations and individuals. King George VI visited Coventry immediately after it was almost destroyed in the Second World War. As he walked among the ruins and spoke to some of the homeless, an elderly woman called out, 'Thank God, your majesty, that we have a king who will come to a place like this!'

Christ's coming to the world at the first Christmas, and his continued loving presence with us, brings courage, confidence and joy to his followers.

Advent 3 *Second Sermon* **Our God is Coming**

'Our God is coming; he will not keep silence' Ps 50,3 (RCL) or 'Behold, our God will come with vengeance; he will come and save you.' Isaiah 35,4 (RCL) or 'Life or death, the present or the future, all are yours; and you are Christ's; and Christ is God's'. 1 Cor. 3,22 (ASB & EP)

Dates

Long ago, many people expected our Lord's return, and the end of the world, when the year one thousand came. In mediaeval times, the year 1000 was regarded with both religious emotion and considerable fear, as being the date when – in the view of many – the end of the world and the Second Coming of Christ would take place. In the present century some of the sect called Jehovah's Witnesses have looked with expectation at certain dates; and the remarkable Catholic Apostolic Church, founded by the great Scottish preacher Edward Irving around 1832, which included in its beliefs the promise that the Lord Jesus Christ would return before the last of the 'Apostles' died – which happened in 1901. Other small groups have looked, from time to time, in the same way, and all have been disappointed.

More Dangerous

More dangerous have been those cult leaders of our own time, who have taught and persuaded their followers that not only is the end of the world coming soon, but it is urgent for those who accept their call to 'leave their bodily containers and go to meet the new life awaiting them in another world' as proclaimed Herff Applewhite in March 1977. Probably accelerated by the appearance of the Comet Hale-Bopp, Applewhite persuaded his followers to commit suicide – 'We are happily prepared to "leave this world" is our conclusion' – he is reported as putting out on the Internet. Cult experts predict that further tragedies will occur as the year 2000 approaches. 'There are always cults and cult-like behaviour surrounding millennial end times,' said Michael Shermer, of the 'Skeptics' Society. 'People are always looking for signs that the end is near . . . for these people, there are just too many weird things going on.' (*Sunday Times*, 30 March 1997).

Christ's Words

If, instead of twisting strange meanings from events in the world or in the skies such folk would look carefully – and prayerfully – at the words of Jesus recorded in St Mark: 'If anyone says to you, "Look, here is the Christ!" or "Look, there he is!" do not believe it. False Christs and false prophets will arise and show signs and wonders, to lead astray, if possible, the elect' (Mk 13.21,22).

Be Alert

Although Jesus warns us against the folly of attempting to fix the date for the 'End of the World', the 'Second Coming', or other events of importance to us as Christians, the Lord does not mean that we are to ignore the reality of the events of the future. We should pray about them, and prepare for their coming, be that soon or distant.

We share with the first disciples various ways in which we experience the Coming of the Lord. We share in the joy of Easter worship, and when we receive the holy Bread of eternal life and the Wine of heaven at every eucharist we take part in; we experience Christ's power in the help and guidance of the Holy Spirit, when we spread out our problems and fears before God; we experience the power of the Lord in the challenge of some great crisis, either in our personal life or shared with others. And finally, we experience the power of the Lord when we are summoned to meet him by death.

In addition, there is the great final Coming of Christ, about which so many people have made – and still make – useless guesses; there is little we can say, because its time and nature is unknown to us, but we should always be prepared.

> *O God,*
> *by whose command the order of time*
> *runs its course;*
> *forgive our impatience, perfect our faith,*
> *and,*
> *as we await the fulfilling*
> *of your promises,*
> *grant us hope*
> *because of your word;*
> *through*
> *Jesus Christ our Lord.*
>
> *(PHG)*

The Fourth Sunday of Advent *Sunday next before Christmas* 21 December 1997 **Blessed is she who believed**

'Blessed is she who believed that there would be a fulfilment of what was spoken to her, from the Lord.' Luke 1, 45 (RCL) or 'Tell out, my soul, the greatness of the Lord, rejoice, rejoice, my spirit, in God my saviour; so tenderly has he looked upon his servant, humble as she is. For, from this day forth, all generations will count me blessed.' Luke 1,46–48 (RCL)

The Artist
Luke is the artist among the New Testament writers. Indeed, his moving concern – in particular for women involved in the Gospel story, his flair for descriptive touches, gives us splendid verbal pictures. Consider too, that The Prodigal Son, The Good Samaritan, the Walk to Emmaus, the Visitation, the Presentation in the Temple, are just a few of the pen pictures which appear in his gospel only.

How the artists have been inspired! Down the ages, from Cimabue to Graham Sutherland, from the stained glass artists of Chartres to Henry Moore, St Luke has given the scene and the actors. Without this, our great Galleries and indeed our whole pictorial life, would be so much poorer. Rightly, St Luke is the patron not only of doctors and physicians, but also of artists.

The Visitation

Today we hear the story of the Visitation, the meeting of the two pregnant women – Elizabeth and Mary. When we visualize the scene, so wonderfully brought before us by Luke, what are the lessons we can learn?

First, obedience to God's will. 'Here am I,' said Mary to the angel who announced the astonishing story of the forthcoming Saviour, 'I am the Lord's servant; as you have spoken, so be it.' It was Mary's 'Yes!' that set God's scheme of salvation for his world in train. Without her willing co-operation the Incarnation could not have taken place; upon her decision rested the whole future of the human race. Well indeed did Elizabeth cry out 'God's blessing is upon you, above all women!'

Mary's Heart

Second, the lesson of a mind fixed upon Jesus. 'Mary kept all these things in her heart' – all the astonishing events that had happened or were to happen – the angels, the shepherds, the Wise Men, Simeon and Anna, the boy Jesus in the Temple. And of course, so many other happenings in the daily life of the family at Nazareth. Like any mother she must have had many memories, some happy, some sad. But unlike others, she must have been very aware of the growing pressure of his great Calling on her Son. We can be sure that she did all she could to smooth his path and help him to take the decisions he had to take.

Do we keep the things of Jesus always in our hearts? Do we look at our decisions in our lives, first and foremost, from the point of view of God's call?

Elizabeth

'Who am I,' Elizabeth cries, 'that the Mother of my Lord should visit me?' Her first instinct is to ask, so unselfishly, for another rather than herself, to show concern for Mary and the other Child rather than for herself. Do we not, ourselves, know persons with that rich gift of unselfishness, who ask after us rather than pour out their own troubles; sometimes we are shamed by their self-giving. Perhaps we can be enriched and changed at least a little to their likeness. Certainly Mary receives acceptance and understanding; even Joseph with his love could not so understand and accept, hard though he tried to cope, no doubt, with tensions in the village folk, as Elizabeth is able as pregnant herself, to understand and accept.

Perseverance

Perseverance and loyalty brought the two women together; perseverance and loyalty brought Mary to be with Jesus in his greatest need. 'By the cross where Jesus hung stood his mother.' When his cause seemed to have failed and his work was ending in a cruel death, his mother was there. Careless of the insults of the soldiers and the contempt of the crowd, she was there, calling upon her innermost strength and the depths of her love.

As we may try to follow the example Mary gives us, so we also may be blessed as she was, if we look to her faith and trust in the love and care of the eternal and ever-loving Creator.

> *Almighty God,*
> *who by your grace called the Blessed Virgin Mary,*
> *and opened for all the door*
> *of infinite mercy and eternal light:*
> *fill us with your grace,*
> *that, through our obedience and faith,*
> *the world may rejoice in your mercy,*
> *and walk in your light;*
> *for the sake of Jesus Christ our Lord.*

(P.H.G. 91)

Advent 4 *Second Sermon* The Spirit of God

'There shall come forth a shoot from the stump of Jesse, and a branch shall grow out of his roots. And the Spirit of the Lord shall rest upon him.' Isaiah 11.1 (RCL & ASB)

14

Ancient Prophecy

The advent of the Messiah was the great happening to which Israel looked forward. This ruler was to be a king, especially plentifully endowed with the indwelling Spirit of God. The Church of the Old Testament might not have any precisely formulated doctrine of the Holy Spirit; but was well aware of the Spirit and recognized manifestations of the work of the Spirit in their midst. When God created man, he 'breathed into his nostrils the breath of life' (Gen. 2.7). When our human breath goes forth, we die; we yield up our spirit. Here is a truth which we believe, shadowed out in the Jewish faith, that God is over us, in the midst of us, and within us.

The New Testament

The New Testament would have us think of Our Lord as having the Spirit of God, not by measure, but without measure, boundless and beyond measure. As St Paul says, 'the fullness of God was in him' (Col. 1.19). Christ's human nature needed and received the sanctifying and enlightening power and influence of the Holy Spirit. This rested upon him from the very first, and from first to last never left him. This is why he could claim, in his address to the congregation of the synagogue at Nazareth, 'where he had been brought up' (Luke 4.16),

> *'The Spirit of the Lord is upon me,*
> *because he has anointed me to preach good news to the poor.*
> *To proclaim release to the captives,*
> *recovery of sight to the blind,*
> *liberty to those oppressed,*
> *to proclaim the acceptable year of the Lord.'*
>
> *(Luke 4.15–19)*

Rejection and Acceptance

Yet, we see that from the very beginning, belief and unbelief, acceptance and rejection, have run throughout the Gospel. 'They that were his own received him not' (John 1.11). Now, here in his 'home town' the response to his message is of rejection and even violence. 'They took him to the brow of the hill, that they might throw him down headlong' (Luke 4.29).

Did the shepherds who received the message of the angels, and ran to the manger, play any further part? They went back to their fields and their sheep; we hear no more of them. No shepherds give their support to the Lord, when he begins his public preaching and suffers contempt and rough handling. Had all memories of the wonders that accompanied his birth, faded away and become lost?

Mary

Unlike the men in the synagogue, whose attitude to Jesus changed so rapidly from 'wondering at the gracious words which proceeded out of his mouth' to being 'filled with wrath' and ready to do murder – was one woman who, 'treasured all these things in her heart' (Luke 2.19). Mary the mother of Jesus, had simply said 'yes' and gave herself freely and openly to the will of God as it was revealed to her. She did not ask to 'see the distant scene' but trusted the Father to reveal in due time the role for which Jesus was destined. May we follow her example, and in humbleness and trust put our faith in God, and with Mary rejoice in our salvation.

Christmas Day Thursday 25 December *At Midnight or Early Eucharist* **'Good News!'**

'Behold I bring you good news of a great joy which will come to all people: for to you is born this day a Saviour, Christ the Lord!' Luke 2.10; or 'Glory to God in the highest, and on earth peace among men with whom he is pleased!' Luke 2.14 (RCL)

Preparation

Welcome to you all; Christmas greetings to everyone here, and indeed to all our relatives, our friends and family, our neighbours and all near to us. We have all been preparing for Christmas, and now here we are, at the climax, the great Day itself, for which our preparations and anticipations have been made, looking forward with joy and happiness.

But, for the first Christmas there was no preparation, in one sense of the word, by the people most closely concerned. Joseph and Mary had travelled far from their home town, and had arrived at Bethlehem in the midst of a vast influx of people, due to the orders of the government. Joseph was not well off, and anyway there was no room in the inn; the stable was not the least idea of what strange things were to happen before sunrise. The innkeeper had no idea that an event of stupendous importance to the whole world, was to take place in his stable. What changes he might have made, what preparations if he had known!

Ready Indeed ...
Yet some of those concerned with the event which took place at Bethlehem, were ready, or had been preparing themselves. Mary, so highly honoured by God, was a young woman of exceptional character; during her early life, she had been preparing herself for something very great, which was revealed to her by the angel Gabriel. Joseph – of whom we know little – yet we know that God did not choose him without reason; and the shepherds – they too were chosen.

Later, there were the Wise Men, who followed the star; and that devout couple Simeon and Anne to whom it was to be revealed that the Child Mary and Joseph brought to the Temple, was a very special Child indeed. Prayer and worship, devotion to God, readiness to accept God's will made known to us – these are ways of preparing ourselves, for what God wants us to do in our own lives of today, our own times and our own positions in the world of the here and now.

God's Preparations
Above all, when we rejoice on Christmas Night, we must remember that the greatest preparations of all for the first Christmas, were not those of any human beings, but the preparations of God himself. God decided to send his beloved Son into our world; he raised up prophets to prepare human minds long beforehand. He chose John the Baptist to 'prepare the way' for Jesus.

At the same time, God was preparing other minds to be receptive of the life and the teaching of his Son – we think of St Paul and all the apostles, we think of those men and women who accepted the teachings of the Early Church in the face of opposition and persecution, even cruel death. And we think of people down to our own times, who set forth the truths and the meanings of our Faith, all too often meeting with hatred, distrust and brutality, yet who press on to succour the persecuted, the poor, those in distress, those in need.

17

No doubt we have things to do, when we get home, things we must do now that Christmas is here; but at the head of our lists of gifts and our preparations, let us stand our resolve to thank God for his Gift in the Coming of the Saviour, and to remember all that it means to the whole world.

> *What can I give him,*
> *Poor as I am?*
> *If I were a shepherd*
> *I would bring a lamb.*
> *If I were a Wise Man*
> *I would do my part.*
> *Yet what I can I give him –*
> *Give my heart . . .*
> *Christina Rossetti (NEH 28)*

Christmas Day Thursday 25 December *In the Day* Christmas Presents

'The Word became flesh and dwelt among us, full of grace and truth; we have beheld his glory, glory as of the only Son from the Father.' John 1.14 or, 'To what angel did God ever say, "Thou art my Son, today have I begotten thee"?' Hebrews 1.5. (RCL (3))

Gifts and Giving

Why do we give one another presents? A small child will begin Christmas Day with an eager look into his or her Christmas stocking – 'What has Father Christmas (or Santa Claus) brought me?' Even much older people feel excited on Christmas Day – do we not? Especially when there is some unexpected and oddly-shaped parcel labelled with our very own name! 'Well,' we say, 'who can have sent this? Let's open it quickly!' It is good to make much of the giving and receiving of gifts at Christmas, because they remind us of our love and affection for people – we want to show that we care for them, and so we give them signs of our regard and affection. Equally, those who care for us send us presents and cards as expressions of the affection they have for us. If the giver of the gift is well-to-do, then the gifts may be quite expensive; if not well off, the gifts will be smaller and less costly – but that does not mean there is less love behind them. Indeed, far more love may come with a small gift than with an expensive one!

Love and Loving
So the first thing the gifts tell us is, about our love for each other. Our gifts remind us of family love, of the love between young people that will ripen into marriage, of the love between old friends over many years, and of love that has survived many years of residence far apart, or has triumphed over temporary quarrels and misunderstandings. St John sees the coming of Jesus Christ into the world as a command to us to love each other – 'If God thus loved us, dear friends, we in turn are bound to love one another' (1 John 4.11).

The second thing Christmas gifts remind us of, is God's love. As well as telling us of the love between human givers and receivers of Christmas gifts, Christmas presents tell us of God's love for us. They remind us of the very first Christmas present of all, and how that present came to us from God himself – the gift of his Son. 'The true light that enlightens every one was coming into the world' (John 1.9) and 'All the ends of the earth have seen the salvation of our God!' (Ps 98.3). And so, at Bethlehem, a child lay in a manger – the greatest of God's gifts to us, the gift of his only Son. That child was born in a stable, amidst cold and poverty, in order that we might be warmed and enriched by his coming.

A tiny child – so tiny that his mother's arms could completely unfold him; yet his power and might reached far beyond the heavens. 'In him was life, and the life was the light of men ... The true light, the light that enlightens every man, was coming into the world' (John 1.4,9) and 'To all who received him, who believed in his name, he gave power to become children of God' (John 1.12).

Love that Lasts
How long will the great majority of Christmas presents that are being opened today, last? Many are not meant to last, but are intended to be eaten, or in some other way to be used up fairly quickly. Many are given into the hands of the young, in the way of toys or equipment for sports, perhaps; and some of these will last only a pretty short time. Even what we might call solid, long-

term gifts can meet with accidents before their period of usefulness would normally be over. At best, our gifts cannot last for ever, but will grow older and shabbier as the years go by.

It is God's gift of his Son to our humanity that is the only Christmas gift that is really permanent and always lovely. This is a gift that will always be with us, in this world and the next. 'In him was life, and the life was the light of men; a light that shines in the darkness, and that the darkness cannot overcome' (John 1.4,5). The wonder of Christmas is that the holy land and marvellous God, who can seem to be so remote and unreachable, has come down among us, is concerned for us, has made his love available to us all through that Child lying in the manger.

> 'Unto us a Child is born,
> unto us a Son is given.'

The First Sunday of Christmas 28 December 1997 The Father's House

'Jesus said to his parents, "How is it that you sought me? Did you not know that I must be in my Father's house?"' Luke 2.49 (RCL)

An Alarm!

Many of us will have gone to various open-air entertainments where children are around in some number; and it is not very unusual to hear a loud-speaker announcement about a child who has strayed from his parents. 'Where is our Nicholas?' or Elsie or whatever the child is named; Nicholas turned up, waiting hopefully in the ice-cream queue – although he didn't actually have any money on him. I think he imagined that any queue was worth joining because what was being queued for was bound to be for free!

There were no loud-speakers to help Joseph and Mary find Jesus when he was lost. At the age of twelve they had taken him to Jerusalem for the Festival of Passover, travelling for mutual help and protection with a group of their fellow villagers from Nazareth. On the first day of the return journey, Joseph and Mary discover that Jesus is not with the party. They had thought that he was with other members of the party, maybe relatives or friends. In some considerable worry, they retrace their steps, and after much searching they find Jesus at last, in the Temple.

Development

If this was the growing boy's first visit to Jerusalem, we can imagine something of what it all meant to his alert, sensitive, inquiring and devout mind. We should remember that he was now moving on towards manhood, and was on the verge of adolescence; and we can understand how his interests were centred on the Temple. We are told how eagerly Christ listened to the learned rabbis of the Temple; he not only listened to their words, but asked them questions of such a character that they were surprised at his insights. So eager was he in his quest for knowledge, that he quite forgot the need to return home; was not the Temple as naturally his Father's house, as the humble Nazareth home from which he had come. We would gather from the story, that even at this early stage of his development he had already seen clearly that he must serve in some great cause which would bring glory to God and blessings to the human race.

Notice too, how in his first recorded utterance, he spoke of his Father, his heavenly Father; and already there was nothing more important to the Son than his Father's business, nothing dearer than his Father's Name.

Adolescence

Every normal and healthy adolescence has in it a resemblance in some way, to the adolescence of the Son of Man. There is, there should be, an awakening to life and a broadening intelligence. Everything once accepted is likely to be questioned; there will be new points of view, maybe different from those of parents and teachers. New ideals are often formed and followed with fervour.

Then again, both in male and female young folk, philosophic speculation and religious doubts appear in some minds. This can lead to cynicism, or on the other hand, issue in lives fired by lofty idealism and an enthusiasm to serve our fellow humans in high and far-reaching ways.

We should not treat young inquirers wrongly; sympathy and understanding is needed, as their minds push out into new territory. Youthful idealism should not be treated scornfully nor lightly; great promise can be there, and the best needs to be encouraged. Ideals should be nurtured until they grow up into maturity, and then they can be a standard to be accepted as a guide in life.

Our Lord Jesus Christ faced all the difficulties and all the problems and perils confronting a growing youth; his commitment to the ways of his Father is the bedrock of his life-story. Mary his mother profoundly accepts the puzzlements and the consternation; but treasures in her heart everything that has happened, and awaits God's good time, when all will fall into place and be made clear.

Christian Life

Our Christian life can be like this: we do all we think we should do – and yet the ways of God cut across, or cut away, our best efforts. Let us remember how on the one hand, Jesus calls us to be about the affairs of the Father; on the other hand, Mary treasuring in her heart teaches us to wait patiently in faith, when we are taken by surprise by our God.

> *Heavenly Father,*
> *whose blessed Son shared at Nazareth*
> *the life of an earthly home:*
> *help us to live as the holy family,*
> *united in love and obedience,*
> *and bring us at last to our home in heaven:*
> *through Jesus Christ our Lord.*
>
> *(ASB)*

First Sunday of Christmas *Second Sermon* **All One in Christ**

'There is neither Jew nor Greek, there is neither slave nor free, there is neither male nor female; for you are all one in Christ Jesus.' Galatians 3.28 (RCL, Second Service)

Fellowship

The whole of our world is suffering from a grave and deep lack of mutual understanding and consideration – what we can call a lack of fellowship. How many things go wrong, cause pain and distress, because so simple a thing as genuine, ordinary, human fellowship is lacking.

The Church itself is set out to be an example, a leading organization, to show, to demonstrate, real fellowship. The demand, the call, is not so much for orthodox teaching, for correct services and ceremonial, for music and colour – important though these are in their own way – but for real fellowship. Fellowship has two great aspects – fellowship with one another, and equality in the service of God and the love and care for each other; and fellowship with God. The New Testament has much to say, much for us to note.

Fellowship with God

Here is the root of the matter; we human beings are created with immortal spirits, capable of fellowship with our Creator. St Paul tells us we are called to fellowship with Jesus Christ (1 Cor. 1.9, Phil. 1.5) as with each other, and he mentions the communion or fellowship of the Holy Spirit (2 Cor. 13.14). We read of our Lord himself holding fellowship with his disciples – fishermen of Galilee, artisans and tax-collectors, men admitted to friendship with him, and women as well (Luke 10.38–42 and John 11, and 20.11–18). Fellowship with Jesus is the secret and source of fellowship with one another; and indeed with all peoples of the world today.

Is not our primary need more real fellowship with God? The Holy Communion is this, surely, if it is to be anything; our prayers and services are not merely asking God for this and that – they should be fellowship with God. The early Christians and the mediaeval Saints found the Eucharist their chief delight. We make a great mistake if we allow our daily work, our social life, even religious duties or Church organizations to interfere with our times of communion with God – our highest privilege and our absolute Christian necessity.

Fellowship with one another

After the great Day of Pentecost, the new converts, we are told, by St Luke, continued in the Apostles' fellowship – 'All who believed were together ... They devoted themselves to the apostles' teaching and fellowship, to the Breaking of Bread and the prayers' (Acts 2,42). Persecutions only made their fellowship the sweeter; this fellowship pervaded their lives. The weekly celebration of the Lord's Supper was not only Holy Communion with the Lord, it was the sacrament of a very real fellowship with each other. As they ate of one loaf and drank of one cup, they were indeed one family – neither Jew nor Greek, bond nor free, male or female, but all one in Christ Jesus. When we get back true fellowship, get over remnants of snobbery and sexual division – as, thank God we are beginning to do – people will again come to our churches, where friendliness and equality and fellowship will make all equally at home in the Father's house.

The Second Sunday of Christmas   4 January 1998   Divine Fullness

'From his fullness have we all received, grace upon grace.' John 1.16 (RCL)

Christ's Work

Our Lord Jesus, by his human nature and the work which he did while incarnate, connects our human needs with the fullness of God. Through his incarnation infinite fullness has been opened to us. Abounding, shoreless, fathomless is the love of God. From the very first experience of Christ, there is fullness; we can rejoice in the thought, like a little child dipping his tiny bucket into the deep and broad ocean. The little child still likes to be enfolded in strong arms; 'underneath you are the everlasting arms' (Deut. 33.27). From our first experience of Christ, there is a fullness – pardon, peace, joy. 'In him we have redemption through his blood, the forgiveness of our sins, according to the riches of his grace lavished upon us' (Ephesians 1.7).

Power

'To all who received him, who believed in his name, he gave power to become children of God; who were born, not of blood nor of the will of the flesh nor of the human will, but of God' (John 1.12–13).

As we come to the presence of the Child, there in the stable, we can dare to acknowledge – in the presence of his weakness, his vulnerability – our own weakness and vulnerability. We too often cover ourselves up; we are too ashamed to allow such things to show – the tensions of busy lives, the worries and anxieties of succeeding in the way the world (our world) thinks of success.

All these things and so many others, become irrelevant in the presence of the Child, the Child who is the sign and symbol of another kind of life. A life of co-operation rather than bitter competition, of peace rather than war, of love rather than hate, of give rather than grab. To pray for our enemies rather than hating and cursing them; to try to understand and try to forgive. As we look at the Christ Child in the stable, and go on to remember – as we must – that child grown into a Man, and that Man hanging upon a cross, yet able to say, 'Father, forgive them, for they know not what they do' – the way of eternal Love is the way of the Cross.

Faith

The essence of our Christmas faith is that Jesus Christ was born, truly son of Mary and Son of God, truly human and truly divine. Generation after generation of believers have striven to express this wondrous mystery in human words; impossible to describe fully our languages. Nevertheless, the introduction to John's gospel which we read today, has been a source of never-failing faith down the generations. We can begin to appreciate something of the Word, the Son, having an eternal life with the Father, yet making himself small, a child from a mother's womb, in order that he might grow up amongst 'All things made through him' and experience the strains and stresses of the human life, the pressures and strains of living amidst his fellow humans. The Lord knew full well that, at the end of his life's journey there would be a cross upon which he would be nailed in a cruel death, the brutal final punishment prescribed by Roman law.

Pessimism – and Joy

'Brief and powerless is Man's life; on him and on all his race,
The slow, sure doom falls, pitiless and dark.' – Bertrand Russell

Such words would be not only pessimistic, but all too sadly true, were it not for a little Child lying in a manger at Bethlehem. It was this Child who was to ignite a spark to give light and joy, future splendour and future power, to what we see as the brief life of us human beings.

The incarnation means for us, for all humanity, Love incarnate, a love which is both immortal and reaching out; it has a power which is beyond our ken, it has a strength that cannot be broken, nor is it confined within any bounds that we can understand. The love of God incarnate is a love so intense that it overflowed – and indeed still overflows – into our world, and showed itself in the love of Christ.

At Bethlehem God made his home in our human hearts and nature, and took upon the divine nature a human heart, so that God could love in a human way; and through this human love lead men and women to reach up to the divine love. 'For God sent the Son into the world ... that the world might be saved through him' (John 2.17) and 'from his fulness have we all received, grace upon grace' (John 1.16) since, 'the only Son, who is nearest to the Father's heart, it is he who has made him known' (John 1.18).

Second Sunday of Christmas   *Second Sermon*   God is Love

'He who does not love, does not know God; for God is love.' 1 John 4.8

Fact

Our chosen text traces love to its very source. 'God is love.' St John is not saying that God loves, but that God is love. It is because God is love, that he loves his creation and all his creatures as he does. This fact rings through the New Testament.

Is it not very striking that however different – and differing – were the intellects, mental attainments, personal characters of the apostles, yet because all had received and absorbed the Spirit of the Lord their Master, all of them – Peter the Rock, James the Brother, John the Son of Thunder, to name but three – all alike represent love as above all else, the chief characteristic of the true follower of Jesus.

Creation

The essence of God is to impart himself, to let his glory and salvation stream out on others; simply because love is his whole essence, his nature through and through. It was this infinite love, his very self, which created humanity; so ordering all forces, all events, that we might come into the world. What God might have made us, and what he had made us, through his creative activity in nature, shows us how great is his love. How wonderfully made, how fearfully developed are we not? The physiologist and the anatomist tell us this about our bodies, and the psychologist about our minds; the more we begin to know, the greater our astonishment at the wonders we carry within ourselves.

Nature

While we start with ourselves, we look outward into the marvels of creation, of the world about us, and see how everything in Nature tells us of God's creative power. All Nature pulsates with life, and all life comes from Him. No tiniest scrap of earth, no drop of water from the sea, but tells of God's providence and love. And as we now look away to the depths of the universe, and see great worlds among the stars, what wonders may there yet be to explore and to understand. What fantastic history has been written in the developments of suns and planets, of comets and stars, of Milky Ways, black holes, nebulas, galaxies and asteroids – we merely gaze at mysteries beyond us, yet all are parts of God's marvellous plans.

Our Lives

In our personal lives, so tiny and remote from the great wonders of the universe yet of immense importance to ourselves, and in God's mercy, to him also – we are striving to put into effect the teaching and the love of Christ day by day. 'All things work together for good to them that love God' (Romans 8.28). It is not always easy to see God's purposes, and evidence of his love, but we must remember Christ's life and death are the demonstrations of God's love; in fact here is the crowning demonstration. 'God so loved the world, that he gave his only Son' (John 3.16) that whosoever believes in him should have eternal life. Here is the heart of the Gospel; all his life was a manifestation of love. His compassion shines in every action, as the glory of the sun is shining in every beam of light. Christ's tears, we may say, were 'the drops of his love'. His life was the incarnate demonstration of his love. His death was the consummation of his love.

What does this mean to us?

Surely, if God's love has been shown to us so conclusively, we must show his love to others. 'He that loves not, knows not God'. Love of others is a distinct way of understanding and displaying God's love. We have seen what God's love is, so we must copy it. Wherever there is a want, we must strive to supply it. Where there is a woe, we must seek to heal it. We must love one another; for love is of God, and God is love.

The Epiphany of Our Lord   Tuesday January 6 1998   King of All Peoples

'Going into the house they saw the child with his mother Mary, and falling to their knees they did him homage.' Matthew 2.11

The Light of the World

'Arise, shine, Jerusalem, for your light has come, and the glory of the Lord has risen upon you' (Isaiah 60.1).

The Church has seen in the visit of the Wise Men, the beginning of that universalism of the Faith, which the Old Testament plainly foreshadows as the purpose of God. The whole world is to be swept into God's redemptive purpose. So in the visits of the Bethlehem shepherds and the Magi to the Christ Child's crib, the whole world is represented as falling down in worship of the world's Redeemer. Who were these strange visitors to the house in Bethlehem? and what was the compulsion that brought them from far, to do homage to a Child whom they saw as a King, though born in a land far from their own? And what was the meaning of the gifts they offered?

The Wise Men

The story suggests that the three strange visitors to the baby Jesus were astronomers or astrologers – perhaps a mixture of both. They became aware of the birth of a new King through seeing a new star or some other heavenly body, and interpreting its appearance in that way. Perhaps it was the climax of many years' study; the great event of their lives maybe. We can be reminded that in diligently performing our everyday duties and our secular work, we fit ourselves to get to know more of God; it is not to idle or careless people that he reveals himself.

Courage
We can only guess at the problems of the journey, as T. S. Eliot does in his verse 'Journey of the Magi',

> 'A cold coming we had of it,
> Just the worst time of the year
> For a journey, and such a long journey:
> The ways deep and the weather sharp,
> The very dead of winter.'

Difficult; and certainly dangerous at the end, when they were in the hands of a cruel tyrant, notoriously suspicious that people were plotting to take his throne, to whom they had talked of 'coming to seek a new King!' In our service of God we must be prepared for self-sacrifice, and for courage in face of danger.

Symbolism
Symbolic meanings are given to the three gifts the Wise Men brought with them. Gold, the King of metals, stands for the Divine Kingship of Jesus. Frankincense, much used in the worship of the Temple, stands for the Priesthood of Christ. Myrrh is used in the East to anoint the dead, and reminds us of Jesus' death for us on the Cross.

And the symbolic interpretation of the whole event, sees it as a great proclamation that Jesus was born to be the Saviour of all humanity. Though he himself lived and preached and worked among the Jews, he set his followers a wider task – to proclaim him to the world, and to rich and poor alike. The Wise Men came from foreign lands to worship Jesus, as fore-runners of the men and women of every nation who have welcomed Jesus as their Saviour.

Prejudice
In New Testament times there were a number of followers of Jesus who honestly believed that his work on earth was concerned with the Jews alone; although this false idea has been long swept away, there are still many Christians who are prejudiced against those who differ from them in colour, in race, in religious outlook, in their social standing, and in even pettier and more foolish ways.

The coming of the Wise Men and their act of worship, which must have put great demands on their faith in view of the strange and lowly place in which they found their King, must speak to us of what is still only a distant ideal. That is, the world-wide kingship of Christ, and the unity of all humanity, men and women together, under his rule. The Epiphany bids the Church work and pray, with this great purpose and objective central to all that is said and done in the Name of the Lord.

INTERCESSION FOR EPIPHANYTIDE

Jesus, Lord of the Church,
You have called us into the family
of those who are the children of God.
May our love for our brothers and sisters in Christ
be strengthened by your grace.
> *Jesus, Lord of the Church*
> *in your mercy hear us.*

You have called us to be a temple
where the Holy Spirit can dwell.
Give us clean hands and pure hearts
so that our lives will reflect your holiness.
> *Jesus, Lord of the Church*
> *in your mercy hear us.*

You have called us members of the Body of Christ,
so when one suffers all suffer together.
We ask for your comfort and healing power
to bring hope to those in distress.
> *Jesus, Lord of the Church*
> *in your mercy hear us.*

You have called us to be the Bride
where Christ the Lord is the Bridegroom.
Prepare us for the wedding feast
where we will be united with him for ever.
> *Jesus, Lord of the Church*
> *hear our prayer,*
> *and make us one in heart and mind*
> *to serve you with joy for ever. Amen*
> > *PHG Epiphanytide, p. 236*

The Baptism of Christ *(The First Sunday of Epiphany)* 11 January 1998 **The Chosen One**

'Thus says the Lord, he who created you, O Jacob, he who formed you, O Israel "Fear not, for I have redeemed you; I have called you by name, you are mine. When you pass through the waters I will be with you."'
Isaiah 43.1,2

'A voice came from heaven, "Thou art my beloved Son; with thee I am well pleased."' Luke 3.22

The Brink of the River

John the Baptist stood by the brink of Jordan, that famous river, talking with a number of quite ordinary men, giving them something in the way of a rule of life – 'Share with those in need; share clothes and share food.' Tax collectors were told 'No unfair collection – take only what is right.' Soldiers were warned off rough treatment, robbery and false accusation – 'And be content with your pay!' In the hearts of many in the crowd, was the question, 'Can this man be the Christ, so long-promised?' John preached good news to them, but carefully pointed out that he was – in no way whatsoever – the Messiah, the Christ of God. No! certainly not. 'I baptize you with water, but he who is coming will baptize with the Holy Spirit and with fire!'

The people were on the tip-toe of expectation.

Jesus

There follows a general baptism of the people, and amidst them is Jesus himself. After being baptized, while praying, there is this striking vision of the heavens opening, and the Holy Spirit descending in the form of a dove. But most shattering of all is the Voice from heaven, declaring that this young man is none other than 'God's beloved Son, with whom I am well pleased!'

Who is this Jesus? Luke answers, The son – as was thought – of Joseph; and gives a long and impressive genealogy including such names as David, Jesse, Judah, Jacob and Isaac, right back to Adam – and God.

The Lamb of God

As John looked into the eyes of the humble young man who knelt down in the water, he had caught a glimpse of the divine fire. This indeed was the one who would baptize with the Holy Spirit and with fire!

'Me baptize you?' he said. 'I need to be baptized by you, with your fire, not with this water.' John had sensed not only the signs of the Spirit's presence, but also the terrible yet glorious purpose of Christ's coming. The incredible truth began to dawn upon him, that this quietly spoken Galilean carpenter was the Agent – and Victim – of the whole world's redemption. Here was the Lamb of God, that would take away the sin of the world; that would restore a lost race to the community of heaven. Here was the Sinless One who would conquer death and sin. Here was the Sacrifice to end all sacrifices; the Lamb upon whom would be laid the sin and sorrow of the world, whose blood would be effective in the greatest of all transactions.

Conviction

These concepts and their implications, only partly understood as yet, of course, flooded into the mind of John. The conviction grew overwhelming, so that the next day he felt compelled to point his own closest followers and friends to Jesus, and watch them go away from him, to follow the Lamb of God.

Here is the picture of the true evangelist. His job is to point us to Christ to preach him to all and sundry, to cry out: 'Behold, behold the Lamb!' But this he cannot do unless he himself has seen the Lamb. For all of us a moment must come, when to our astonishment we see Jesus as he is, not as some overwhelming figure of super-human grandeur – but as the most human of all men.

'Son of Man'

For is not that the inner meaning of the title 'Son of Man', which the Lord himself so frequently insisted upon using? Human and humble, but – God-with-us, going to his awful death rather than modify one word of his Gospel; meeting the full onslaught of human wickedness, ignorance and stupidity, identifying himself with us to the last breath of his tortured body. The jeering bystanders mocked him: 'He believed in God, let God deliver him! Let God take him down from the cross and we will believe!'

But God did not save him from death; God did something infinitely greater. He raised him from the dead, thereby proclaiming for ever the conquest of sin and death. Thus is the eternal purpose fulfilled in Christ; that is the work of the Lamb of God.

The First Sunday of Epiphany   *Second Sermon*   Newness of Life

'If we have died with Christ, we believe that we shall also live with him.' (Romans 6.8) or 'We were buried with him by baptism into death, so that as Christ was raised from the dead by the glory of the Father, we too might walk in newness of life.' (Romans 6.4)

The Holy Spirit

At Christ's baptism he was anointed by the Holy Spirit, the same Spirit that drove him onward to announce the Good News of the Gospel, to the world. The Spirit was the directing force of the Messianic mission; the baptism of the Lord was the beginning of the public proclamation of the coming of the Kingdom of God; a kingdom which was to change completely the lives of all those who accepted its rule.

So we can begin to understand why the service of Baptism is designed to be celebrated as a group activity, as a celebration of the whole Christian community. No longer ought it to be performed in an otherwise empty church, on a Sunday afternoon perhaps, but it should take place as a part of the main service, at which the whole community welcomes the newcomers, children or adults as they may be.

> *'We welcome you into the Lord's family.*
> *We are members together of the Body of Christ;*
> *we are children of the same heavenly Father,*
> *we are inheritors together of the Kingdom of God.'*
> *(ASB)*

The community welcomes the newcomers, knowing that through their baptisms the Kingdom of God is extended. Each newly baptized Christian is initiated into the same task as Christ himself began – and in each person's own way, he or she is to carry that task onwards and forwards. By our Christian character and our Christian life, we are all called to spread the Good News of the Kingdom.

Light

Baptism has been called 'The Feast of Light'. Christ told his followers, 'Let your light so shine before men, that they may see your good works, and glorify your Father in heaven' (Matt. 5.16) and, 'By this my Father is glorified, that you bear much fruit' (John 15.8) and if we indeed do this, putting the work of the Kingdom first, before all else, then Christ can truly say to us, 'So you prove to be my disciples' (John 15.8).

The Spirit, through the ages, is guide and protector of the Mystical Body of Christ, as he was of the Christ on earth in long-ago Palestine; and we Christians are all under his influence and his guidance.

With Christ we are baptized with water and the Spirit; immersed in the holy font we die to ourselves, are buried in the cleansing waters, and rise again to our new life. United with Christ, our sinful humanity is washed in the waters of Baptism, made holy by the Lord who is himself all-holy.

Not Slaves . . .

'We know that Christ being raised from the dead, will never die again; death no longer has dominion over him . . . The life he lives, he lives to God. We must regard ourselves as dead to sin and alive to God, in union with Christ Jesus' (Romans 6.9, 11).

> *Grant us, O Lord,*
> *not to be taken up with earthly things,*
> *but to love things heavenly;*
> *and even now, while we live among things*
> *   which are passing away,*
> *to cling to what is eternal;*
> *through Jesus Christ our Lord.*
>
> *(PHG)*

The Second Sunday of Epiphany   18 January 1998   The Sign at Cana

'This, the first of his signs, Jesus did at Cana in Galilee, and manifested his glory.' John 2.11

Principal Characters

At every wedding the principal characters are, of course, the bride and the groom. At the wedding at Cana in Galilee, even the presence of Jesus did not distract attention from them; Jesus was still at the very beginning of his ministry. And we may think that he was there, because of his mother, Mary; Mary was well-known, we may be sure; particularly now, as a widow – for we may be pretty well certain that Joseph had passed on – she would play a considerable part in the social life of the area. Mother Mary would be ready to arrange for refreshments, for waiters to serve the guests, for flowers to be brought, and so on. She would have the time now, with her Son starting off on his teaching and preaching; the carpentry and woodworking business would have been sold, no doubt, when Jesus made it clear that his future was in a different calling indeed; a future of service and evangelism, over the country.

A Disaster

What a jolly scene it must have been; friends and neighbours gathered together, with the blushing bride and the awkward, shy groom at the centre; something like the famous painting by Brueghel – 'A Country Wedding' – a crowded scene of merry-making, with trays of pies, plates of tarts, dishes of meats being rapidly emptied, with mugs and pipkins of wine circulating happily. But then, what a disaster!

Something had gone very wrong – the wine had run out! Were there too many guests? All those young men Jesus had brought with him? Or had someone miscalculated? Whatever the reason, it was most embarrassing for the young couple and their families.

Mary saw what was happening; she caught the attention of her Son. His reply to her words seems blunt; we may read into it a protest at being asked to do something that will provoke astonishment at himself – and thus take away the impact of his message. He did not want to be publicized as a magician or miracle-worker!

35

But in response to his Mother's appeal, and wishing to save the young couple and their families from disgrace on this their special day – the Lord performed his very first miracle.

'Do Whatever He Tells you!'
We cannot do better than to follow Mary's words to the servants – 'Do whatever he tells you!' We are his servants, just as much as the waiters at the wedding feast. Let Mary's intercession be our guide, and our inspiration.

The Second Sunday of Epiphany   Second Sermon   Riches of Grace

'Grace was given to each of us, according to the measure of Christ's gift.'
Ephesians 4.7

Unity and Diversity
The unity of the Church of Christ, although that unity indeed means the real equality of all faithful believers, yet is consistent with great diversity of gifts, of influence, and of honour. St Paul clearly teaches that – to use his favourite illustration – the Church is like the human body; our bodies are made up of many organs and parts, with differing functions. We are not all an eye nor all an ear, for instance – diversity of function is consistent with unity of body; and indeed is essential to that unity. The body is not one member, but made up of many members; in every organism a diversity of parts is necessary to the unity of the whole.

The Creator determines the function and the position of each part of an organism. One small part of the developing child, for instance, becomes the eye; another the ear, another the tongue, and so on. Just the same is true of the Church – gifts and functions are determined by Christ. This is the teaching of St Paul when he writes, 'Grace was given to each of us, according to the measure of the gift of Christ' (4.7). There is therefore a diversity of gifts among the followers of the Lord; and the distribution of gifts is in the hands of the Lord Jesus. Some of us have more, some of us less; but all are part of the Church, the Body of Christ, the building up of which is our aim and joy.

We each have our different and differing capacities, and these are to be used to the best of our ability, our time, our capacity, in the service of Christ. We are to grow in Christ in the same way as we grow in nature, growing to full and mature humanity, fit and strong, knowing our capacities, our skills and the areas in which we have developed. Just as this means we are of help and encouragement to our fellow human beings, in our daily life, in our occupation, so St Paul tells us, we are to be in the spiritual aspect – 'mature humanity' and 'mature spirituality' also. 'Speaking the truth in love, we are to grow up in every way into him who is the head, into Christ' (v. 15). Paul points out that of course, in the spiritual world as in the physical or human, some have more capacity than others, some have more gifts than others; we are not to think jealously or regretfully, for the gifts vary as God's love has decided.

But we are to make the best we can of what we have. We cannot all be archbishops, we cannot all be athletes of the spiritual world; but we can all do everything in our power in our small patch – 'Our poverty can be transformed' as the Collect puts it; 'by the riches of God's grace' and we, part of the 'whole body', 'joined and knit together' will grow in grace and love. Each one of us is to be content with the position assigned – not envying others above, nor despising those we consider below. Remember too, that sympathy is the rule of the common life. If one member suffers, all suffer; and if one rejoices, all can rejoice. The important thing is that 'in the renewal of our lives, God will make known his heavenly glory.' (Collect for today) 'And through us the light of God's glory may shine in all the world.' (Post Communion)

Third Sunday of Epiphany   25 January 1998   Good News

'The Spirit of the Lord is upon me,
because he has anointed me to preach good news to the poor.
He has sent me to proclaim release to the captives,
and recovering of sight to the blind,
to set at liberty those who are oppressed,
to proclaim the acceptable year of the Lord.'   Luke 4.18–19

Privilege

It is a privilege to be a bearer of good news; and that privilege is given to each one of us. There is all too often plenty of bad news, but there is good news as well. Notice what happens on the TV: after all the tensions in the world at large, and the troubles at home, the newscaster will finish off with something cheerful and if possible something good. Disturbing news must be reported, of course; we don't live in a make-believe world – often the news will give us to think about how we should – as Christians and good citizens – be acting.

But a bit of good news – especially about our fellow human beings – can lift up our hearts, and make us realize just how *much* good news there is in this battered world. And it meets a human need, for it is true that – as the poet Pope has it – 'Hope *does* spring eternal in the human breast'; and good news of good people, or of good actions, tells us that hope can be made real. Look for the good things in life, and try and tell those you meet that there *is* good, there *is* hope.

The Message of Hope from Jesus

Jesus has returned to Galilee after his time in the wilderness – that time of testing, of deep thought, and of decision – and here he is at Nazareth, where he was brought up, and in the synagogue, which he knows well, is being asked to give a reading, and then to speak to the congregation about it. He knows the Bible, and uses Isaiah's words as his own. 'Today,' he says, 'this scripture has come true!'

We too are anointed at Baptism and at Confirmation; we too are sent to announce good news to the poor – poor in spirit, as well as poor in the worldly sense. We too are to proclaim release to those held prisoner by their sin; we too are to open the eyes of those blinded by ignorance or by hatred. And today, now, is the time appointed, to make it come true.

Good News

Here is the good news of God's love, to us and to all people. It is for us to proclaim by our words and demonstrate by our lives, that 'good news', that release from sin, that new sight to the blind, the freedom that those tied down by sin and fear can experience. Here indeed is the Christian Hope – the Spirit of the Lord that has come upon us. And with that Spirit inspiring us, we can afford to be optimistic – gloriously optimistic.

Why? Because there is no limit to the power of God!

If we believe that God indeed came down from heaven, to be born as a tiny Child for us, and then to teach us and to redeem us – be sure that he can use you and me, for his divine and wonderful purposes.

Let his power and love flood through us, fill us all with joy and peace, through our faith in him – until, by the power of the Holy Spirit, we do indeed 'overflow with hope.'

> Jesus Christ is the light of the world:
> *light no darkness can quench.*
> Stay with us, Lord, for it is evening:
> *and the day is almost over.*
> Let your light scatter the darkness:
> *And fill your Church with your glory!*
> *(Patterns for Worship: 63.2)*

Third Sunday of Epiphany   *Second Sermon*
Leading our Lives

'*You were bought at a price; do not become slaves.*' 1 Corinthians 7.24

A Paradox

The sciences of today have brought us all closer together than human beings have ever been before. We can fly oceans in hours, we can speak across our world in seconds or less, by radio, by telephone, by the internet – and yet we are somehow as far apart as ever, divided by ideologies, race, colour, class and creed. We are separated by Iron Curtains, Bamboo Curtains, barriers of caste, segregation and the invisible frontiers of snobbery and fashion and 'one-up-manship'.

The sense of defeat gives to the modern age its sense of loneliness and restlessness. Our art and music, our poetry and drama, all express violent discord, spiritual strain and loneliness.

We reach each other only by way of symbol and picture, and

we are defeated, for we cannot fully express what we feel; we can only hope that others will not hopelessly misunderstand what we are trying to say.

St Paul

St Paul goes to the heart of this strange loneliness of the individual. In effect he acknowledges that every man and woman sees themselves as the centre of their own world. Our words, even at their best, are inadequate to communicate our real condition. It is to this dilemma that St Paul speaks precisely.

What St Paul says is, 'Each one has what the Lord has given him or her, and they should continue as they were when God's call reached them' (v. 17). He has already stated that in his own view, marriage is to be preferred; partners belong to each other. Now he adds, 'Only, let every one lead the life which the Lord has assigned to him or her, and to which God has called them. This is my rule in all the churches' (v. 21).

Again, where a convert to the Faith has been circumcised, that is, he is a Jew, he should stay as he is and not try to disguise his past. Circumcision or non-circumcision means nothing; what does matter is to keep God's Law. So in general – and not only with regard to marriage – each one of us is to remain before God in the condition in which he received his call.

Fellowship

'I in them and thou in me, that they may be perfected into one.' This is the secret of unity. Only then do the barriers go down. Christianity was able to reconcile Jew and Greek, slave and free-man, rich and poor, noble and humble, into a new community. In this space age into which we are going, it is still the one power which can reconcile humanity, if we are prepared to let God come into our lives, and to go his way. This is what we mean when we say that our crucified Lord has broken down the walls of partition. He sets the prisoner free. He helps us to enter the lives of others; he is the great Reconciler. Will you let him into your life?

The Fourth Sunday of Epiphany   1 February 1998   Dedication

'When the time came for their purification, according to the Law of Moses, they brought him up to Jerusalem to present him to the Lord, as it is written in the law of the Lord: "Every first-born male shall be deemed to belong to the Lord".' Luke 2.22,23

God's Child

From very ancient time, the Jews considered that God had a special claim upon the first son born in a family, and that one of the boy's duties to his family in later years, was to be its spiritual leader. Perhaps this custom was a relic of early days, when each family had a family priest; or it may be a memory of the escape from Egypt, when the first-born of the Egyptians were killed by the awesome Angel of the Lord – but the firstborn of the Israelites were spared.

So it was that Joseph and Mary with the Child Jesus, made the short journey across the hills of Judaea to Jerusalem and the Temple, to fulfil the Law's demand. They do not seem to have been accompanied by any relatives or friends; presumably they were still away in Nazareth. Being poor folk, the least expensive and smallest sacrifice allowed was their choice – two turtledoves or two young pigeons.

Regulars ...

There were a number of regular worshippers in the Temple, as well of course as visitors and pilgrims, often from far away. Some men and women who have the time – perhaps retired – and who love the Lord, come to daily services and also spend time in prayer and devotion, in our own churches; and the Temple was the same. Amongst these faithful who came daily to the Temple were an elderly man, Simeon, and an aged widow, Anna. In some way, the Holy Spirit drew the attention of these two devout folk, to the little group of Mary, carrying Jesus, and Joseph, as they entered the imposing great building.

Simeon and Anna came up to the family and pronounced their blessings on the child, and foretold a great future for him. Simeon's words must have cast a shadow over Mary as he pronounced that

41

'a sword will pierce your own heart also'. That shadow, we know, was the shadow of the Cross . . .

Divisions

What Simeon prophesied would happen, did indeed happen. Salvation, and a light for revelation to all people – yet became a source of divisions, enmity, and hatred. Still today, arguments, hostility, intrigues centre upon the Christ, as they have done since his birth, two thousands years ago; or even before that. Why is this? Why should one who came in peace and love, preaching concern and love for our neighbour, and who gave his life for his beliefs, be a cause of dissension?

The answer must be, that because of how human nature – fallen humanity – is, then dissension, anger and hate are inevitable. Sin spoils and ruins our ideals, and there are unbelievers, enemies of religion; those who dislike or even hate the Christian faith, who will do what they can to discredit or pervert or destroy that faith.

Love

All of us tend to fight for the things we love when they are threatened; it is natural enough that those who love Christ and believe he is the Truth and the Light, will fight to preserve that Truth and that Light – not necessarily by violence but by every legitimate means.

The martyrs down the ages are the witnesses to this. They refused to worship a lie; they fought for Christ by giving up their lives. 'Eighty and six years have I served him,' said St Polycarp, 'and he has done me no wrong; how can I now blaspheme the king who saved me?'

The Sword

Mary experienced this division within herself; the attacks upon her Son drove the sword through her heart. She saw him become indeed 'a Sign spoken against' as she stood beside the cross with shouts of derision and cries of blasphemy echoing round her. When she presented him in the Temple, she was making an offering of her child to the Father; and what she did at the beginning of his life she also did at the end.

The dying Christ and the sorrowing mother were united in suffering, and in acceptance of the Father's will. That acceptance did indeed involve the piercing of two hearts – the one by a soldier's lance, the other by the sword of Simeon's prophecy.

Fourth Sunday of Epiphany   *Second Sermon*   The Temple of God

'What house will you build for me, says the Lord?' Acts 7.49

Stephen's Speech

To the Jewish nation, the Temple of God in Jerusalem was the great and God-given place of worship, the centre of Hebrew life and thought and religion. We think of the way in which Jesus himself, as a young lad, could find nothing better and more natural, than to make his way to the Temple; to worship there and to join in the theological discussions, and hear the words and explanations of the doctors of the Law, 'sitting among the teachers, listening to them, and asking them questions' (Luke 2.46).

But Stephen takes a different point of view. In the long speech he makes before the Council, defending himself from accusations made on the basis of what he had been debating with the 'Synagogue of Freedmen' (Acts 6.9), he makes clear that his view of the history of the people of Israel is very different from the official version.

Was Moses Rejected?

Stephen presents the story of the Book of Exodus as a repeated national rejection of Moses and indeed of all that he stood for. The worship of the Golden Calf is not a mere temporary aberration, but the climax of the rejection of Moses and the True God, and the substitution of what Stephen calls 'the worship of the host of heaven' (v. 42); meaning the worship of foreign idolatrous gods mixed up with astrology. Stephen goes further: he quotes the prophet Amos:

> *'You took up the tent of Moloch,*
> *and the star of the god Rephan,*
> *figures which you made to worship'* (Amos 5.25)

Stephen argues from this and other quotations, that Jewish worship could not be claimed as according to the will of God.

Was the Temple not itself in accordance with the wishes of the Lord?

> 'Heaven is my throne,
> and earth my footstool.
> What house will you build for me,
>   says the Lord?'
>
>   (Isaiah 66.1,2)

Stephen is saying that the Temple should never have been built, and that the history of the Hebrew nation had been consistent rejection of the Lord, and of those he had sent as prophets to bring the nation back to the truth. In particular the betrayal and murder of the 'Righteous One' – that is, Jesus – was the last stage in a long story of betrayal, 'of heathenism at heart and deafness to the truth' (v. 51).

The Reporter

Did St Luke deliberately compose this speech? – so very different from, for example, the style of St Peter, who is not only moderate but always ends with the good news that God's pardon is always available, and indeed is offered here and now. The scholars tell us that Luke includes a number of words and idioms not his usual, which may well suggest that he is drawing upon some source he had access to, rather than composing the text himself. May this therefore be, in fact, the reminiscence of someone who was actually present? Would it be quite impossible that the reporter could have been 'the young man named Saul' (v. 58)?

We know that Paul and Luke were often together (e.g. 2 Tim. 4.11, 'Only Luke is with me') to say nothing of their travels together (as in Acts 21,27 and 28) and we can surely believe that they would have discussed how they each came to Christ. Was the experience of the martyrdom of Stephen the first shaking of the strict Pharistic upbringing of Paul, the first cracks in the breaking of barriers which brought the leading opponent of the Faith, to become its chief protagonist and leader?

> *Almighty God,*
> *help us so to proclaim the good news of your love,*
> *that all who hear it may be reconciled to you;*
> *through Jesus Christ our Lord.*
>
>   PHG (adapted)

The Presentation of Christ in the Temple *(Candlemas)* 2 February 1998 **Light of the World**

'The parents of Jesus took him up to Jerusalem to present him to the Lord.' Luke 2.22

Light of the World

The old name of this festival – 'Candlemas' – reminds us of the great truth of Christ's coming as the Light of the World.

Even in our age of electricity and swift power, the symbolism of the candle is still strong. We use candles on birthday cakes, we use them at Christmas on our Christmas Trees, we use them on special occasions of pleasure or rejoicing. For us the candle is a symbol of pleasure, happiness, joy and remembrance. To the older world, however, the primary meaning of a candle was simply essential light.

We find it difficult to realize the difference a few candles could make, to the drab darkness of a cottage, or a house, in olden days. So what a powerful symbolic action is the distribution of candles at the Eucharist, declaring the way in which Christ our Lord is to be regarded as the true Light, to enlighten the nations of the world, and how the light of his glorious gospel is to dispel the darkness of ignorance and unbelief.

The Old Law

The family bring the first-born to the Temple, as a punctual compliance with all the conditions and terms of the Law. Everything is carefully noted by St Luke; his teaching is that what is to be superseded must first be observed. He that is to be King of all humanity, must first be presented to God; as a true Israelite he is declared holy to the Lord by the same rite used upon every son of every Jewish mother. The Virgin devoutly submits her Babe and herself to the ancient customs, willingly obedient to the Law under which she had been born and had lived. The offering made is that of a poor family, the least that is acceptable for the priest to declare them 'clean'; a pair of turtle doves or two young pigeons. So far, nothing to distinguish this particular couple and their infant from the many similar couples on an occasion which must have resembled a busy Sunday afternoon of baptisms in a large city church today.

A Difference ...

Suddenly, however, there is a difference. In the Temple, besides the throngs of pilgrims and visitors, there were a number of older worshippers who spent much time in the sacred courts. We may think of them as just like those dutiful members of our own flocks, who come to church for the daily eucharist and offices. How thankful we are for their support and devotion. So, among the people who came daily to the Temple were the old man named Simeon, and the widow named Anna. First Simeon, as we hear in our gospel today, sings God's praise over the Child; then Anna also gives thanks, and preaches a prophetic sermon. Both give thanks; but the shadow of the Cross casts its warning of pain and sorrow to come – 'A sword shall pierce your own soul also!' – so Simeon predicts, as well as light and glory.

We must remember the close connection between the Presentation of the Child, and the Crucifixion of the Lord – the one is the consummation of the other. Our Lord's whole life, we must remember, was one continued act of offering. This was what was meant, when on the Cross he cried out – to those there, and also to the whole world, and to all generations – 'It is finished!' Once and for ever he completed that great and perfect Sacrifice, to which he had pledged himself by his wondrous Incarnation.

Our Offering

In the collect we pray that we may be presented to God with pure and clean hearts, by Jesus our Lord, who made expiation for the sins of us all. 'Through him we offer you our souls and bodies, to be a living sacrifice' as the ASB has it in the second Thanksgiving Prayer; or in the Book of Common Prayer rite, 'We offer and present unto thee, O Lord, ourselves, our souls and bodies, to be a reasonable, holy and lively sacrifice.' The words are magnificent and the thought is wonderful; it may be easy to utter the words, but we must really mean them with all our hearts, and carry them out in our lives.

We too were dedicated to God, each one of us. We were brought to our parish church, as babies, to be baptized. (Most of us, that is; a few were baptized later in life). So we, like Jesus, began life with an early dedication to God and his service. Are we mindful of the promises made on our behalf at our Baptism? Are we mindful of the promises we made ourselves at our Confirmation? Those promises should remind us – rather, inspire us – to keep in the forefront of our minds that we are dedicated soldiers and servants of Jesus, dedicated to follow him, to obey his commands, to take with us his example of love and service in our daily lives, and in all our doings.

The service of God is a call to the highest and best we are able to give or to perform; submitting to the will of God means opening ourselves to all possibilities, and doing our best in whatever circumstances we find ourselves. We are called to perform the highest service we are able to give or to perform.

The Presentation of Christ in the Temple
(Candlemas)   Second Sermon   **Signs**

'The Jews said to him, "What sign have you to show us for doing this?" Jesus answered them, "Destroy this temple, and in three days I will raise it up".' John 2.18,19

The Coming of the Saviour

In New Testament times, many of the thoughtful Hebrew people were constantly looking out for the coming of the Saviour, whom the Old Testament declared that God would send to them. They made many guesses as to how this 'Coming' would happen; often these ideas were not based on anything in the Bible, but were strange ideas of their own invention. One idea for instance, was that the Saviour would suddenly descend from heaven in a miraculous way; some thought he would make this descent into the courtyard of the Temple itself – what an appropriate spot for the occurrence!

This was in fact, the force behind one of our Lord's temptations in the wilderness. If he had gone to one of the pinnacles of the Temple, thrown himself down, and miraculously been unhurt, the crowds who were always coming and going in the precincts, would hail him as Messiah. It would have been a wonderful short cut to winning popular respect, interest, devotion – and to getting his message to the people.

Rejecting a Short Cut

But as we know, Jesus did not obey the tempting voice which whispered to his inmost self such thoughts. Indeed, he visited the Temple several times, and some of these visits are referred to in the Gospels, but he never did anything to gain favour with the people by sensational means. On the contrary, the talks he gave were such as to arouse the hostility of the authorities – and sometimes of the ordinary people also, if he seemed to be attacking what was regarded as traditional customs.

There had grown up near the Temple what was in effect a cattle market, selling oxen and sheep and pigeons for sacrifice, as well as changing ordinary money into the special Temple money, in which everything bought on the sacred area had to be paid for. Apart from various shady practices – the changing of the money, the bargaining over prices – and the noise all this created – Jesus saw the whole business as an abuse on the sacred premises. He voiced his disapproval emphatically, drove out the men who sold the cattle, upset the tables of the money-changers, lashing out with a whip of cords, and ordering the traders to 'Take all these away; you shall not make my Father's house a market-place!'

The Temple of Stone – and the Temple of flesh . . .

The traders and the authorities intervened, saying, 'What authority can you show us to justify your actions here?' Jesus replied, using – as he sometimes did – expressions and words which bore metaphorical or unusual and higher meanings – 'Destroy this temple, and in three days I will raise it up.' They were taken aback, and said, 'It has taken forty-six years to build this Temple, and will you raise it up in three days?' (We may notice how Jesus, as reported in this gospel, uses on occasion, words which in addition to their usual meaning as understood by the people, have a metaphorical or higher sense – e.g. 'New birth', 'Bread of life', 'Living water' – thus giving an opportunity to show and expound a higher or metaphorical sense.) Certainly the disciples remembered what Jesus said, and when he was raised from the dead, they understood what he was meaning on this day when he cleared the Temple court.

The Third Sunday before Lent
(*Septuagesima*)   8 February 1998   'Fishing'

'Jesus said to Simon, "Do not be afraid; henceforth you will be catching men".' Luke 5.10

A Different View

We are told by those who have travelled to the Holy Land and visited the Lake of Gennesaret, that sometimes the conditions of wind and water are such that it is possible to see some way under the surface from one viewpoint, while from another all that can be made out are ripples, wavelets and the baffling reflections of the bright sun in a clear sky.

Probably this is the explanation of Jesus' suggestion to Peter – 'Put out into the deeper water, and let down your nets for a catch!' It reminds us perhaps of the old proverb – 'The outsider sees more of the game.' And the co-operation of two boats to bring in a heavy catch was – and still is – a regular practice.

The Sequel

The sequel to the episode is summed up by the words of Jesus: 'Do not be afraid: henceforth you will be catching men.' For as soon as they had begun to bring their catch in, we are told that Simon Peter, astonished at what had happened, fell on his knees with the words, 'Depart from me, for I am a sinful man, Lord.' Some kind of fear came upon this simple fisherman – was the catch so unusual that he felt there must be some supernatural power involved? Then came the words from the Lord; and Peter knew he was at a turning-point in his life. With James and John, his partners in the fishing firm – and now his partners in the new life – they left everything and followed Christ.

A New Life

Imagine if Peter had never followed Christ. He would have remained, no doubt, as a simple, hard-working, honest and pious fisherman, busy every day with his trade, working with his partners and dealing with all the many calls of daily life. His religion meant a good deal to him already; Sabbath by Sabbath he would attend the synagogue, listen to the readings and the sermon, pay his dues and live a modest but useful enough life, observing the

49

festivals and fasts, and doubtless – like so many – looking and hoping for the promised Saviour. Instead, he was pulled out of all that his skills and training in his work had made him; exposed to the limelight, tested in ways he would never have thought possible. Tested indeed – and failed; but recovered only to fail again – and recover under the loving care and forgiveness of the Lord.

The Rock
Peter's personality grew and toughened under the strains and stresses; it became eventually rock-like in faith and love, so that Jesus could say 'You are Peter – the Rock; and on this rock I found my Church.'

And in the end, we may believe, with the traditions of the Church, that Peter died, died for the love and the truth that Jesus had shown him; died in bitter martyrdom, but with supreme faith and trust in his Lord, through the agony and horror.

Not that all the times were times of success. Peter must have looked back often to that dawn occasion when 'they had toiled all night and taken nothing!' It was indeed a warning that there would be long, unsuccessful times – but with the promise of amazing success if they were faithful, and persevered, and were not afraid.

Third Sunday before Lent   *Second Sermon*
Our Offering
'Whatever you do, in word or deed, do everything in the name of the Lord Jesus, giving thanks to God the Father through him.' Coloss. 3.17

Offering ourselves to God
St Paul tells us, in our reading from his letter to the Colossians, that we are to seek those things that are above, not on things on earth; and sums up what he has in mind with advice that we must put on, as God's chosen one, compassion, kindness, lowliness, meekness and patience . . . forgiving one another, as the Lord has forgiven us, so we must also forgive. The call of Christ is 'Follow me' like his call to Peter (Luke 5.10). This does not mean that we

should drop everything, leave friends and families, and devote ourselves solely to the great task of evangelizing the world. Indeed, to this some are called; they know their calling, it is insistent and overcomes all opposition. Those who have such a calling or vocation, know it; we thank God for them and their work – missionaries, teachers, preachers, clergy.

Daily Life

For most of us, however, we are involved in the ordinary business of living – earning, bringing up families, 'maintaining the fabric of the world' as the Bible puts it (Ecclus. 38,34). This is our vocation and calling, and this is how we fulfil God's will. Our lives are to show the love and power of God, day by day, to those we will meet and come in contact with, in office, shop, works or daily converse and daily life. St Paul puts it well: 'Whatever your task, work heartily, as serving the Lord and not men, knowing that from the Lord you will receive your reward; you are serving the Lord Christ' (Colossians 3.23,24).

The Gospel

The best *preaching* of the Gospel, is *living* the Gospel, it has been said. The more we try and follow Christ in our daily lives, copying his example of love, care, tenderness and consideration, the better we are proclaiming the Gospel he came to teach.

As Christians we have been called to build the Kingdom of God; we must try with all our might to develop the Kingdom in ourselves and in the world around us, until that day comes when we will see its glory fully revealed at last. And then we shall shine in the kingdom of our Father (Matt. 13.43) and celebrate the heavenly wedding of the Lamb (Rev. 19.7) with joy and happiness that will be eternal.

Education Sunday

The Church's task and opportunity!
Copies of the Church's Education Sunday leaflet 1998
can be had from:
The Promotions Secretary
National Society, Church House,
Great Smith Street, Westminster, London SW1P 3NZ

The Second Sunday before Lent
(Sexagesima) 15 February 1998 'Creation'

'Who then is this, that he commands even wind and water, and they obey him?' Luke 8.25 or 'The Lord God formed man of the dust from the ground, and breathed into his nostrils the breath of life; and man became a living being.' Genesis 2.7

Early Days and Today

Until the 19th century, it was the general belief that God had created the heavens and earth, and all plants and living creatures, just as is described in the Book of Genesis. Charles Darwin and his theory of Evolution challenged that belief. There was much argument, much conflict and bitterness on both sides. But the ever-increasing weight of factual evidence, produced by geologists from rocks and fossils, and by biologists from the immense variety of living things, has led to acceptance that the Bible story is of moral and poetic truth, rather than truth as in a scientific text-book.

Today, we all generally accept that Creation is not to be thought of as a single act, or series of acts, away in the remote past, but as a continuous and continuing process of evolution. This has been going on for many millions of years; it is going on now, and – unless we foolish humans blow up our fragile planet Earth with its cargo of life – it will go on for millions of years to come.

The Future

Who can tell what wonders and immense changes there may be for our world, and for humanity, in that vast period of time ahead, when so much has been accomplished in the (comparatively!) short period since mankind struggled out of the primeval jungle?

It is a future we can barely guess at. But one thing we know, and can cling to with confidence – God will be with us. For, as we have stopped thinking of God by a single great miracle creating the world, shaping it, making the plants and animals and finally making humanity – then standing apart from it, or at the most, occasionally stepping into human history and making changes by his supernatural power – we must today see God as working through the continual process of living and adaptation.

God is Close

Surely then, God is for us infinitely near; not only is he the great Maker of the stars and vast inter-stellar spaces, but also the author of the smallest creatures, and indeed of the very structure of the tiny particles that make up all life and all creation. St Paul tells us, 'He holds all things in unity', speaking of Christ 'the image of the unseen God' (2 Cor. 4.4). So we should try to understand God as in, and through, and beyond, all time, present, past and future. He is infinite; and 'infinite' is that outside of which there can be nothing; so God is *more* than the universe, beyond all matter and all space.

And yet, while our God transcends all that we can ever observe with our clever instruments, or know as human beings – yet, he is nearer to us than our breathing or our very private thoughts.

Mystic

This begins to take us into the realm of the 'mystics', those people who share some of the experience of poets and prophets. Consider our English Dame Julian of Norwich, who saw the whole universe as a tiny nutshell, but safely held in the hand of God. Her message is 'All shall be well, and all shall be well' – a message of hope, and trust, and love.

We place ourselves, in love and trust, in the hands of our Creator. The beginning of life and the process of evolution, the drive of life and its energy, implies an end, a goal. What can this be?

'In Christ,' writes St Paul, 'all things are to be reconciled, through him and for him, everything in heaven and earth, when he made peace by his death on the cross' (2 Cor. 5.19).

We look ahead then, to that almost inconceivably remote time, when the goal of our evolution – and the goal of the entire world – will be accomplished; a complete harmony of united humanity and a redeemed universe.

Second Sunday before Lent   *Second Sermon*
Faith

'Do not be anxious about tomorrow, for tomorrow will be anxious for itself.' Matt. 6.34

Ourselves

We know ourselves well enough to know and admit that we are each a mixture. We are to some extent selfish, preoccupied with our own troubles and worries; we are at all times proud, idle, lustful, angry, greedy, jealous, grabbing. But – it is also true that men and women are capable of great acts, of heroic unselfishness, stoic bravery, great love, compassion and understanding, and self-sacrifice.

We are a mixture of good and bad, sometimes well mixed, sometimes hardly mixed at all – so slabs of good and bad can lie side by side in the same character. As Jesus tells us, it is what comes out of a human being that defiles; it is from within that evil and sin emerge.

Nature

In the wonderful passage we have just heard, Jesus tells us to look at Nature. What lovely things there are there, flowers, the birds of the air, plants – all beautiful, marvellous works of God's creation. Why should we worry ourselves – we are all in the hands of God!

Yet we are all self-centred; we bring with us the over-hang of our primitive evolutionary past. We feel guilt at our self-centredness and aggression, since these drives were essential at every stage of the long process that has made us what we are, human – and we inherit this self-centredness. But if our primordial ancestors had not been self-centred, we should not be here today.

After all, what is more self-centred than a baby? But when babies have grown up, and become mature human beings, enough to know the difference between right and wrong, only then do we have responsibility for sin. This responsibility is part of what it means to be 'made in the image of God'. For God gives us freedom; freedom to sin if we so choose – but also freedom to respond to his love.

Children of God

If we grow up in an atmosphere where love is known and experienced, we feel safe and secure, and want to share that life and love with others. We are 'children of God', as St John puts it.

If we do not experience love as children, or if we have not experienced the reflection of God's love in the love and security of a family, we become insecure. We try and bolster ourselves up with substitutes for true living, real life – we go for drugs, sex, drink, cruelty – we snatch from others, try to gratify ourselves at the expense of others; we jeer and hate our fellow humans because they are 'different' – in colour, or style, or race. 'Whoever hates his brother is a murderer.'

Real life means real love. If we close our hearts, how can we claim that we love God?

The Sunday before Lent *(Quinquagesima)*
22 February 1998   The Transfiguration

'This is my Son, my Chosen; listen to him!' Luke 9.35

A Critical Time

Christ's Transfiguration came at a critical moment in his life. In the early days of his ministry, the crowds heard him gladly; but his teaching inevitably sifted the serious from the sensationalists. His idea of Messiahship was not theirs, and it was his own convictions regarding his mission, that led him to tread the path that inevitably led to the Cross. Many therefore could see what the future would be like, and turned away. The Transfiguration came at a time when circumstances were mostly discouraging, and when the prospect was becoming day by day nearer to a fatal and terrible end.

So, a theologian has said, 'If the Son must needs go down into the valley of the shadow of death, the Father's face shines upon him for a moment before he enters it, with a brightness which will not be obscured.'

Glory

The Transfiguration has inspired the genius of many artists down the years. Perhaps the most outstanding is the painting by Raphael, in the Vatican. This picture is the work of a man of ardent faith, and presents Christ as gloriously triumphant and inspired in Divine power. Fine though it is, this painting gives us an external presentation of this great event, omitting the terrible end. The gospels give us something of the significance the Transfiguration had, to Christ himself and to the 'chosen three' who witnessed it.

The subject on which the two great figures from the Old Covenant
– Moses and Elijah – came and conferred with Christ was the death
which he was to die; 'his departure, which he was to accomplish at
Jerusalem' (v. 11).

Peter and the others were heavy with sleep, we are told, but
they saw Christ's glory; Peter's remarks seem like the confused
talk of a man not clear of the mists of the night, but well-meaning
in a disjointed way.

The Voice
The Divine Voice authenticated Christ and his mission; if his disciples were not yet accepting or completely understanding, the
future was shown by the external splendour on the mount. Our
Lord's glory emanated from within, showing the essence of his
Divine being, and the utter dedication and courage with which
he was ready to face even death. The Vision was not prolonged,
but it was good to have seen it and to have shared in it. It is good
to see the glory of the Lord; the Transfiguration cheered the Son,
and taught the disciples.

The words 'Listen to him' are evidently intended for the disciples; and so we are taught that it is not enough to behold Christ
in his glory – we must listen to the teaching he gives and obey
his commands. And we must also be prepared to suffer with him,
knowing that Jesus is most glorious in freely giving himself up
for the world's salvation.

Coming Down to Earth *(if the second reading is used)*
After the Transfiguration, with its strange and wonderful message,
the Lord and the three disciples had to come down the mountain-
side – and were met with the noisy crowd. Wanting this, wanting
that, wanting healing, comfort, the unveiling of God's love and
will; in the middle the distraught father, so desperately worried
about his epileptic son. The disciples have been unable to help;
here is a sudden change from the quiet peace and glory of the
mountain top, to the sorrows and tragedies of daily life. How
relieved the nine must have been, when they saw Jesus returning;
even Jesus felt the weight and the faithlessness unable to cope.
'How long am I to be with you and have to bear with you?' he
reproachfully asks. But he heals the sick boy and gives him back
to his father.

Months later, confident in his own life undestroyed by death,

Jesus was to assure the disciples of his uninterrupted presence with them, saying 'Peace to you!' (Luke 24.36). In the inspiration of moments of vision we are to carry on in faith and grateful memory, knowing that he is always with us, through days of humdrum duty, or in passing through dark valleys. Let us be glad for moments on the mountain top, and rejoice in the divine promises.

Sunday before Lent *Second Sermon*
The Wheat-grain that falls into the Ground

'Unless a grain of wheat falls into the earth and dies, it remains alone; but if it dies, it bears much fruit.' John 12.24

Fruition

Jesus says that in order for a seed to come to fruition, it must die itself. It is sown in the hard, cold earth, and is seen no more in the shape of a seed; but in due time reappears above the surface of the soil, as a new green shoot, full of life and promise for the future.

It is significant that Jesus said this when he was told that some Greek visitors to Jerusalem had asked for an interview with him. The idea which Jesus states in his parable of the seed which is sown, dying to obtain new life, would be very familiar to Greek philosophers; it was an important feature of the mystery religions. Greeks, too, were familiar with the idea of sacrifice as a part of religious practice.

What would have been new to them, was the thought of self-sacrifice, especially self-sacrifice for the sake of others.

Sacrifice

It is not surprising that, having spoken of the death of the seed, Jesus should go on to speak of his own death, which was now only a day or two away, for the Cross is the greatest piece of self-sacrifice which the world has known or indeed will ever know. Jesus himself furnishes us with the greatest example of what he proclaimed.

'Now is my soul troubled.' All the gospels record a moment

before the final conflict when Jesus seems suddenly to have had a moment of irresolution. He contemplates a prayer to the Father for safety – but no, for this is the very moment for which he has been born. 'Father, glorify your name!' To *this* prayer came the response from above – 'I have glorified it, and will glorify it again.' Jesus was not some kind of made-up copy-book 'sample human'; he was a particular man, a Galilean, son of a carpenter, now a travelling preacher and rabbi, living under the conditions you and I live our lives – at the mercy of time, place, other people, events not of our own choice or will. He became our Saviour by offering up to God a perfect human life; something that we, you and I, can never do. That is, he offered up through all his life, full obedience to the will of God. This life culminated in the Cross upon which he met his death. That crucified Figure, 'lifted up from the earth', still draws all men to himself (John 12.32) and will continue to do so, through the ages ahead as it has done in the ages past. Here indeed is the Victory of the Cross; here is the overwhelming proof of God's love for us all, when he showed mercy to his sinful people in offering up his own Son on the Cross for our salvation.

Ash Wednesday *(The First Day of Lent)*
25 February 1998 **Sackcloth and Ashes**

'Blow the trumpet in Zion; sanctify a fast; call a solemn assembly, gather the people . . . Between the porch and the altar, let the priests, the ministers of the Lord, weep and say, "Spare thy people, O Lord" . . .'
Joel 2.15 – 17

Ancient Symbols
Sackcloth and ashes – ancient symbols of sorrow, of penitence, of abasement of ourselves before the power, the truth and the holiness of God. In the pages of the Bible we read of the old kings and patriarchs, prophets, priests and leaders, putting aside all their finery; and with their robes, all their claims to rank and privilege. All clothed themselves in sackcloth, coarsest of fabrics, and sprinkled ashes on their heads, humbling themselves alongside the meanest of their people.

So here today – in many churches the hangings are changed for sackcloth – the Lent Array – or for penitential purple. All ornaments and finery are put away or covered over. The ashes placed on the foreheads of the faithful are symbolic of our common mortality – 'Ashes to ashes, dust to dust' as says the burial service; a sign of penitence and abasement before God.

Take Stock
Penitence for what? For our falling short so often; for the missing of our aims, for our failure to reach the standards that we recognize – our sins, that is to say. Abasement – before the majesty, the purity and the holiness of our God. Confronted with his pure light, pierced by his keen gaze, we cannot bear to see ourselves revealed as we really are.

> *'O would some power the Gifts give us,*
> *To see ourselves as others see us . . .*

Lent is a time to take stock, to put ourselves into better order, clear out the rubbish and dirt, and try to see ourselves as others see us. And the most important 'other' is, of course, God. How do we measure up against the standards of God? How can we in Lent, this Lent, come to see ourselves more clearly?

The Bible
First, to measure ourselves against the standards of Christ, let us take out our Bible, and in particular the Gospels. This year, we are reading St Luke in our churches – a good start would be with him. Try a different translation; get hold of a commentary. The Bible Reading Fellowship leaflets are excellent, but there are many others. Read the Gospels slowly and meditatively; let the words of Christ sink into your mind and soul. Visualize the scene, the people, the action.

The Eucharist
Second, seek Our Lord's spiritual strength. In prayer – 'More things are wrought by prayer than this world dreams of' – so let us get our spiritual life into a better shape this Lent. Attend the Eucharist – try and get to a daily celebration on at least one weekday. Not necessarily at this church; maybe there is a church or house-group near your place of work.

Self-discipline

The Lord Jesus went into the desert and fasted. Exactly what form of self-discipline our own selves will benefit from most, is for each of us to decide. Come and talk about it, if you feel this would help. Jesus said, about evil spirits, 'This kind goes not out except by prayer and fasting.' If we give up smoking, sweets, certain foods or drinks – what we save will go to our Lent Box (or Missionary Project etc. as the church has arranged).

Reconciliation

Fourthly, seriously to consider the use of the Ministry of Reconciliation. The clergy are not psychologists, but there is much to be gained by talking over problems with another person, upon whose trust and absolute discretion you can rely, and whose spiritual standing you can respect. More important than this, however, is the assurance of forgiveness that a priest can give, as the accredited representative of the Body of Christ, the Church. Many find great relief and comfort by availing themselves of the Sacrament of Forgiveness.

Looking Ahead

So it should be, that this Lent we should turn to Christ; Christ with us, and we with him, to consider ourselves in his light and his love. As we can bring ourselves into conformity with his standards, use his strength to supply our weakness, so we can become more fully instruments in his hands, for the spreading of his Kingdom.

The First Sunday of Lent (Sixth before Easter) . 1 March 1998 The Wilderness

'Jesus, full of the Holy Spirit, returned from the Jordan, and was led by the Spirit for forty days in the wilderness, tempted by the devil.' Luke 4.1,2

Turning Points

In every human life there are turning points; times when we realize that we have made important decisions, or taken definite steps perhaps, which will influence and indeed make, our whole life from this point onwards. Jesus was no exception. His baptism in the river Jordan by John Baptist was a very important event. The Voice from heaven and the descent of the Holy Spirit at the riverside, made it clear to him that here was his vocation. Was he to follow it? Was he indeed being called by his Father to a special work? And where was the power and strength needed for such a future?

So immediately after the baptism Jesus went away, alone, into the lonely silence of the desert to work out, with intense prayer and deep thought, what he was to do and how he was to do it. The accounts in the gospels are demanding our special reverence, because they must represent what Jesus himself told his disciples about this period, and his own intimate experiences of soul and mind, as he struggled with the ways in which he could bring human souls to the Kingdom of God the Father.

Fasting and Praying

To be thrown out into the harsh bleakness of the desert seems to be an inevitable part of our own call to God's service. To feel isolated, to be for a time incapable of forming real communion with God or man, seems to be a part of our Christian training. The reason must be that for most of us, our faith has been so shallow; we skate on the surface, rather than penetrate. It is superficial, unreal – and so we can seem lost, isolated in the wilderness, like the Children of Israel in the desert long ago.

In fact, new powers of communion are being built within us; our growth in strength of spirit is proceeding – we are being trained to be the sort of people God wants us to be.

Temptation

Satan comes to us. We are tempted to give up, to despair, to be cynical. Tempted not to help others when we know we can, and know we ought – when we think, what's the use? And behind these temptations is the temptation to disbelieve in what we really are, vessels of God's spirit.

Here is the great temptation, to deny that it is 'the Spirit himself that bears witness with our spirit' (Rom. 8.16). God is with us and in us. His Spirit is our spirit.

Our Lent
So here is our Lent, our going out into the wilderness with Jesus. Let us apply then, some words we have heard from St Paul: 'No one who believes in him will be put to shame' and 'every one who calls upon the Name of the Lord will be saved' (Hebrews 4.15). And from St Peter: 'Rejoice in so far as you share Christ's sufferings, that you also may rejoice and be glad, when his glory is revealed' (1 Peter 4.13). Our temptations, our sufferings, in so far as we can offer them to God, are a sharing in Christ's temptations and sufferings.

This Lent, let us accept our wilderness. If from today's readings we can realize what our own Lent really means – then the angels will indeed bear us up, and minister to us, as they did to the Lord. In other words, we will find moments when giving for love's sake alone really satisfies, really makes us feel alive and in fellowship and communion. At such moments Christ's glory is revealed, and we can rejoice and be glad. Lent, we discover, is really Easter in disguise.

First Sunday of Lent *Second Sermon*
The Humble and the Self-Righteous
'Two men went up into the temple to pray; one a Pharisee and the other a tax collector.' Luke 18.10

Friend of Sinners
St Luke seems to take particular pleasure in recording those incidents in our Lord's life, as well as conversations and discussions, in which Jesus appears as 'The Friend of Sinners'. So we may say that this parable takes its place alongside the story of the 'Prodigal Son'. Certainly because of this characteristic, it seems that the Gospel of St Luke, of the whole four, is the one which will most cheer the downcast, give hope to the penitent, and encourage sinners to turn to a better life.

Resemblances and Differences
Both the men who go to the Temple are alike – both dependent upon God's grace and love, both human beings no doubt, with the usual dependants of family and relatives, we may suppose;

and the daily struggle to succeed in their work and problems.

Both, also, seem to be in the habit of going often to the Temple, the centre of their worship, their religion, and their nation. Both profess to draw near to God 'in his holy dwelling-place'; both address him in his holiness and his divinity. Yet, the very points of resemblance are the marked differences between the two. This shows in their attitude and their prayers. In their attitudes – one confidently strides ahead, close to the holy place, takes up an attitude of piety; the other takes a more remote place, away at the back, and dare not raise his eyes, but strikes his breast in repentance.

Reality
In their prayers, one compares himself with his fellow human beings, sinners that they are, unlike himself. He thanks God for his own good behaviour, his careful keeping of the Law, what he does but says nothing about all he has left undone. The other is all too aware of his own state as a sinner in the sight of God; he beats his breast, not daring to look up, but only asks for the mercy of the Lord.

Christ's Comment
Jesus' parable points the need for all of us to be in contact with reality. We must take care that we do not fall into the sad state of error of the Pharisee: imagining ourselves to be in God's favoured regard, because we do all that is required of us by our human – dare we say, ecclesiastical? – standards; we go to church, take our part in the services, read the Bible, give to the good causes and the Church needs. But in fact, though we do not want to see it, we may well be in the state of the 'tax collector', trading in doubtful ways (for the 'tax collector' of the ancient times was a shifty crook, using bullying and force to squeeze the poor, and bribe the hated occupying Roman power).

This man still retained something of his religion; knew his faults and sins, and in his heart was horrified at the wretched tricks and bullying he had to get up to, and begs God's mercy upon him. Hence, he is praised by the Lord as being realistic, whereas the other, the 'good man' is dismissed as living in a false world.

The Second Sunday of Lent 8 March 1998
Sorrow for the Future

'O Jerusalem, Jerusalem!' Luke 13.34

Our altars carry in the centre, a cross; and the cross is the general symbol of our faith, of Christianity. Yet the cross and suffering of Christ have always been difficult to understand – difficult for his disciples then, and for us in our day. So it came as something of a shock when – after the warning from the Pharisees that it was not safe to stay there, for Herod the king wants to kill Jesus – that Jesus should decide to go on towards Jerusalem, even though this would mean the imminent possibility of death.

More than that, the Lord seems to be saying that in fact he will be killed when he goes to Jerusalem; is he then looking for death, after spending three more days in Galilee, casting out demons and healing the sick?

Judas
It may well be that this decision by the Lord, may have set in train the mind of Judas on the course of disapproval, disbelief and despair that in the end led to the betrayal of the Lord. It could not be that Jesus was going to abandon all hope of an earthly kingdom, surely? Judas had belonged to a group of what we might call 'Resistance Fighters' – their aim was to rid the Holy Land of the invaders and set up a strong Jewish government and rule, and they had no hesitation in using assassination to further their cause. He had been attracted, we may assume, by the preaching and character of Jesus; and maybe laid aside the programme of murder and brutality that his group took as their contribution to the future free nation and land. In place of bloodshed and cruelty, Judas looked to the preaching and teaching of Jesus to bring him the support of the majority, and place him upon the throne of his ancestor David, as the King of a free and just Holy Land, swept clean of heathens and non-believers, and looking back to the great days of long ago.

The Way of the Cross
But now all this is being thrown away. The Lord is seeing ahead of him, not a reign but the horror of death. He sees himself as one of the prophets and holy men of the past, who were killed or

stoned when they tried to reform the faithless nation. St Paul takes up this point in his letter to the Philippians – where he pours scorn on faithless Christians, who abandon their beliefs and live as enemies of the cross of Christ (3.18). They even make a point of glorying in their shameful conduct and loss of faith. St Paul looks forward to the coming of the Saviour, who 'will change our lowly body to be like his glorious Body' – the Body of victory over death and destruction; to be looked for and to be stood firm for, against all opposition.

Indeed, the way of the cross has been hard and difficult for the disciples then to understand, as indeed it is still hard and unpopular for us in our day and age. In this time of Lent, let us try our best to unite ourselves with the sufferings and pain of Christ, and the sufferings and pain of the world about us. We, as followers of Christ, are called to follow him in the Way of the Cross; bearing in our bodies the dying of the Lord Jesus' (2 Cor. 6.9).

Second Sunday of Lent *Second Sermon*
Bearing the Cross

'Whoever does not bear his own cross, and come after me, cannot be my disciple.' Luke 14.27

The Symbol

Most people do not know, and those who do know usually forget, the significance of the cross as a badge in the early days of the Church. Its choice was like selecting a gibbet, with a rope and noose hanging from it, as a badge. In Roman days, criminals were crucified, and it was so prolonged and painful a way of execution, and regarded as so disgraceful an end, that to be put to death by some other means was a privilege of some value.

So the symbol which marked men and women as Christians was a sign of deep disgrace. It is no wonder that the first Christians were looked upon as very eccentric people. What a strange Leader they followed and worshipped – a condemned criminal!

Meanings

When we see any object being used as a symbol, whether it is religious or not, we should try and look beyond what we see with our eyes, and discover the message it is meant to convey. We should be on our guard, too, lest an inspiring meaning should have been cheapened by constant use as a symbol, or even distorted and changed for the worse.

We see something of this kind in such things as postage stamps – where at one time there used to be a portrait of the Queen on our British stamps, nowadays the portrait is reduced to a little design up in a corner, and all sorts of other symbols or designs are the main feature – sometimes interesting and even historic, but sometimes too rough and ready, or commercial.

The Meaning of the Cross

The Christian cross tells us first of all, about our Lord's sufferings – not only about the agony of the long time he hung upon the Cross itself, but also of the physical and mental suffering he endured in the hours beforehand; and above all, it tells us of his death.

The fact that such a strange symbol came into general use so speedily among Christians, should remind us of why he died. We are all sinners against our fellow human beings, and – more important – against our Creator; and deserving of punishment. But by laying down his life in such a terrible and shameful way, Jesus has atoned for our sins, and opened to us the gateway to salvation.

We have ourselves therefore, in love and thanks for what our Lord has done, to follow in his footsteps. Loyalty to Jesus must take precedence over all other loyalties – Luke expresses this very strongly in this section – 'Count the cost first!' Perhaps these words were spoken by way of encouragement at a time when the disciples were faltering – as indeed might be expected when the Lord spoke so firmly and freely about his possible death in Jerusalem (vv. 33,34).

> *O Christ, you call me and every disciple to follow you*
> *You are my way to God,*
> *You are the life of my soul,*
> *You are my resurrection from the dead:*
> *You are the pattern for my life.*
> *All I have to do is to follow.*

Because you are with the Father,
You are with him in every place,
With every disciple as with me,
O Master and Lord.

(G. A.)

The Third Sunday of Lent   15 March 1998
'Time for Repentance'

'Let anyone who stands, take heed lest he fall.' 1 Corinthians 10.12

Repentance

Jesus is told, on his way towards Jerusalem, about the brutal slaughter by Pilate of some pilgrims from Galilee, on the very road that Jesus would be taking. In almost the same breath, comes the news of the accidental collapse of a tower, involving the death of others, dwellers in Jerusalem. All the territory of Israel, including both Galilee and Jerusalem, has been hard hit. Is this because the people were sinners? which is the common opinion put forward in the saying, 'It is an act of God!' which implies that those who suffered were sinners, sinful enough in fact to deserve death.

Jesus refuses this in both cases; the issue is not whether the people who died were sinners, but rather that all who dwell in Jerusalem or Siloam are sinful enough to deserve death. And he tells his listeners that they must repent – or perish in their turn.

The Fig-tree

Jesus goes on to tell the parable of the fig tree. 'Here is this fig tree, year after year still barren, producing no fruit.' Anyone would agree that such an unprofitable tree could certainly be cut down – why, it has been there for three years, and still nothing in the way of figs. 'Cut it down,' says the owner; but the gardener suggests that they should leave the tree for another year, and in the meantime he will dig round it and feed it with manure. Then, if it produces figs, well and good; if not, cut it down.

Our Lord does not follow such arguments, especially when we are really talking of human beings. The Son of our loving God and Creator is aware that many people need time, patience and help; and then, with such encouragement, will become, will grow into, good and useful members of society.

Temptation

St Paul tells us a similar story, looking back at the Old Testament days. He recalls the famous and historic escape from Egypt under the great leader, Moses. Yet, although the people had supernatural food and drink, they did not all survive the rigours of the passage towards the Promised Land. We then, in our time, must be careful not to allow evil to take us over – some of the ancients fell into idolatry, others sins of the flesh. Repentance is not often found in the collective sinfulness of society, is it? Yet God in his mercy extends time for us to give up our sinful ways; and he will not give us up, despite our many failures.

Take heed of the lessons of history; take heed of the need for repentance. God is gracious and willing; moved by his love, he leaves us free to choose what is the best for ourselves – if we will only take notice of the standards of love and care, honesty and truth in our lives.

Third Sunday of Lent   *Second Sermon*
The Lamb of God
'Behold the Lamb of God!' John 1.35

We think of innocence when we hear the expression 'Lamb of God'. The innocent who is the victim; the sacrificial victim *par excellence* in the Bible; its gentleness, its innocence, its youthful exuberance – all combine to make the lamb the very image of the gift of new life. There is the reference to the Passover lamb, sacrificed at the annual festival, and representing the Messiah, giving his life for the people.

For John, Jesus *is* the Lamb of God – 'Behold the Lamb of God!' he calls out to the two disciples with whom he watches Jesus walking by (v. 36). This has the result that the two disciples leave John and attach themselves to Christ; thus becoming the first two disciples of Jesus (Andrew, and perhaps, John, son of Zebedee)

Andrew brings his brother, Simon, whom Jesus re-names Cephas (Peter) from the Greek for 'rock', and he also follows him.

Then follows the strange story of Philip and Nathanael. A fig-tree plays a part in this story, rather mysteriously; Jesus tells Nathanael that he, the Lord, has seen him 'under a fig tree'. This is – surprisingly – enough to make Nathanael at once acclaim Jesus as 'Son of God' and 'King of Israel'. Jesus tells him that he will see 'Heaven opened, and the angels of God ascending and descending upon the Son of Man.' This vision seems to reflect the story in Genesis 28, of the dream or vision of Jacob. Jacob dreamt that he saw a ladder, reaching from heaven down to the earth, and the angels of God were going up and down upon it. When Nathanael saw Jesus, it was as if the true Israelite saw the true Israel in heaven, with his true counterpart on earth. The vision emphasizes what (for John) was an essential feature of the title 'Son of Man' – someone whose destiny was to be carried on, both on earth and in heaven; a mediator, in fact, between humanity and God. Not at the last day only, but always – to the eye of faith – Jesus unites God and man.

The Fourth Sunday of Lent   22 March 1998
Two Sons – and their Father

'Let us eat and make merry; for this my son was dead, and is alive again; he was lost, and he is found!' Luke 15.23

Happy Ending

The story of the Prodigal Son ends with a surprise party. When the prodigal's elder brother was returning home from his day's hard work, he heard the sound of music and dancing coming from his father's house.

He could scarcely believe his ears!

Life had been pretty quiet since that disreputable jackanapes had left home. 'What can my father be up to?' he must have asked himself – then questioning the servants, he found out.

That wretched brother had returned and to welcome him, this party was in full swing. Well! No wonder the elder brother was furious. Here he was, slaving away doing at least two men's jobs, and *he* never gets a party – but let this wasteful dissolute fellow come back penniless, and a party is laid on for him.

How Unfair

Unfair indeed – yet, how unfavourable the elder's rankling grievance compares with the striking love and generosity of the father. Not only had he gone out to meet the returning prodigal – instead of holding back, as would befit his dignity – he had not even waited to hear his son's submission and repentance, but straightway led him home, clothed him, and set in train the feast.

What joy! Here we can read off a general lesson by Jesus, about the nature of God's forgiveness, compared with the rules and regulations laid down by scribes and Pharisees. No conditions, no reparations, no testing for genuineness – the son simply returning to the father's arms. 'What joy in heaven over one sinner who repents!'

Grim and Gruff

The elder son can't see it this way at all.

The rewards given to the younger son are inappropriate and completely unfair. *He* has in contrast gone on working the estate for his father's benefit – even though it was technically his own property – while his brother, by squandering his inheritance, has deprived the father of the elder son.

We sense something of the nature of the elder son.

The prodigal is certainly easy-going, probably foolish, but an engaging personality; the elder seems a sour person. His years of 'slaving' have turned him in on himself, and he is now embittered, a prisoner of his own restrictions. We must feel sorry for such, unable to 'loosen up', to enjoy the ordinary pleasures of life, shut up behind walls of their own making.

Critics

Jesus' critics – from whose opposition this and the preceding parables stem – are united in condemning him because he 'welcomes sinners and eats with them'. In orthodox Hebrew religious thought, penitence was valued and a truly repentant person would be welcomed back into the company of the faithful. He must repent first, and only then could he be welcomed back, by God or his fellows.

Jesus' offence in the eyes of the strictly religious, consisted in not waiting for signs of renouncing the bad ways. For Jesus, repentance is not simply a way of making amends so as to rejoin the ranks of the just and pious, and take a front pew in the synagogue again. Repentance belongs to a different order of things altogether; it is a complete change, and it is a complete joy.

Fourth Sunday of Lent   *Second Sermon*
Exhortations
'Be steady, endure suffering, fulfil your ministry.' 2 Timothy 4.5

Take Courage
St Paul is imprisoned in Rome and expecting death by execution very soon. Today he is renewing his encouragement and exhortations to Timothy, his disciple, and the Christian at Ephesus.

'Take courage', Paul writes, 'take your share of suffering as a good soldier of Christ Jesus' (2 Timothy 2.3). Struggle to maintain the truth in the face of heresy and moral corruption. Be sure to hand on the faith to trustworthy ministers in turn. Fulfil your ministry; despite your undoubted faith you need to bestir yourself to face your difficulties as a Christian leader. Leave aside timidity and hesitations.

There is little enough time left for Paul to say more. First and foremost comes the preaching of the Word, all the more pressing as the time is coming when few will listen ('itching ears' to hear new ideas! How like today).

Martyrdom
Paul's martyrdom is imminent; he looks back with confidence as well as sorrow; he knows himself what a strong fighter for the Gospel, what a good runner in the race – the marathon, we might say – he has been. Now he looks forward to the heavenly reward promised by Christ, and has no fear of death, and what lies beyond.

In spite of the short time available, he hopes Timothy will manage to come and see him soon; Paul is lonely and alone, mentioning the names of those who have gone. 'Luke alone is with me' – the continual companion who has been with Paul on so many voyages and journeys, taking notes and keeping his diary, which we now have in the form of Luke's 'Gospel' and Luke's 'Acts of the Apostles'. What a great debt we owe to this Greek – or Greek-educated – writer and physician; and how little we know about him.

Personal Notes

More notes – about those who have helped the Apostle, or those who have been in opposition, like Alexander the coppersmith. Here was a strong opponent, who seems to have almost prevailed against the Apostle himself (v. 15), who 'was rescued from the lion's mouth'! which sounds very desperate.

But his final words, in this letter, that is, are strong and full of hope. He mentions his 'first defence' – this would be the trial which ended his first imprisonment in Rome with an acquittal, and made further missionary work in Rome itself possible (perhaps this was when Onesimus, the runaway slave, came to him and acted as his secretary; it may well be Onesimus whom we have to thank for preserving – probably in drafts and first copies – the letters of Paul which we have in our Bibles now). However, Paul must feel that the second arrest and trial will not turn out so well; as he says, 'I am already on the point of being sacrificed; the time of my departure has come' (v. 6).

The Apostle

If Peter was the Apostle to the Jews, Paul was the Apostle to the Gentiles, that is, the rest of the world. Let us not forget that Paul, like Peter, was a repentant sinner. He was as we know from his own letters, converted from being the persecutor of the infant Church to being its greatest missionary.

Paul has left the stamp of his powerful personality upon the Church, and upon the theology of the Church, by those letters of his. He instructs, warns, begs, orders, implores, threatens, opens his heart, weeps tears. He takes the first giant steps into the mysteries of Redemption – many have followed, but Paul was the first. He was the strategist who saw what was needed to ensure the development of the Church of Christ, as the Church of All Nations. Paul enabled the Gospel message to break out from its confines amongst the Hebrew people, and to reach – with its transforming power, every race and every country in the world.

Mothering Sunday   22 March 1998   Mothers

'Simeon said to Mary his mother, "Behold, this child is set for the fall and rising of many in Israel, and for a sign that is spoken against and a sword will pierce through your own soul also".' Luke 2. 34,35 or 'Jesus went back with them to Nazareth, and continued to be under their authority; his mother treasured all these things in her heart.' Luke 2.51

Mothers' Day
Today is 'Mothering Sunday' – that's the old name, and the proper name, for it; or 'Mothers' Day' if we prefer to keep up with the card-shops and the florists. (And how right it is, to remember our mothers and bring them a present – a gift or some flowers – there are flowers here today for the children to take to their mothers – as tokens of our love and our respect).

What a good and happy thing it is, to remember our mothers, their love and their care, on this special day in the year.

The Centre of the Home
In our early years we keep close to our mothers, and mother is the firm base and strong centre to the home, to which we return. Later, as time goes by, and we leave the nest, so our visits no doubt become rarer. But still, our mothers are the great figures of our lives; and there is a special pleasure for mothers – and fathers too – in seeing their children grow, and grow up, to become unique and individual persons. As the fledglings grow in strength and knowledge, so the role of mother and father reduces itself; advice rather than commands, tact rather than compulsion, a broadening of horizons all round, with understanding taking the place of rote and rule.

Sadness
There is bound to be sorrow as the bonds of home, and the ties of affection, diminish; decisions are no longer – if indeed they ever were – the laying-down of law, but rather become sweetened and transformed into advice, into helping comments, and the widening of horizons all round. We must be clear, that if this did not happen, the children would never grow up and become individual people in their own right. We cannot be Peter Pans.

The sense of peace and security which a truly happy – and

Christian – family gives, will remain with its members all their lives, because it springs from a deep-down joy and love.

Threats

There are threats to the family of various kinds. Humanistic philosophies of our day would destroy the family all too easily; a mechanistic outlook on life will render it – and indeed all our human relationships – of no effect and valueless. Yet so long as the family survives – and we believe it will survive, being one of the fundamental institutions of humanity and human society as God has planned it – a vital institution for the perpetuation of the human race, the citadel of freedom, and the school of virtues without which there would be no real freedom, no sense of community. Sometimes, indeed, times may be hard and circumstances adverse, contributing to the break-up of a home. Yet the real thing behind a broken home is personal guilt; the strength of any home is in such personal virtues as love, truthfulness, understanding and patience, unselfishness and forbearance.

Thank you, Mother

So today, on Mothers' Day, Mothering Sunday, we thank our mothers for their love, their care, and their concern. Truly, we acknowledge the pain mothers suffer as we leave them, but that pain can be sublimated through the joy of realizing the thought of the new individual who has come to full stature. Here is how the family and the race are carried on, part of the great plan of God, in which we are allowed to play our parts, and which – one day – we will be able to understand and appreciate more fully.

> *Lord, we give you thanks because*
> *you make husband and wife one flesh;*
> *you put us together in families,*
> *to grasp your love and forgiveness,*
> *care and protection, respect and authority,*
> *reflected in those around us.*
> *And, as we grow, you prepare to bring us*
> *into the glorious freedom of your children,*
> *as brothers and sisters of Jesus Christ.*
>
> Gen. 2.24; Romans 8.17,22 *(Patterns for Worship p. 193)*

The Annunciation   25 March 1998
Image of the Church

'Mary said, Behold I am the handmaid of the Lord; let it be according to your word.' Luke 1.38

An Image of the Church

Down the ages, loving hearts have seen in Mary, the Mother of the Lord, an image or a prefiguring of the Christian Church itself.

This image is clearly seen in Mary's response to the angel's message at the Annunciation – the Church exists to say 'Yes!' to God, and to accept his message and to do his will. No doubt Mary by no means realized fully the implications – especially for herself – of her 'Yes!' She must have had an inkling later, when Simeon in the Temple, told her that her child would be a sign which the world would refuse to acknowledge, and that a sword would pierce her own heart also.

Pain

She must have known, and lived with, the knowledge that the future held not only joy, but also pain for her; and that her child would be the cause of her own deep suffering.

Light and darkness were to be the symbols of Mary's life, just as well as that of her Son. His presence would be marked by the power of the Holy Spirit, which like fire, can both inspire and divide, warm into life or burn with pain.

Grace

'Full of grace' is another way of putting it; grace means the indwelling presence of the Almighty in a human being. With Mary, all this was indicated, and more, when the angel said to her that the Child 'will be called the Son of the Most High'. Mary with her Child is a foreshadowing and a revolution of what our human nature can become under the supernatural influence of God.

Mary suffered and experienced the trials of life, trials that are not only a normal part of the experience of humanity and human life. But in her case, they were in a higher degree of pain and suffering than most; and still she continued steadfast in love and faith and trust.

Consent

The Almighty even asked her consent to what was being proposed; his messenger came not with a command, an order, but with a request. At first Mary did not understand – 'She was greatly troubled at this saying' we are told. She asked questions.

But it was Mary's 'Yes!' that set in train the redemption of the world.

'Rejoice, so highly favoured! The Lord is with you!' Luke 1.28

The Fifth Sunday in Lent *(Passion Sunday)* 29 March 1998 **The Shadow of the Cross**

'Jesus said, ''Let her alone, let her keep it for the day of my burial''.' John 12.7 or 'I count everything as loss, because of the surpassing worth of knowing Christ Jesus my Lord.' Philippians 3.8

At Bethany

The house at Bethany, where Jesus was a welcome guest of Lazarus 'whom Jesus had raised from the dead' and his two sisters, Mary and Martha, formed a place of quiet and repose for the Lord Christ. He must have looked forward to his visits here – a peaceful small village where he knew that (within reason) he would be unapproached, and could relax without crowds pressing round asking for healing, asking for miracles, asking questions, trying to 'catch him out' with tricky quotations. No, here his resort to the quiet affection of the home at Bethany, shows something of the very human need for support that the Lord was feeling at this crucial point of his life.

A Touching Gesture

Something is different, however, at the house – the atmosphere is strange and strained. A modest feast has been arranged and is served, no doubt much as on previous occasions, with Martha busy keeping all at table well supplied. Mary, however, does something unusual – she anoints the feet of Jesus with a costly and rich ointment, the kind of material used for the anointing of the bodies of the dead in Hebrew burial rites. This action seems to be intended as a kind of foreshadowing, or rehearsal perhaps, for the anointing which should have been given to the body before its burial. Judas makes his questioning comment, as the 'treasurer' of the little band, at the waste of this expensive material; and John takes the opportunity of blackening Judas' character – he is a petty thief, stealing from the common purse.

But Mary's action of extravagant devotion to Jesus is taken by the Lord as pointing towards the inevitable climax of his life, his sacrificial offering of himself upon the cross.

Fulfilment

'Thus it is written, that the Christ should suffer and on the third day rise from the dead' (Luke 24.46) – so Jesus explains that his death is necessary to the fulfilment of his mission. When Jesus, in his life on earth, came to know that he was truly God as well as truly man, he did not use the divine side of his nature to escape the sufferings of our human life. He lived his life under the conditions you and I live ours; at the mercy of time, place, other people, events not of our choosing nor willing. He drew on the same resources of God that are open to us all; and it was *thus* 'he became to all that obey him, the author of eternal salvation' (Heb. 5.9).

His Perfect Offering

Jesus became the Saviour by offering up to God a perfect human life. 'Although he was a Son, he learned obedience through what he suffered; and being made perfect he became the source of eternal salvation' (Heb. 5.8).

He is the Saviour because he did what you and I could never do. That is, he offered up through all his days, a life of full obedience to the will of God, and this life culminated in his death upon the Cross. That Figure upon the Cross still 'draws all men unto him' (John 12.32) and continues to do so, from one millennium to another, and away into the future ages ahead, as it has done in the present and in the past. So indeed we may triumph in the power of his victory, as our Collect tells us, for this is truly the Victory of the Cross.

Fifth Sunday of Lent *Second Sermon*
The Passover

'Jesus sent Peter and John saying, "Go and prepare the Passover for us, that we may eat it".' Luke 22.8

Its Theme and Conduct

Passover or Pesach is the best-known of Jewish festivals, and plays an important part in Jewish life. The theme of the service is remembrance of the Exodus (in our Bibles, Exodus 12) when the angel of death 'passed over' the Israelites, but struck the first-born of the Egyptians (v. 27) with the result that the people of Israel were able to go forth from Egypt, under the protection of this threat recurring. Their haste was such that the dough, made ready for bread, was not leavened; hence the eating of unleavened bread was one of the customs or directions ordered to mark the yearly Passover celebrations (Exodus 13.3).

In the afternoon the Passover lambs were slaughtered at the great altar in front of the Temple. After sunset – which in Hebrew calculations meant the beginning of a new day – the people assembled by families or small groups of friends to make a solemn meal, consisting of roasted lamb, herbs, and unleavened bread. During this meal the miraculous deliverance of Israel out of captivity would be recited. As joining together in a formal meal, the members of each group were bound together by table-fellowship, signified by sharing the bread and wine blessed by the host.

'The Last Supper'

Luke tells us bluntly how Judas went off and made his arrangements for the betrayal of Christ. What were his motives? Luke mentions money; some commentators suggest that, in fact, Judas had become disenchanted with the style of Jesus, and the 'spiritual' rather than 'actual' kingdom that the Lord seemed to be preaching. We may remember that Judas 'Iscariot' had been a member of the vicious extremist Jewish group, known as the 'Sicarii' or 'Daggermen', whose object was the assassination of people considered enemies of the Hebrew nation, or betrayers and double-dealers (compare Acts 23.12–31). Maybe, money was not the chief aim of Judas after all.

The man 'carrying a jar of water' would be an unusual sight in most Palestinian cities; such work would almost invariably be regarded as that for women. Perhaps this was a sign or 'pass-word' so that Peter and John would know a friend at once.

The Upper Room

The 'Upper Room' is possibly to be located in the house of Mary, the mother of John Mark (see Acts 12.12). Mary may have run a kind of hostel for pilgrims to Jerusalem – there must have been many of such places, considering the number of visitors and pilgrims through the year, especially about the festival times.

The 'young man' who followed Jesus, 'with nothing but a linen cloth about his body' (Mark 14.51) has been thought to have been perhaps the young Mark; did he know Jesus and his followers from previous occasions, as visitors to his family home? Perhaps he served them at meals, maybe even assisted at the Last Supper; he would have been very lucky indeed knowing the men and women about Jesus; and he would have seen, and probably spoken with, the Lord himself. This would explain perhaps, how he was set afire with the Christian message, and – full of promise – came to be taken with Barnabas and Paul on a preaching mission in Cyprus and Asia Minor (see Acts 15, 37–39) which did not turn out too well. But he made up for any faults later (Paul in prison praises him as 'a comfort' as well as 'a fellow-worker' (Col. 4.11 and Philem. 24).

> Grant us your light, O Lord,
> that the darkness of our hearts being done away,
> we may be brought at the last
>   to the light which is Christ.
>
> (Bede: PHG)

Palm Sunday (The Sunday next before Easter) 5 April 1998 The Way of the Cross

'Bearing the human likeness, revealed in human shape, he humbled himself, and in obedience accepted even death – death on a cross.' Philippians 2.7,8

Palms and Popularity

A favourite event of our Church Year is the re-enactment of the Entry of Our Lord Jesus Christ into the holy City of Jerusalem. It is a good thing to go out into the fresh air, to walk in procession about our neighbourhood – with fellow Christians of other churches whenever possible – and display publicly something of our belief in, and love for, Christ – our Redeemer and King.

Our little dried palm-leaves – or, as our ancestors used to take, sprigs of fresh green stuff – remind us of the fleeting nature of the welcome that Jesus received, on that first Palm Sunday so many years ago in the hot Palestine sun; for if the palms are not dried now, they will be faded soon. Just so, the enthusiasm of the crowds, as they surrounded and cheered the Lord, seated meekly on a donkey – the sign of peace, not war – changed and faded. On Good Friday he was crucified, and many of the same people were in the crowds that mocked and insulted him, as he followed his Via Dolorosa, his Way of Sorrow.

What Happened?

Of course, we may blame the pervasive influence of the High Priest and the Jerusalem politicians, for the change in popular feeling. They – rightly enough from their own point of view – wanted to save the Jewish state and nation from falling into yet another bitter and destructive religious war. So many similar risings, always brutally crushed, had happened in the past.

Was it not simple political common sense, that one man should die for the people? So, every cog of the party political machine went into action. Public opinion was turned round by propaganda, by smears, by judicious threats and bribes also, no doubt. But would that have been enough? No, there must have been a genuine popular revulsion, to achieve such a violent alteration in so short a time. What happened?

True Colours

Jesus was revealed in his true colours; the crowds that surrounded him on his entry into the City were calling out 'Hail to the King!' They saw the entry of Christ as the beginning of a new reign – the restored Kingdom of David; the hated oppressors would be thrown out by supernatural powers, and the Hebrew nation would once again be free.

When Jesus made it clear that he was not concerned with power politics but with individual souls – and as this realization spread – the disappointed masses turned from hope and praise to disgust and hatred. This is really why the crowds deserted him and changed their cry to 'Crucify!'

Rejection
The priests and doctors of the Law, the elders and scribes, had hated him from the beginning; but the people would not have changed so soon, if they had not been deeply disappointed. Yet, it was this crucified Man who before long was to be the spiritual magnet for souls from all nations and from all countries.

'I, if I be lifted up, will draw all men to me' (John 12.32).

Christ's death was the supreme example of giving and sharing love; love was lifted up on a cross, so that everyone, each of us, might be united with that wondrous offering. In that lonely death on the cross, Jesus brought salvation to all who are abandoned – 'He humbled himself,' as St Paul told us (Phil. 2.8–11) 'and became obedient unto death, even death upon a cross. Therefore God has highly exalted him, that at the name of Jesus every knee should bow, and every tongue confess, that Jesus Christ is Lord.'

Palm Sunday   *Second Sermon*   Rejection
'The stone which the builders rejected, has become the head of the corner.'
Luke 20.17

The Vineyard
The stone rejected (Ps. 118.22) by the builders, is based upon the beautiful words of Isaiah we heard as our first lesson (5.1–7). In the son of the story, thrown out of the vineyard and killed, we see Jesus, the victim of hate and brutality; the servants, bringing their master's messages, are the prophets sent by God, violently treated and turned away, wounded or beaten up.

In this grim parable, Jesus pictures how little attention was paid by Israel to the prophets sent by God, and how – when the climax came and God sent his Son, the long-awaited Messiah, he was hated by many, and put to a cruel death.

It is a sad reminder to us, not only of the actual events which brought our Lord's ministry to a sudden end, but that we all take a share in those events to some extent, by rejecting some of the things that Jesus taught then and stands for now. Let us not make the mistake of seeing this parable simply as allotting blame to those immediately responsible for our Lord's death. To all of us, it puts a question – which in various ways and in various words, Jesus put to a number of people during his ministry here on earth: 'What is your real attitude to me?'

Our Answer
How will we answer this question?

It is all too easy to turn Jesus away, and to turn away *from* Jesus; not necessarily by violence like the men in the parable, nor like the Jews and the Romans to whom the parable alludes, but by our own indifference, our own love of self, or our own lack of the courage needed to follow him in the temptations of daily life.

Maundy Thursday   9 April 1998   *(Principal Service)*   'Love one another'

'A new commandment I give to you, that you love one another, as I have loved you.' John 13.34

Simple yet Difficult
One of the simplest statements in our Bible is our text – 'Love one another, as I have loved you.' Yet, it must be one of the most difficult to grasp.

To obey truly these words of our Lord Jesus Christ, spoken to his disciples on this solemn night of the Washing of the Feet and the Last Supper, requires a pastoral and loving heart. We need to have a feeling for people, a feeling which means that we share their joys and their sorrows, their problems and their pains, however much of our time and our energy may be required.

'Churchy' Church
Naturally the statement about 'Love . . .' is vigorously upheld and preached about, for Jesus Christ himself said it. But if we read a Church paper or the minutes of a Synod meeting, loving one another does not seem to come over as the deepest compulsion

of us Church people today, in our time. We seem too concerned with 'efficiency', with how much money can be raised for this or that cause, with 'how much' the parish can contribute; sometimes 'loving one another' seems to have become a sort of pious notion, for which there is scarcely time in the busy hurly-burly of Church life.

Early Christians

The first Christians, who were mostly Jews, found it just as difficult. They were used to a Law which codified human relationships; if you kept the rules, all was well, your conscience was clear. Into this situation had come Jesus, saying those wild things about 'loving your enemies', and 'pray for those who persecute you', and 'Love God and your fellow human beings' and everything else would fall into place. Very disturbing!

And still today, some of us regard 'Love one another, as I have loved you' as just one of those things Jesus said – and not at all too seriously to be taken. But for the early Christians it was different; to love one another as Jesus had loved them, was no old text, no pious platitude. They came to see that the Old Law was the *real* soft option, because it was far less demanding, far less wide-reaching; and every case was covered by a ruling long handed down, and thus requiring no new thought, or concern, or care.

Today

To try and apply Christ's words to the varying, moving, constantly changing pageant of the world and its people as they pass by, and as we pass along with them, is very different. 'As I have loved you' – the disciples knew what that meant. Each of them must have been aware of an individual personal love, as they journeyed round the countryside, with Jesus walking and talking with them, learning something of their thinking and of their problems, making each feel his deep affection and care. He made it very clear that each of them must have the same love for each of the others.

And the Lord followed up that final command with the famous words – so often seen on our war memorials – 'Greater love has no man than this, that a man lay down his life for his friends' (John 15.13). Christ is himself about to make just that sacrifice himself; our mutual love should be such, that we too can do the same, following the Lord's example.

Life and Love – a Summary

'If you are Christians, then your Jesus is one and the same Jesus
as on the throne of his Glory; the same as Jesus in the Blessed
Sacrament, received into your hearts in Holy Communion; Jesus
mystically with you as you pray – and Jesus enthroned in the
hearts and bodies of his brothers and sisters, up and down the
land. And it is folly – madness – to suppose that you can worship
Jesus in his Sacraments and Jesus on his Throne of Glory – when
you are passing him by, in the souls and bodies of his children.
It cannot be done! Go out and look for Jesus in the ragged, in the
naked, in the poor, the oppressed, the sweated; in those who have
lost hope, in those who are struggling to make good. Look for
Jesus! And when you have found him, gird yourselves with his
towel, and try and wash their feet . . .' (Bishop Frank Weston)

Maundy Thursday *Second Service* Atonement

*'He shall bear all their iniquities upon him.' Leviticus 16.22 'Why, what
evil has he done? I have found in him no crime . . . But they were urgent,
demanding that he should be crucified.' Luke 23.22,23*

Ancient Customs

The three great annual festivals of the Hebrew people were originally fixed by farming and agriculture, and the dates they were
held on depended on harvest in the locality and not some definite
calendar. Later, the dates were fixed and related to the decisive
events in the history of Israel. Passover commemorated the
Exodus; Weeks (Pentecost) the giving of the Law on Mount Sinai;
and Tabernacles – the wilderness wanderings.

The Day of Atonement

The Day of Atonement is a fast, the only one commanded in the
Mosaic Law; it was held on the tenth day of the month Tizri, five
days before the Feast of Tabernacles. It is the climax of all
ceremonial cleansing, and was the only occasion on which the
High Priest was permitted to enter the Holy of Holies; he was
vested in plain linen vestments, not the rich and colourful as used
on other occasions. Special sacrifices were made for the High Priest
and the other priests; then, for the sins of the people, two he-goats

are brought forward. One is 'for the Lord', the other 'for Azazel' – the choice is made by lot; the first goat is sacrificed to the Lord; the second is brought before the High Priest. He places both his hands on the head of the goat, and confesses over it all the sins of the people of Israel, 'all their transgressions, even all their sins' (Lev. 16.21) thus transferring their sins to the goat (Scholars tell us that in early religions the idea that evil can be transferred, both in the sense of misfortunes and also of moral evil, is common and well attested). But this goat is not properly a sacrifice; it was not offered upon the altar, but driven away into the wilderness. A man – usually a non-Israelite – follows the goat at a distance, to make sure it will be quite successfully lost (and the sins of the nation with it) when the wretched creature falls down a precipice or over some steep rocks.

The Scapegoat

This goat is of course the 'Scapegoat', a familiar animal, we are told by the experts in ancient religions. It will also, no doubt, be familiar to those who know the famous painting by Sir Edward Burne-Jones, entitled 'The Scapegoat in the Wilderness'. One cannot help but sympathize with this wretched animal, driven out into the harsh waterless desert of savage rocks and deep precipices, where the goat will surely perish before long. It limps pathetically towards its fate ... 'Azazel', the scholars also tell us – although thought at one time to refer to one of the 'Fallen Angels' – actually means 'jagged rocks'. The Scapegoat is not a sacrifice to God nor to Azazel; the animal has simply been chosen by God to provide a means of getting rid of the sins of Israel.

With sacrifice, washings and cleansings, all taint of sin is declared removed from the people, and with the end of the Day of Atonement – the great penitential day – the 'Sabbath of Solemn Rest' is ended, and a new beginning has been made for the nation.

O God, the God of Abraham and Isaac,
  of Moses and Elijah, of the Kings and the Prophets,
  open the eyes of your Chosen People
  that they may understand the fullness
  of your love and your truth;
  and so come to see and confess
  that the Lord Jesus is indeed Messiah and Saviour;
  and that so believing,
  they may return from exile;
  and with all your Church
  glorify your Holy Name and further your Kingdom;
  through Jesus Christ the Lord.

Maundy Thursday *(An Alternative Service)*
A Political Trial

Gospel: Luke 23.1–25
'Pilate released the man who had been thrown into prison for insurrection and murder; but Jesus he delivered up to their will.' Luke 23.25

Pressures

It is clear that when there was an official formal meeting between the Roman Governor, Pilate, and the Jewish high priest, Caiaphas, as many Jewish dignitaries and public figures as possible were drummed up to attend; thus giving importance and credibility to the High Priest. His arguments would be backed up with as much noise and fuss from the claque as possible (23.1). Even more important was the widespread knowledge that Pilate was in a difficult and delicate political situation – he had brought the standards of the legions into the Temple, causing riots which had brought sharp condemnation from Rome, and a warning that the Jews and their beliefs must be handled with kid gloves – or else!

So Caiaphas makes his entry at the Praetorium, supported by the whole Sanhedrin (who of course have, as the highest spiritual

Court, condemned Jesus to death for blasphemy – Luke 22.66–71) and a surging crowd of the people.

Accusations

The accusations against Jesus now produced, are those that would strike home to the Roman authorities. He is a seditious person, a resistance leader; and against all loyalty to Caesar, he calls himself a Messianic King. Pilate has had all kinds of strange characters brought up before his judgement seat; he calmly asks Jesus if he really is 'the King of the Jews'? Jesus replies, 'That is what you have said' (23.3). Pilate finds this reply inoffensive, and the demeanour of Jesus – we may assume – dignified and rational. 'This is no criminal,' he says to the accusers (23.4). He is half-way to dismissing the case.

'Is He a Galilean'?

So, the accusers now relate noisily (v. 5) how Jesus has caused unrest in all Judea, and in Galilee, and even as far as Jerusalem. This should stir up Rome! Pilate catches the word 'Galilee'; here is a way out! If Jesus comes from there, he should be handed over to its ruler Herod Antipas – who by good luck is actually right now here in Jerusalem for the observance of the feast. (Not only is this a possible way out for Pilate, his action will go some way towards healing a rift between himself and Herod.) So, to Herod Jesus is sent, under Roman guard, and accompanied by the accusers. Herod certainly turns out to be interested in Jesus – as he was in John Baptist (Luke 9.9) – and he hopes to see some miracle. But Jesus refuses to answer questions, nor gives any 'sign'. The priests renew their accusations, and Herod – disappointed, sets his guards to mock at Jesus, has him dressed up in some gaudy robe, and sends him back to Pilate (one result of this episode is, that Herod and Pilate get back on good terms with each other again).

Release?

Jesus is back again before Pilate; the governor is tired of playing games, he wants nothing more to do with this wretched, difficult, business. He will follow the long-standing custom of marking the Festival by the release of a prisoner. 'This man (Jesus) is not guilty of any of your charges, and certainly does not deserve capital punishment. Herod and I are agreed upon that! Therefore I will have him flogged and let him go.' But the clergy and the people, stirred up by the verdict of the Sanhedrin that Jesus is a blasphemer, continue to demand furiously the death penalty; and the release – instead – of the captured guerrilla leader, Barabbas, who is already in prison, and under sentence of death.

Pilate is conscious-stricken, and tries a third (and final) attempt to set Jesus free; but he is beaten back by the threat of complaints being sent up to the highest level – 'You are not Caesar's friend!' (John 19.12). Pilate cannot afford the blackmail of disloyalty and the all-too-likely ruin of his career, so he hands over Jesus to the crowd, and orders the release of Barabbas. Murderer Barabbas may be, but he saves Pilate's skin.

> *O God, you sent your Son to redeem the world*
> *by his obedience, even to death; give us grace*
> *so to remember his sacrifice, that we may take up*
> *our small crosses and follow him, dying daily*
> *to sin and living to faithfulness, and thus*
> *glorifying your holy Name and your love. Amen.*
> *(P.H.G.)*

Good Friday   10 April 1998   The Cross

'We have not a high priest who is unable to sympathise with our weaknesses, but one who in every respect has been tempted as we are, yet without sinning. Let us then with confidence approach the throne of grace, that we may receive mercy and find grace to help in time of need.'
Hebrews 4.14–16

The Green Hill

> *There is a green hill far away*
> *Without a city wall,*
> *Where the dear Lord was crucified*
> *Who died to save us all.*

That familiar hymn reminds us that the Crucifixion took place at a particular spot on earth; that it took place at a particular time, we are told in the Creed – 'he was crucified under Pontius Pilate',

Roman Procurator of Judea from AD 26–36. But the act accomplished there and then is not to be thought of as confined to one, far-off, small, local time-and-place.

The real value of what happened, and its true significance, is not away amongst the things of time; the Crucifixion is not a slowly fading memory of an event that once happened, and is now no more.

Calvary

The Incarnation is emphasized by the early Christian Fathers of the Church, for they see clearly that the Passion derives all its value from the Person of him who suffered and died upon the Cross. 'The Son of God has become the Son of Man – that the sons of men might become the sons of God' said St Athanasius.

What was to be seen on Calvary was a divine Act, which however immersed and displayed in the outward, brutal and sordid circumstances in which it took place, has its origins and cause in the Mind and Will of the Eternal God, Creator of all things. A divine – yet no less a truly human – act, embraced by the human mind of Jesus, accepted and freely chosen, and humanly carried out.

> 'Lo, I come to do thy will, O God . . . a body hast thou prepared for me'
>
> (Hebrews 10.5–7)

A Free Offering

No necessity or compulsion blurred the perfectly free acceptance and offering of Calvary. What was done *to* the God-Man, must not be confused with what was done *by* him. 'I lay down my life that I may take it again. No one takes it from me, but I lay it down of my own accord . . .' (John 10.17).

It is a travesty if we envisage an angry Father condemning an innocent and unwilling Son, to the death of the Cross. Jesus was born and took our nature so that he might accomplish the purpose that was no less his than that of the Father. The Agony in the Garden reveals not a conflict between the divine and the human wills, but the tension that is natural, between the sensitive and human soul of Jesus and his higher, rational mind . . . 'The spirit is willing, but the flesh is weak' (Matthew 26.41). However courageous a man, confronted with crisis and danger, there is a natural, sensible repugnance and fear from whatever evil threatens – but the steadfast resolve to endure, rather than lose integrity or fail the purpose set before him – that is what carried him through.

Sacrifice

What Christ did was to offer himself, wholly and entirely, as a sacrifice expressive of the worship, praise, honour, thanksgiving, love, obedience and service, that man owes to his Creator and Lord.

Because Christ is acting as High Priest and representative of humanity – not only as created but also as our humanity actually *is* – sinful and separated from God, so his sacrifice becomes one of propitiation, reparation, intercession, atonement and reconciliation. Because it was all for God, a perfect and complete rendering of all that humanity owed to him, it was all for humanity. The Resurrection is the sign that the Sacrifice has been accepted on high, and of the promise that its effects are within the reach of all of humanity who shall desire to receive them.

And both act and effects are due to the fact that it was not 'a man' who suffered and died upon the Cross, but the God-Man, whose divinity gives an infinite value both to the act itself and to its effects, which enable us to do what we had no power to do of ourselves.

In Christ

The full meaning of the Cross, on which hung the human body of Jesus, is not really disclosed, until what he began there, and consummated in the fullest manner, is seen to be carried on in his mystical Body, the Church. The whole of St Paul's teaching, for instance, centres round the truth which he constantly repeats, that to be a Christian is to be 'in Christ'.

So, he can say, 'I live, yet not I' – that is, the I that I was – 'but Christ lives in me,' and, 'I help to complete, in my poor human flesh, the full tale of Christ's afflictions still to be endured, for the sake of his Body which is the Church' (Col. 1.24). St Augustine writes, 'Christ continues still to suffer in his members, that is, in us . . . The full measure of the Passion will not be complete until the end of the world.'

Christ our Lord's Passion does indeed go on, in the members of his Body upon earth, not only by sharing in the eucharistic offering, but also in all sacrifices they make, and all the sufferings they endure. So, what Christ did for humanity is done in – and by – humanity itself, united to its Head.

Good Friday *Second Sermon* The Title Over the Cross

'Pilate wrote an inscription to be fastened to the cross; it read "Jesus of Nazareth, King of the Jews".' John 19.19 or 'Through him God chose to reconcile the whole universe to himself, making peace through the shedding of his blood upon the Cross.' Colossians 1.20

Titles for Jesus
In our Scriptures we find Jesus referred to in various ways, and given various titles. Some references describe our Lord's work in general terms; others draw our attention to certain aspects of his nature, and to particular happenings in his life. For instance, at Christmas we often hear the words of the prophet Isaiah, calling the Messiah to come 'The Prince of Peace'. On the other hand, at Ascension tide, we hear St Paul telling of Jesus 'leading captivity captive'. On Good Friday we find some titles for Jesus specially fitting: in Isaiah, the prophet's words about 'The Suffering Servant', or in St John's gospel 'The Lamb of God'; a symbol of sacrifice, reminding us of Christ's sacrifice of himself, upon the Cross.

The Roman Titles
Two titles of Jesus are specially appropriate today, because they were first used upon Good Friday. One came from an unknown centurion in the Roman army; the other from the Roman governor, Pilate.

The centurion, having watched Jesus die upon the cross, was greatly moved by the Lord's death, very different no doubt from the deaths of criminals and rebels; so much so, that the centurion describes Jesus as 'Truly, this man was a son of God,' a striking comment on the nobility that shone through the agony and pain. Pilate's inscription was officially ordered to be painted on a board, taken to Calvary, and nailed above our Lord's head. It read, 'Jesus of Nazareth King of the Jews,' and is recorded by John, Matthew and Mark in slightly varying forms.

Pilate's Motives
Why did Pilate have this inscription set up, which so greatly angered the Jewish authorities that they appealed to him to alter the wording?

We may well think that Pilate took this opportunity to have revenge for the way in which his authority had been undermined by threats to report him to Rome (John 19.12 – 'If you let this man go , you are not Caesar's friend!') and his attempts to save Jesus frustrated (Matthew 27.24 – 'When Pilate saw that he could prevail nothing . . . he took water and washed his hands, saying, "My hands are clean of this man's blood; see to that yourselves!"') To show his anger and his contempt he picked his words carefully, in particular knowing that the title 'King of the Jews' would be extremely infuriating both to the religious authorities and to the anti-Roman resistance groups.

Truth – by Accident
Whatever his motives for writing what he did write about Jesus, Pilate displayed a great truth – Jesus *is* the King of the Jews; since the days of Pilate the Hebrew people have produced a wonderful number of great men – and women – in science, music, the arts, in commerce and business, but not one has influenced the world as Jesus Christ has done.

As for the centurion's recognition of Jesus as 'Son of God', we may recognize his interpretation of all excellence and heroic achievement as manifestations of the Divine. We should note that Jesus used the direct, intimate Aramaic 'Abba' for 'Father', as in the original version of the Lord's Prayer, in place of the usual Jewish sign of respect – 'my father'. Jesus' unique revelation of the Father springs directly from the knowledge that God is *his* Father. This relationship is profoundly important not only for the nature of Christ, but also for the nature of the Church; for God is Father of the disciples because he is the Father of Jesus. Jesus was bringing humanity into a family which transcended the limits of blood relationship, because he was claiming them as *his* brethren (Matt. 25.40).

The Spread of Christ's Kingdom
Many of the world's great kings spread their dominions widely; sometimes by war, sometimes by diplomacy. Their motives were often pride or greed. Not for motives like theirs, nor in ways like theirs, Jesus also seeks to spread his kingdom. His methods are not violent, his motive is not self-glory, but love for humanity. Many things in this life on earth exemplify this love, but nothing more than what we remember on Good Friday – his death for us on the Cross, which proclaims to the world his love for all who dwell in it.

Easter Day   12 April 1998   The Glorious Event

'On the first day of the week, at early dawn, the women went to the tomb, taking the spices which they had prepared. And they found the stone rolled away from the tomb, but when they went in they did not find the body. While they were perplexed two men stood by them in dazzling apparel, and said to them, "Why do you seek the living among the dead? He is not here but has risen".' Luke 24.1–6 or 'Christ has been raised from the dead, the first fruits of those who have fallen asleep. For as in Adam all die, so also in Christ shall all be made alive.' 1 Cor. 15, 20–22

The Light of Christ
Today we celebrate the greatest and most glorious event of our Christian faith, the raising to new life of our Lord Jesus Christ. Deserted by his disciples, betrayed, arrested and interrogated, beaten and tortured, he died the death of a common criminal; and by all human reckoning, he and his story and his followers should have faded away into the dark limbs of time forgotten.

Then Victory
Instead, what a change! What an unexpected triumph! What a stunning reversal of a lost battle and a lost cause!

No wonder the disciples found the tidings difficult to believe, when the women brought their story. No wonder they were afraid, as St Mark tells us; gradually the truth began to dawn upon them.

Like the breaking of a soft and beautiful Spring dawn, the light increases and grows and spreads until finally it fills the whole sky. So it was with them; they heard the story of the Emmaus road, then the Lord himself stood amongst them, and said 'Peace be with you!' (Luke 24.13–36). A new light shone, and in that light they saw their surroundings, their companions, and finally themselves, revealed, and fresh, and new like the first light of God's First Day.

The Light of Christ
Indeed light is a favourite symbol of the new life of the Risen Christ, that new life to which we are all called. Christ himself said: 'I am the Light of the world', and Christians have delighted to expound this theme down the ages from the earliest times, in preaching and verse, in art and in the liturgy and life of the Church itself.

The Vigil
In this church (*or*, in many churches) ancient custom is followed, and the Resurrection is symbolized by the blessing of new fire in the darkened church followed by the lighting of a special large candle – the 'Paschal Candle' – which is taken to a place of honour in the sight of the assembled congregation. It becomes the focus of the 'Easter Vigil Service', in which scripture is read, psalms and hymns sung, prayers made, expounding the message of God's salvation offered to all humanity down the ages, and above all is the saving Sacrifice on the Cross.

'Pass on the Light'
The most dramatic moment of the Vigil is surely when the little candles, held by the people, are lit from the Easter Candle. From one to another the light spreads as each passes to his or her neighbour the flickering flame; the lights divide and spread until the whole church is a mass of small bright flames. In that light we begin to see our neighbours and companions, and finally ourselves – lit up by Christ's new light as our lives should be by his new life.

And the point is, that the Light of Christ, like the flame of the little candle, only reaches us by the assistance of other people, who pass on their light. Our job is to pass it on again. Christianity is caught, not taught, as the old saying has it.

94

Undivided

Nor is our light diminished by passing it on; we lose nothing ourselves, our light continues as strong and bright as ever it was. What a gift, that we can pass it on, give it away, and still retain it ourselves! 'How far that little candle throws his beams! So shines a good deed in a naughty world' . . . said Shakespeare, echoing, as it were, that much greater Poet and Artist, our Lord himself, who told us, 'You are the light of the world' (Matt. 5.14), and 'Let your light so shine before men, that they may see your good works and give glory to your Father in heaven' (Matt. 5.16). We are to be light-givers, not huddling together and hiding our flame.

Our Task

Here then is our Easter task: the torch is handed on to us, we are to hand it on to others. The light we receive from Christ is to be shared. However much we may devote ourselves to worship, to our religion, however firmly we hold our faith – unless we are doing our best to share with others, that worship, that faith, is largely useless.

This is the message of the Easter gospel; St Matthew has, 'Do not be afraid. Go and take word . . .' St Mark, 'Go, and give this message . . .' St Luke, 'Preach to all nations . . .' St John, 'Go, and tell . . .' Let us make a firm resolve, as we celebrate the wonder and the joy and the glory of Easter, a resolve to share the Risen Life and the New Light.

Easter Day   *Second Sermon*   **The Risen Christ**

'I delivered to you as of first importance what I also received – that Christ died for our sins in accordance with the scriptures, that he was buried, that he was raised on the third day in accordance with the scriptures, and that he appeared to Cephas, then to the twelve.'
1 Corinthians 15.1–5

The Resurrection is True!

St Paul bluntly tells his flock at Corinth that 'if Christ has not been raised then is our preaching in vain and your faith is in vain'. Less than thirty years after the Crucifixion, he has to remind them of the historical facts about the Resurrection. He quotes the tradition which he received from those in Christ before him – Christ had died according to the Scriptures, and was buried. He had been raised on the third day, according to the Scriptures. He had appeared to Peter, then to the Twelve; then to about five hundred Christians, to James, to the Apostles, and last of all, to Paul himself.

These facts are so important that he lists them out at length.

Not a Vision . . .
Let us notice particularly that Paul does not begin by quoting his *own* experiences. The Risen Lord had indeed appeared to him (1 Cor. 15.8) but St Paul does not start from there. Instead, he quotes tradition which can be checked and confirmed by others. The implication therefore is, that St Paul's experience of the Risen Christ was not a private mystical vision, like the one he describes in his second letter to the Corinthians (12.1–5). No, it was like the experiences of the others, who believed that Christ *was* risen *because* they had seen him.

. . . but Fact
So, St Paul provides early and valuable evidence that Jesus *had* appeared to his followers three days after his crucifixion; and that it was on the basis of *those* appearances that they preached his resurrection from the dead.

The Empty Tomb
St Mark, the earliest gospel writer, speaks of the women at the empty tomb, but does not record appearances of Christ. (The scholars generally agree that the last part of the last chapter of St Mark is not part of the original.) On the other hand, the tradition of appearances quoted by St Paul, certainly implies that the body was not in the tomb. The women were not at first believed, according to St Luke; and there were rumours that Jesus' own followers had stolen the body (as St Matthew tells us). The very weakness of the evidence suggests strongly its historical probability.

Hallucinations?
Might not the appearances reported of Jesus, have been hallucinations, or some kind of hysterical fantasy?

An important point in this connection must be the undoubted fact that the disciples were not expecting the resurrection (Mark 9.32). It is therefore in the highest degree unlikely that they made 'a mental projection' of their own wishful thinking, and thus 'saw' Jesus. We are plainly told in Matthew and John that some doubted the Resurrection – the disciples were not a group of credulous and uncritical simpletons. Rather, they were wrestling with events and trying to understand them – full of wonder and fear.

A 'Happy Ending'?
There is no hint, even, that they have invented a 'resurrection' as a 'happy ending' to a tragic story of the martyred hero, beloved teacher and miracle worker. From the start what they proclaim is not a tragic hero, but the Cross and Resurrection of Christ; and on the Cross and Resurrection is founded the earliest Christian witness.

It is on the basis of two things – the empty tomb and the witness of his closest friends – that the followers of Jesus came to understand that God had raised him from the dead. But these two things – on their own – were insufficient to lead the disciples to believe that Jesus *was* risen; it was rather through their readings of Scripture and their communion with the Risen Lord, that they came to realize that he had indeed been raised 'according to the Scriptures'. Here is the point of the Emmaus event.

History – and Power
There is no way in which History can 'prove' the resurrection truth. History can only point us in the right direction, and show us that the Christian claims are not without foundation. But to know the power of Christ's Resurrection, we need more than history, we need faith as well. And that faith can only be faith in the Living God, who 'kills and makes alive, who brings down to the grave and brings up again'. It is this God who gave his Son for our sins, and raised him for our justification.

The Second Sunday of Easter 19 April 1998 The Gladness of the Resurrection
'The disciples were glad when they saw the Lord.' John 20.20

Joy!

How joyful were the disciples when Jesus appeared in the midst of their little company – doors locked for fear of some raid upon their meeting, yet here he was! The extreme dejection of the previous days was swept away, into the joy of knowing that the Master was alive.

Notice that: Three times in the reading for today, the Lord says 'Peace be with you!' This is not some polite form of welcome or greeting. It is an offer of grace, of that peace of which he spoke at the Last Supper: 'Peace I leave with you; my peace I give to you; not as the world gives do I give to you' (John 14.27). Three times in today's reading he speaks the words to his disciples; first when they were hidden away behind locked doors and frightened; then again when they had recognized him by his wounded hands and side, and were glad to know it was indeed the Lord. With that knowledge strengthening them, Jesus disperses their fear, and by his presence imparts a deep-down calmness of spirit, so that they are able to receive his commission to go forth, and the gift of the Holy Spirit, together with the power of absolving or retaining sin.

Belief

Then with Thomas, later, known as 'The Twin', who refuses to believe without incontrovertible and tangible evidence, Jesus offers peace; and receives from Thomas the wonderful and significant confession of faith – 'My Lord and my God!' In Jesus, they had seen and known as much of God as humanity is capable of knowing in this world; yet to all the followers of Christ he gives his blessing. Faith is the response that must be given to Christ's offer of peace. Here is the open door to peace, peace of the soul; the antidote to tension, restlessness, confusion as to the meaning of life, and the insecurity which brings unhappiness. Finally, at the end of the chapter, John sums up the whole intention of the book: 'Written that you may believe that Jesus is the Christ, the Son of God, and that believing you may have life in his name' (20.30).

The Task

How marvellous, the cessation of fear, the security of knowing that all was well once again, and Jesus was once more there and in control. The fragments could be picked up, the great task could recommence, and the nightmare of their apostasy be forgiven and forgotten. But no; that fragile sense of security is shattered by the words of the Lord himself:

'As the Father has sent me, even so send I you!' (20.v.21)

A few minutes before, it had been a case of waiting for a fateful knocking on the door, that would mean arrest, and probably death at the hands of the authorities. Now, however, it was the disciples who were the ones who would knock, knock loudly and insistently on the doors of the world, with the message of the Gospel that stemmed directly from the Cross and the Resurrection.

> Eternal Giver of love and life,
> your Son Jesus Christ our Lord,
> has sent us into all the world
> to proclaim the gospel of the Kingdom.
> Confirm us in this mission,
> and help us to live the good news we bring,
> through Jesus Christ our Lord.
> – Patterns for Worship

Second Sunday of Easter   *Second Sermon*
Walking Home
'That same day two of them were on their way to a village called Emmaus, which lay about seven miles from Jerusalem; and they were talking together about all these happenings.' Luke 24.13

A Sad Conversation
On Easter evening two of our Lord's followers were walking home together from Jerusalem to the village of Emmaus. On their walk they were – very naturally – discussing the events which had just taken place in Jerusalem and had – so sadly – ended with the death of Jesus. The Lord's death was probably the reason they were leaving the city; there was no reason for them to stay now their Master was dead. They had heard some rumour that he had

actually been seen alive by some women the morning after, but though companions had visited the tomb and found it empty, there was no sight of Christ, dead or alive.

The Other Traveller

Then another walker overtook them and joined in their conversation. He explained to them the true significance of the death of Jesus, and his words changed their mood from one of despair, to a measure of renewed faith and hope. It was not until he shared a meal with them at Emmaus that they recognized him as Jesus, and knew that he had really risen from the dead.

So, as soon as Jesus left them, they did not lose a minute – late though it must have been by now – in hurrying back to Jerusalem with their good news. Doubtless they were taken aback to be greeted by their friends with the very same good news they had walked so far to bring – 'The Lord has risen indeed!'

Talking about Jesus

The Gospel does not tell us why Jesus selected these two disciples from a wide choice of so many despondent followers. It is significant, however, that when he joined them on the road they were deep in conversation about him, his life and his death.

Everyone is so busy today, are we not? We constantly grumble about the hurry and bustle of modern life, and how difficult it is to fit in all they have to do. We believe that there is no time in our lives for some things which ought not to be left out of anyone's life; and one of these things is surely our relationship with Jesus.

Busy People – Joyful People

What took place on the road from Jerusalem to Emmaus indicates that Jesus is most likely to reveal himself to those who think of him often, and seek him regularly. We must make time in our hearts and lives for Jesus to come to us and take the rightful place in our hearts. What a joyful return journey those two people from Emmaus must have had, and how they must have explained what had taken place to their friends and neighbours: eagerly and happily and all because they were thinking and talking about Jesus.

The Joy that Jesus brings . . .

The visit of Jesus brought joy into their hearts. He came to them with that object in mind, and he has the same purpose for each of us. There are inevitably moments in everybody's life when sorrow is uppermost; but the followers of Jesus should have joy and thanksgiving in their hearts as much as possible.

Whatever the ups and downs in our own life, we have so much to rejoice in, at the Resurrection of Christ, and all that it means to us and to all the world. Let the words of Jesus and the teaching of the gospel be in our hearts and minds always.

> *God of our salvation,*
> *you have restored us to life,*
> *and brought us back into your love,*
> *by the triumphant death*
> *and resurrection of Jesus.*
> *Strengthen our faith*
> *as we go to live and work*
> *in the power of your Spirit,*
> *to your praise and glory.*
> *(Patterns for Worship 52.17 adapted)*

Third Sunday of Easter   26 April 1998
Recognition
'It is the Lord!' John 21.7

Starting a New Life?
Seven of the remaining eleven disciples had gathered together, in their own well-known surroundings at the lakeside. Three of them – Peter, James and John – were fishermen; Thomas and Nathanael were in the same occupation, for we do know that Zebedee ran a fishing business. We know nothing of the identity of the other two. Why had they come together? Were they sad and disappointed men who had lost their hopes for the future, and were disillusioned now their Leader had gone? There is almost an eagerness in their response to Peter's 'I am going fishing', which is practically an invitation to restart their old lives. 'We will go with you' has a ring of acceptance of the situation; back to the old jobs. The visions and dreams have gone – beautiful but shattered.

Disappointment

Having decided to take up again their old calling, the seven set to work with a will. Alas, disappointment is their lot. They toiled all night, but their nets were empty. Did this fruitless effort remind them of another night of effort unrewarded (described in Luke 5 – 'We toiled all night and took nothing!')?

Some see in this incident an illustration of what we may expect when we try to toil on alone. Too many of us like to feel that what we accomplish, we do in our own power – and so, when unexpected credit is gained, it is by our own unaided efforts. We need always to put our trust in the hands of Jesus and follow what he may put into our minds.

With Christ

It was the dawning of the day, and in the dim silvery light an unrecognized figure called to the boat from the shore: 'Have you lads caught any fish?' A casual, friendly enquiry. When the answer was 'No!' – a grumpy tired-out response – the speaker gave instructions as to where the net should be re-cast. (We are told by tourists who have visited this very place, that in certain lights, the fish can be far more clearly seen by a person on the shore, than by the fishermen in their boat.) Although the person giving directions was not as yet recognized, the catch was amazing.

Recognition

The first to recognize the man on the shore as Christ, was his Beloved Disciple – John. 'It is the Lord!' This is a cry from the heart uttered by countless Christians down the ages, who come to recognize the Saviour's presence and guidance, and acknowledge him with reverent faith.

There are many of us by whom Jesus is unrecognized today. Some do not recognize his aid through unbelief; their lack of vision and belief is a barrier to deeper knowledge of him. Yet, the time may come when he *is* known; then the cry of faith will go up – 'It is the Lord!'

After Breakfast

'When they had finished breakfast', the evangelist tells us, Christ repeats to Peter his question: 'Do you love me?' – 'Do you love me?' The scholars tell us that here is the Lord's way of wiping out the three times that Peter denied his Lord; now Peter, on the ground of his love, is installed as shepherd. Peter, moreover, will not only be a pastor, he will be a martyr; and glorify God by the obedience and faith shown in his death. It may well be that verse 18 is proof that Peter had already suffered martyrdom by crucifixion.

> Jesus, Son of God, you entrusted your sheep to
> Peter, because of his love for you; deliver your
> Church from all evil and keep her in peace. May
> she glow with love, be strong in hope, and shine
> with holiness; for your Name's sake. Amen.
>
> *(Ancient Prayer)*

Third Sunday of Easter   *Second Sermon*
Resurrection

'Jesus cried with a loud voice, "Lazarus, come out". The dead man came out, his hands and feet bound with bandages, and his face wrapped with a cloth.' John 11,43,44

A Strange Story

The story of the raising to life by Jesus of the brother of Mary and Martha is a strange story to our modern ears. Lazarus had not stopped breathing just that minute. He had been dead for four long days; and Martha's blunt words imply that some decomposition had actually begun, as indeed it would in the fierce heat of Palestine. Some of the early artists when depicting this miracle, show the bystanders holding their noses or putting a cloth across their faces.

Miracle

Such homely and down-to-earth touches are a hall-mark of the gospel according to St John. He is the evangelist above all to whom we look for details about times and places, names and dates. He tells us, for example, that Jesus loved Mary and Martha, and their brothers; the Lord knew them well, and doubtless valued the times of peace and quiet and comfort that visits to their household gave to him. In the midst of the noise and demands of life on the dusty roads, how great a relief to encounter something of a respite, a time to draw on the power and grace of his Father, and the gentle service and care of the family. With this very detailed information and evidence goes also the extraordinary conviction that what Jesus did exceeded the bounds of possibility. We are face-to-face with the living power of Jesus, the Word of God.

The Event
Martha, meeting Jesus, is even now not without hope; she quotes the belief of Pharisaic Judaism, that the dead – or at least the righteous dead – will rise again at the Last Day. Jesus tells her that he is the Resurrection and the life: it is the Son of God who has life in himself, and gives life to the world; and Martha makes her statement of faith – Jesus is the Christ, the Son of God, the Saviour.

The story moves on; Mary joins the entourage, falling at the feet of Jesus and weeping, which moves him greatly – so much that he too is in tears. Then at the grave, the tomb which has been constructed already, is removed; Jesus prays to the Father, then calls in a loud voice, 'Lazarus, come forth.' And the man does so, still wrapped in the linen strips which had been bound about his body.

A Sign
An astonishing miracle. But also a 'sign', that is to say, a proof of the power and person of Jesus. This sign is to be completed, and fully clarified, by his own resurrection. As Lazarus was the same person who died and then was raised to life, so Jesus, who rose from death to life, is the same Christ who was crucified. The resurrection is a triumph over death.

Of two things only can we be sure and certain: we live; and we must die. The Saviour too was a man who lived and died – and then rose from the dead to prove that a life such as his, could indeed conquer death.

The Fourth Sunday of Easter   3 May 1998
The Good Shepherd
'My sheep hear my voice, and I know them, and they follow me; and I give them eternal life, and no one shall snatch them out of my hand.' John 10.28 or 'The Lord is my shepherd, I shall not want.' Ps 23.1

A Quarrel in the Cold (John 10.22–30)

In rough weather, especially cold and windy days, there were several places in Jerusalem where philosophers and teachers could collect their pupils or adherents, and continue with instructions and discussions. 'Solomon's Portico' seems to have been on the eastern side of the Temple; it is mentioned in the Book of Acts as where a striking healing took place, of a lame man by Peter and John (3.1–10). Such places were also used as courts of law; and the incident today seems to suggest a law-court, with the Jews surrounding Jesus like a meeting of the Sanhedrin, or even an army encircling a besieged city.

Challenge

The challenge is, for Jesus plainly to declare himself the Messiah. This he refuses to do on the grounds of the opposition and unbelief of his judges; but he says that his works give an answer – 'bear witness to me'; and he adds 'I told you and you do not believe, because you do not belong to my sheep.' No matter how openly Jesus speaks, those who are not his sheep will not believe him; no matter how obscurely he speaks, those who are his sheep, whether Gentiles or Jews, will understand. Out of the mutual understanding comes the gift of eternal life, and the assurance that 'no one shall snatch them out' of Christ's hand (v. 28).

Authority

This authority, and this security, are the authority and security of God himself; say 'Jesus' and you have said 'God'; 'I and the Father are one.' This enrages the Jewish crowd, and they threaten to stone the Lord. But he whom God has commissioned and sanctified cannot be accused of blasphemy when he asserts a relationship with God, for which God himself is responsible.

Fourth Sunday of Easter   *Second Sermon*
Witnesses

'You are witnesses of these things; and behold, I send the promise of my Father upon you.' Luke 24.48,49

Recognition

The Lord Christ, when he appeared to his disciples, was not always recognized. Peter, on that post-resurrection fishing trip, could not recognize the voice he heard, calling from the shore. Mary Magdalen, weeping in the garden, thought he was the gardener, until she heard him say her name. The two disciples who walked with him to Emmaus, talking all the way, did not recognize him until the breaking of the bread. Today's account of Jesus' appearance, just after those two had told the others, caused startling and fright even when he spoke. They thought he was a ghost, until he showed them his hands and his feet and urged them to touch him – 'A spirit has not flesh and bones, as you see that I have!'

Joy and Wonder

They continued uncertain, even if full of joy and wonder, until he went to the extent of asking for food, and actually eating some cooked fish, before them. Then he 'opened their minds', and they were able to understand that all was for the best, and that the Scriptures had given a true and accurate prophecy of what was to happen and would indeed be fulfilled (v. 44).

The summary of the Gospel is, that Christ was destined to suffer and rise again, and in consequence of this, repentance and forgiveness of sins are to be proclaimed universally. The preaching of this world-wide message is to be given in Christ's Name, and the apostles are commissioned as witnesses, and will be given the Spirit as power from on high. As in the case of the Gospel itself, so the starting-point for the Church's mission, in the power of the Spirit, will be Jerusalem, where they are to stay until they are 'clothed with power from on high'.

Our Task

Today, as in the time of the apostles, Christ relies on the witness of his disciples for the spread of his rule over the hearts and lives of humanity. We should be ready to count on the action of the Holy Spirit in the hearts of others, as well as in ourselves. The Holy Spirit works in unison with our efforts; we are not alone. We should therefore speak out plainly and with courage about our faith, without exaggeration – but also without concealment. Today, in our own times, as in the time of the Apostles, Christ relies on the witness of us – his disciples – for the spread of his rule over the hearts and lives of humanity.

Lord God,
thank you for the unity you give us in your presence:
draw your Church together
into one great company of disciples,
together following our Lord Jesus Christ
into every walk of life,
together serving him in his mission to the world,
and together witnessing to his love
on every continent and island,
in the power of your Spirit,
to your praise and glory.

(Patterns for Worship 52.29)

The Fifth Sunday of Easter   10 May 1998
Unity

'Behold, the dwelling of God is with men. He will dwell with them, and they shall be his people.' Rev. 21.3 or 'A new commandment I give to you, that you love one another; even as I have loved you, that you also love one another.' John 13.34

All one in Christ

The search for unity amongst Christians has abandoned the attempts to 'convert', and today we are not trying to shake others from their creeds, but trying to listen to what God is saying to us through these others. This was the conclusion forced upon Peter when he saw that the Holy Spirit was given to Cornelius and to his household. Peter recognized – and it had been a hard struggle – that all believers, whether Jews or Gentiles, and whatever their nationality or colour, are united in Christ. Each is given particular gifts, from God, and each, with their gifts, is to serve the Church and the world on equal terms. It took time and a special revelation to convince Peter of this!

Diversity

'You who were once far off have been brought near in the blood of Christ', says St Paul (Eph. 2.13). We must understand that unity is not diminished nor impaired by diversity; and much has happened in every denomination to bring back the emphasis upon participation by the whole people of God, the Body of Christ, week by week, in the worship of the Church. We have begun to understand that we are all celebrants together, not watchers of something done for us. We all share in the Priesthood of God's People, as we 'proclaim the Lord's death till he come', and all eat the Bread of Life and drink the Cup of the Lord.

Love above All

If we are indeed the People of God, we are to show that which is the great principle of God, namely, love. We are born to love, to show love to others, to receive love ourselves. Jesus our Saviour shows us the power of love, the love we should have for one another. When Judas had left the Supper, on that last evening together, Jesus gave us his last words; 'A new commandment I give to you, that you love one another; even as I have loved you, you also must love one another. By this love you have for one another, everyone will know that you are my disciples' (John 13.34,35).

Life

It may take us all our lifetime and more to learn what this means, and to carry it out; but here we have the meaning of life. And we shall understand the description of the new world, given by St John in his Revelation; the holy city where God is ever-present with his people; no tears, no death, no pain any more, for the world of the past has gone, and all things are new.

Fifth Sunday of Easter   *Second Sermon*
Triumph

'O sing to the Lord a new song, for he has done marvellous deeds! He has revealed to the nations his saving power.' Ps. 98

Daniel and the Lions
The scholars suggest that the Book of Daniel was written – or compiled, rather, as it is a collection of stories of different dates – during difficult times for the Jewish nation, as encouragement for the present and hope for the future. The figure of Daniel seems to be that of a legendary hero, like the other legendary 'righteous man' Job, or the example of righteousness from ancient days, Noah.

Encouragement
Stories of faithfulness to duty, of great courage, and of successful resistance to tyrants, can do much to encourage those who hear them, then as now. Most of us take pleasure in stories and TV series, about 'Occupied Europe' and the bravery of Resistance men and women against Nazi tyranny.

And there are tyrannical dictators in too many countries today; unlike King Nebuchadnezzar they may not set up golden images, but they enforce brutal regimes or persecute religion, as well as depriving their people of freedom and justice.

Trust in God
In these countries and in others, there are Christians who need help and encouragement in the face of oppression and persecution. We should do all we can to work and pray for them, put pressure on our own Government to impose sanctions in trade or monetary rulings, these 'prisoners of conscience' and all who are oppressed and under threat of life, freedom and liberty.

Prayer and trust in God can be great supports, and the stories of Daniel and his adventures can help by reminding us all of our duty to be faithful to God, as well as pointing to the strength that men and women, down the ages, have found in putting their trust in him.

Bravery
We may remember – or be reminded of – the brave followers of Jesus who took it upon themselves to do all they could for their Lord, after the crucifixion. Joseph of Arimathea took courage and went to Pilate and begged the body of the Lord; the women – Mary Magdalene, Mary the mother of James, and Salome – bought spices to anoint the body. It was these who were granted the first knowledge of the amazing story of the Lord's Resurrection; and

rightly, their story is here in our hands in the Bible, two thousand years later, and we venerate them still.

The Sixth Sunday of Easter   17 May 1998
The Promise of the Spirit

'The Counsellor, the Holy Spirit, whom the Father will send in my name, he will teach you all things, and bring to your remembrance all that I have said to you.' John 14.26

The Guide

In today's Gospel, we hear Christ telling his disciples that although he himself will leave them, the Counsellor, the Holy Spirit, will be sent by the Father in Christ's name to teach them all that they will need to know, and will bring to their remembrance all that Christ himself had said to them. What is most important is, the love between the Lord and his followers; if this is maintained, all will be well – The Father will love them, and with Jesus will come and make their home with their disciples.

We are at our best when we love, because love is a purifying and uniting force. True love, in other words, makes for the perfecting of the individual soul.

The Spirit of Love

All true love results from the coming of the Holy Spirit, the Spirit of Love. And the power of the Spirit does not cease at the limits of the human heart, within a human being. No, it radiates outwards; it transforms our everyday activities and our ordinary human relationships, enriching them by his presence.

The presence of the Holy Spirit enables us not only to face up to the harsh realities of life, those bonds that press upon us all the time, but also to understand their true worth and purpose.

The Spirit of Truth

All true love results from the coming of the Holy Spirit, the Spirit of Love. And the power of the Spirit does not cease at the limits of the human heart, within a human being. No, it radiates outwards; it transforms our everyday activities and our ordinary human relationships, enriching them by his presence.

The presence of the Holy Spirit enables us not only to face up to the harsh realities of life, those bonds that press upon us all the time, but also to understand their true worth and purpose.

The Spirit of Truth

We are also told that the Spirit is the Spirit of Truth.

It is the Spirit that gives life – true life – that life of which Christ so often spoke. Worldly lives have been described as looking at things and seeing them, but only seeing their market value. The spiritually minded looks also, but sees the eternal values.

'Two men looked into a pool – one saw mud, the other stars . . .'

Let not your Hearts be Troubled

Christ said, 'Peace I leave with you; my peace I give to you; not as the world gives do I give to you. Let not your hearts be troubled, neither let them be afraid . . . I go away and I will come to you.' The world was not to see him, but his disciples were to see him. We, like the disciples, can see Christ, because we have with us that Spirit who inspires us with the vision of faith.

Sixth Sunday of Easter *Second Sermon*
'Lo, I am with you always' (*Matt. 28.20*)

'We do not walk alone' – Many people would disagree, perhaps strongly. A loved one has died – parent, husband, wife, close friend; now they are alone. But the words of Jesus affirms that loneliness may be God's opportunity.

No one can walk alone once they realize their unity with other members of the human race. There is a very memorable Bible phrase 'bound in the bundle of life' or, 'bound in the bundle of living, in the care of the Lord' (1 Samuel 25.19).

We are all bound in together, and Jesus is with us. To truly 'join the human race' requires an act of will, a deep interest in the concerns of others – and a belief in the grace of God.

Jesus our Friend

We need never walk alone, for the Lord's own words tell us that we have God with us, for our friend. Jesus came to create community and to call us into community. That community is the dynamic, transforming community of God's love. For untold numbers of people the striking verses from St Matthew's last chapter 'Behold, he is going before you to Galilee; there you will see him. Lo, I have told you!' (from the angel) and, 'Lo, I am with you always, to the close of the age!' (from Jesus himself).

That wonderful mystic of our own time, Simone Weil (1909–43) was led to direct experience of God, and singularly complete devotion to Christ, although in fact she never received baptism. In one of her books she tells us how 'Jesus himself came down and took possession of me . . . I felt in the midst of my suffering the presence of love, like that which one can read in the smile of a beloved face.'

Let us remember Christ's own words and affirmation – 'Lo, I am with you always' – Matt. 28.20.

The Church

We experience God's friendship in Christ, within the community of friends that we call the Church. In this community we can be given release from the prison of the moment, and from the jail of our solitariness, and enter into the unbroken 'Communion of Saints'. Let us be clear that 'Saints' means the members of God's family, not images in stained glass of people of long ago, nor stuffy and sometimes starchy 'good' people.

In the New Testament a saint is a Christian on the road to Christ-like-ness. On the road, walking along the same dusty track that the Lord himself knew well. And with us as we go along, is indeed Christ, Christ beside us, Christ with us always.

Ascension Day 21 May 1998 Ascension Joy

'He led them out as far as Bethany, and blessed them with uplifted hands; and in the act of blessing he parted from them. And they returned to Jerusalem with great joy, and spent all their time in the Temple praising God.' Luke 24.50–53

Joy!

A special feature of the event we call 'The Ascension', is the joy that filled the hearts of the disciples when Christ withdrew from them. They seem to be fully aware that they would no longer see him 'in the flesh', and departures usually involve sadness, but this brought great joy. 'With great joy, though this Jesus, from whom all their joy was sprung, was departed out of their sight. With joy, because that Jesus had claimed his right as the Christ, because he had shown that he had come from a Father, and had done the will of that Father. With joy, because Death and Hell were shown to be the Father's enemies, and they had been vanquished. With joy, because being delivered from these enemies, they could serve God without fear, in holiness and righteousness all the days of their life.

Open!

Christ's ministry had been in public; his crucifixion had been all too public; his burial had been public also. The resurrection had been public – witnessed by the guards at the tomb, though they fled in terror. The Lord appeared in public several times after his resurrection – for instance at the lakeside. Is it not natural therefore, that the Ascension should take place in broad daylight. The group which he led out to the Ascension Hill was not composed merely of the Eleven (see Luke 24.33) – there was a good number of disciples. St Paul tells us that on one occasion Christ 'appeared to over five hundred brethren at once', and he says that most of them were alive at the time he wrote (1 Cor. 15.6). We may reasonably suppose that a large number actually witnessed the Ascension.

King!

When we say in the Te Deum 'You, Christ are the King of glory!' we are declaring our faith that Christ exercises with the Father, supreme domination over the whole of Creation. We repeat our belief every time we say in the Creed – 'Through him all things were made.' This is indeed the Kingship of God. There is, however, a more direct sense in which Christ is King. In the words of the great modern mystic, Teilhard de Chardin, 'The incarnation means the renewal, the restoration, of all the energies, all the powers of the universe. Christ is the instrument, the Centre and the End of all creation. Through him everything is created, is hallowed, is quickened. This is the constant general teaching of St John and of St Paul.' When St Paul wrote that God was in Christ reconciling the world to himself (2 Cor. 5.9) he is not confining this merely to personal relationship. Of course this is included, but St Paul's sentence concerns the very nature of the entire cosmos – the universe – and points to its potential future in the light of Christ. Today, as we consider the Ascension, we are led to contemplate the mystery of how Christ, in his true manhood and perfect humanity, has been exalted by his Father, acknowledged as the Son, and enthroned beside his Father in heaven.

Ascension Day   *Second Sermon*   King of the World

'Worthy is the Lamb who was slain, to receive power and wealth and wisdom and might and honour and glory and blessing!' Revelation 5.12

A Test Case?

What can we make of the Ascension story, in our modern times? Can we cope with the old outlook, the antique view of the universe, which we find in the Bible? The Bible uses the language of 'up there, down here'; it assumes the antique view of the world as a kind of three-decker sandwich; heaven above, earth in the middle, and hell down below. All within easy reach of one another, as shown in beautiful mediaeval paintings, stained glass, carvings; and written about so astonishingly, by – for example – Dante in his wonderful 'Heaven, Purgatory and Hell' better known as 'The Divine Comedy'.

In Our Day

We in our day of space-travel, of telescopic and radio-telescopic probing, away into the vastnesses of a huge and apparently uninterested universe, have a very different world-picture. We know now that the earth is a tiny speck in an immense vastness; we know it is not the centre of the physical universe. Instead, it is the third planet of an insignificant fourth-rate star on a rather remote fringe of a great galaxy, itself only one of a vast army of galaxies that extends away and away into infinity.

No longer can we believe comfortingly in our earth as the mid-point around which all else revolves, nor the stars as bright pin-holes in the floor of heaven above.

A Question
We are forced, therefore, to ask what can we make of the Ascension story? What is it really about? What was the Ascension?

The New Testament
First, the Ascension is not an account of a movement in space. The difference between an astronaut and Jesus is not that the astronaut came back to earth, while Jesus went on. For us to say 'He ascended into heaven' cannot be a statement to be taken literally, but must be understood theologically and spiritually.

The Ascension is the assertion of Christ's *ascendancy*, of his claim to passing over to a higher order of things. He who walked this earth with the men and women who became his followers, came to be recognized as the Eternal Son of God; he who is one with the Father; he who is the Lord of Glory. His is the Name beyond all names, so that at the Name of Jesus 'every knee shall bow, whether in Heaven or Earth or under the earth' (Phil. 2.9). It is just because Christ is who he is, that our Faith offers us the power to live truly and as God wills. What is more, countless thousands have found the gift of power is real, is true, is wonderfully and utterly effective.

Power
All down the ages of the Christian Era, his followers have been aware of the permanence of Christ, that he is always at hand, that we can enter into his presence, that we can communicate with him, and that he can and does communicate with us. This is what is meant when we say that he is at 'the right hand of power' (Mark 14.62) and that from thence, he is the source of power to all who believe in him.

The Seventh Sunday of Easter *(Sunday after Ascension Day)* 24 May 1998 'That they all may be one'
'That they all may be one.' John 17.21

Unity

Years ago, if we took an unbiased look at the Christian Churches – in this our own country, in Europe, in so many parts of the world – the idea that they all might become 'one' would have seemed impossible, even ridiculous. Why? Because each church was hardly in touch, even, with its neighbour. All were separated and without even the most formal contact in most cases.

A great change has taken place; the churches are now aware of each other as never before. Mixed groups of Christians meet together; the leaders of the Churches speak together, make their pronouncements on the questions of the day together. There are 'shared churches' – Anglicans worship with Methodists, share premises with Roman Catholics, with United Reform; Presbyterians share with Episcopalians; we remember how, in a time of trouble with the Liverpool football fans in Belgium, the two bishops – Roman Catholic and Anglican – travelled together to do what they could to demonstrate sorrow, and to work towards a better understanding. Not so long ago, the Pope himself visited this country, and attended a service at Canterbury Cathedral where he met the Anglican bishops – and they greeted each other with embraces and every sign of joy.

'That they may be one'

Jesus, on the night of his arrest, prayed with his disciples; as St John tells us, it was a long and wonderful prayer, full of love, of sorrow, of hope and of – above all – unity. Unity between the Lord and his Father; unity between Jesus and his disciples; unity in the community of the Church, whose unity of faith and love should set forth to the world, the wonderful love of God the Father, he who has sent his Son to show to the world his love. 'As thou, Father, art in me, and I in thee, that they also may be in us, so that the world may believe that thou hast sent me' (John 17.21).

The implication of this relationship between humanity and God, is a new unity amongst the human race; and this is to be embodied not only in the original disciples, but in all subsequent generations of Christians, to the glory of God.

Glory

The references to Jesus being glorified nearly all occur in St John's Gospel as our Lord's death on the cross draws near. Jesus speaks of it as Judas left the room, in order to go and betray his Master.

It has been said that 'The martyr wins for himself the crown of glory; but also by his death he gives glory to God. So, in higher degree, the Son of Man wins glory by his obedience unto death, but therein also gives glory to God whose love was supremely shown, by giving him for the saving of the world. When we confess him as Lord, we do it 'to the glory of God the Father'.

The Seventh Sunday of Easter   *Second Sermon*   'Exalted'

'He who descended is no other than he who ascended far above all the heavens, so that he might fill the universe.' Ephesians 4.10

The Resurrection and the Ascension
St Paul rightly sees the Resurrection of Jesus Christ as the essential point upon which the whole of the Christian Faith hangs. It is in the light of the Resurrection that we look back to see the significance of Jesus' earthly life – but we also look forward because the Resurrection has opened up the possibility of new life for all of us.

As an event, the Resurrection faces us with some historical problems. The Resurrection may not be proved, but it must be open to historical investigation, just because Christianity is not a myth, but a religion in which God reveals himself in and through historical events. The Crucifixion was a public event; it took place – historically speaking – 'under Pontius Pilate'; but the Resurrection is in the last resort, a matter of faith.

Raised by God
We have to remember that the Resurrection is not a possibility simply within the realm of human experience. We are born and at the end of our lives, we die; but the Resurrection is part of the freely willed activity of God. Jesus did not raise himself, he *was* raised by God. If the Resurrection is talking about the 'final' activity of God (that is, about what for us is still 'future' life) then it is not surprising that it remains controversial, and difficult to explain solely within the limits of our human experience.

Not the Revival of a Corpse

The Ascension develops the idea of the Risen Christ further. Christianity does not assert the revival of a corpse – Jesus does not rise from the dead in order to die again. He is, in the language of theology, 'exalted' – 'enthroned with God'. The Ascension points the Resurrection in a Godward direction. Humanity is now taken into the very life and being of God himself. As a result of the Incarnation, the Resurrection, and the Ascension, life within the Godhead is different. Through these events, the possibility of our sharing in God's life, is opened up to us.

Completion

The Ascension, seen as the completion of the whole Incarnational process, also helps us to achieve a more balanced doctrine of the Person of Jesus. It isn't that God 'becomes flesh' and that is just that – for if we overemphasize the Birth of Christ, that is what we end up with. Whereas seeing the Incarnation as completed in the Ascension, reminds us that Christ's own nature is One 'not by the conversion of the Godhead into flesh, but by the taking of humanity into God' (see the Athanasian Creed).

All this has consequences for the Christian life. Christians do not believe in the (Greek) doctrine of the immortal soul which survives death; but in a God-given different life which transcends – but does not avoid – death. We believe in a God who brings life from death ('Resurrection') and takes that life and makes it part of his own ('Ascension'). And both of these become possibilities for us, when we are incorporated into the dying, risen, ascended Lord through our baptism, and then sustained and held in him by our life in the Church.

AT THE ASCENSION

Thanks and praise be to you, Lord of heaven,
for Jesus Christ your Son our Lord.
You gave him the name above every name,
so that we say;

Jesus Lord of all,
We worship and adore you.

King of righteousness, King of peace,

enthrones at the right hand of Majesty on high,
Jesus, Lord of all,
We worship and adore you.

Pioneer of our salvation, you bring us to glory
through your death and resurrection:
Jesus, Lord of all,
We worship and adore you.
                              (Patterns for Worship, 65.10)

Day of Pentecost *(Whit Sunday)* 31 May 1998 The Giver of Life

'They were all filled with the Holy Spirit.' Acts 2.4

Pentecost

The Holy Spirit of God was always at work in this world of ours, in all that is noble, and beautiful, and true. But in Old Testament days, the Holy Spirit is thought of as being given to special people, to perform special tasks; however, there grew up the expectation that the time would come when the Holy Spirit would be available to all – 'The day shall come when I will send out my Spirit upon all humanity; your sons and daughters shall prophesy; your old men shall dream dreams and your young men shall see visions . . .' (Joel 2.28).

In our day, we think of this as happening at Pentecost, as the result of the Ascension of Jesus: 'You shall receive power when the Holy Spirit has come upon you,' said the Lord (Acts 1.8), and 'They were all filled with the Holy Spirit' (Acts 2.4), when the Day had come, and we read of the courage they showed in preaching Christ straightway.

The Comforter

The Lord Jesus told the disciples, when he left them, that he would send them what he called 'Another Comforter': 'It is expedient for you that I go away, for if I go not away, the Comforter will not come unto you: but if I depart I will send him unto you'. (John 16.7). His promise was: 'I will not leave you comfortless: I will come to you'. (14.18). The Spirit is to be what the Lord had always been to them, only in a different way.

As we commit ourselves to Christ, the Holy Spirit builds up in us the very life of Christ. Our life is to be one of union with Christ – he lives in us. We are brought, through the Spirit, into this most loving relationship with God.

Strength

Our need is for help, for strength. The word 'comforter' includes the Latin word *fortis*, 'strong'. Out from our weakness, the Holy Spirit makes us strong; brings power, the divine grace, the very life of Christ.

All our life there is a struggle between 'the flesh' and the Spirit; the flesh is life that is self-centred. It is this which has to be crucified, and this is a painful process. St Paul gives a terrible list of the 'work of the flesh' in his letter to the Galatians: 'impurity, indecency, enmity, jealousy, envy' to name but a few! But he contrasts this with the lovely fruit of the Spirit: 'love, joy, peace, patience, kindness, goodness, fidelity, gentleness, self-control.' Our weaknesses can be taken up and we can be made strong and true, revitalized to take our proper part in the life we live, to the glory of God and the growth of the Holy Church, the Body of Christ on earth.

Day of Pentecost *Second Sermon* Life – not Law

'The new Covenant, not in a written code but in the Spirit; for the written code kills, but the Spirit gives life'. 2 Corinthians 3.6

'To Live Life'

The great characteristic of our Faith is not the laying down of laws, but the teaching of how to live life. Our Lord Jesus Christ came with his chief objective not to reveal a higher moral ideal, but to seek and save that which was lost, to give life, and to give it more abundantly (John 10.10). High moral standards are not only valuable, but necessary; human life cannot advance without them. But, they go only a little way towards the salvation of the world. St Paul has come to realize that the 'Old Covenant', the Law of Moses, in which he had been brought up as a faithful Hebrew – indeed, as a Pharisee who must have and keep the highest standards of conformity – had no power to save. 'The written code kills' is the sad conclusion the apostle draws; only in the new covenant, or new relationship, under which the law of God would become a spontaneous motive of conduct, written on the pages of the human heart, rather than in letters incised into stone tablets. Nor does the new covenant imply any special qualification or authorization; it is God who has qualified us to be ministers of the new covenant, in the Spirit, not in letters of introduction.

The Old Law and the New Law

Moses was the agent of the old Covenant; and that Covenant was of such value that Moses' face shone, and he had to keep a veil over his face, having seen the splendour of God. Yet, the divine revelation turned from law into legalism, as Paul puts it, 'the dispensation under which we are condemned', and the glory faded. A new dispensation is now in effect, and what a radiance must be on the face of the messenger who brings this message! A radiance which will not fade, but will continue, as we behold the glory of the Lord – that is, the Spirit; and where the Spirit is, there is freedom, in which we now live. For we Christians have the Spirit with us continually. Cleansed in baptism through the Holy Spirit, the Christian soul shines with the reflected glory of God; and cured of the old insensitivity of our minds, we can read the Scriptures aright, and are released from the old slavery of the Law. Here then is the wonderful influence of the Lord who is Spirit.

O God, by whom the meek are guided in judgement, and light riseth up in darkness; grant us, in all our doubts and uncertainties, the grace to ask what thou wouldst have us do; that the Spirit of Wisdom may save us from false choices, and that in thy light we may see light, and in thy straight path may not stumble; through Jesus Christ our Lord.
William Bright (1861)

Trinity Sunday 7 June 1998 Mystery and Authority

'There is still much that I could say to you, but the burden would be too great for you now; however, when he comes who is the Spirit of truth, he will guide you into all truth.' John 16.12,13

All Truth

If there is one thing that psychology has persuaded us generally to accept, it must surely be that human beings are more complex than they appear. We cannot assume that the surface we see, is really the whole of a person. We humans are more complicated and have – each one of us – more strands or facets to our characters than is apparent at a glance.

Of course, this isn't exactly new; aspects of character or make-up have always been noted, and changes of character or personality have fascinated people down the ages. And, do we not know – when we look into ourselves – that there are very different sides to our own personalities; maybe even those near and dear to us sometimes have no inkling.

God's Image

We are made in God's image. Humanity is a reflection, or if you prefer, a model, of the nature of God. A small model, of course; and a limited model – and all too often a distorted image due to human failings and faults. But all the same, the varied aspects of one single human nature does surely have some relevance to the nature of God our Creator – as far as we may be permitted, and able, to approach such a subject.

Complexity

Let us try and appreciate something of the complexity of the nature of God. In some ways, we are not much helped by the Bible – or at least the Old Testament. This presents us with an idea of God which certainly on the whole tends to be primitive. 'I the Lord thy God am a jealous God' – in some churches this is read at every Communion service, and must suggest that God is an arbitrary God, a figure of wrath; to be appeased as we read further, by sacrifices of animals, burnt offerings, and so on.

God's Nature

Gradually the concept of a God of love and truth emerges. 'Thou delightest not in burnt offerings' – 'The sacrifice of God is a troubled spirit, a broken and contrite heart' – says the Psalmist. 'He is gracious and merciful, slow to anger and of great kindness' writes the prophet Joel. It is true to say, I believe, that this view of God is basically still the view largely held and expounded by the Hebrew synagogue; but tends towards a legalistic and precise obeying of the ancient rules.

The Muslim Faith

Our Muslim brethren emphasize obedience to God's mighty powers. 'Islam' means obedience, and a Muslim is 'one who obeys'; that is, he obeys the mighty God, the Ruler, all powerful and remote; and in a sense untouched by the sorrows and pains of life.

Hindu Wideness

By contrast, what an immensely wide approach is that of the Hindu religion. All-embracing, it allows for belief in many gods, for belief in one god, for belief in none. Calm meditation and varied ritual find their places, as do the most profound philosophies and the most primitive worship of sex and nature.

Buddhism

The teaching of the Buddha avoided speculation about God, his nature or even his existence. The Buddha seems never to have pronounced upon whether or not he believed in God. Such a question, he taught, is unimportant; we are to live our lives by the great precepts: detachment from the world; the ideal of poverty; concern for the welfare of all life; chastity and truthfulness.

Our Christian Belief

We can learn a great deal about God from other faiths, especially when they lay emphasis on aspects we have forgotten or never learnt. But we can surely claim that it is only in Christianity – in the teachings of Jesus – that we can find a concept of God that truly satisfies the whole of our being, all aspects of our human personality. The many strands that make up a human being find their reflection in the three-fold conception of God as developed in Christian thought and tradition.

The Father

We have the concept of the Ruler and Creator, the God who made the universe – and yet is infinitely close to each one of us, not remote but a relationship as close as a child and its father. 'Abba' – 'Daddy', is the word Jesus chose to describe his God and our God; a God of intimate and personal love and knowledge.

The Redeemer

We believe we cannot lift ourselves by our own bootstraps; we need a Redeemer. And that Redeemer is Jesus Christ, the instrument for the redemption of all humanity and the universe itself; and the symbol and example of God, suffering with his suffering creation.

The Spirit

And we have God at work amongst us, and in and through us; the Holy Spirit in our hearts and minds; and blowing like a mighty wind, through all peoples, all nations, and the world itself. A wind of change, a wind of the Spirit.

May this three-fold God bring us to that eternal kingdom, where we may enjoy for ever his might, his wisdom and his love.

Trinity Sunday *Second Sermon* The Kingdom of God

'In truth, in very truth, I tell you, unless a man has been born over again he cannot see the kingdom of God.' John 3.3

'He came to Jesus by night'

Nicodemus was a learned man; a well-known theologian and teacher, and a man looking for the Kingdom. He has been impressed by Jesus – his words and works – but he is not prepared to accept him openly; hence the night-time call. Jesus accepts the diplomatic opening of their conversation, but confronts his visitor with his real needs for entrance into the Kingdom of God. Nicodemus was aware of rebirth by water, from John's preaching and practising of baptism; yet, 'birth of the Spirit' seems to be new to him, even astonishing (v. 9 – 'How is this possible?').

Baptism

Baptism – rebirth by water – happens on earth; but rebirth is also 'from above' and is an introduction to the divine world above, revealing the heavenly things, restoring the union between earth and heaven. And it is Christ who can do this, for he alone unites the two worlds; he is the unique link between heaven and earth – 'No one ever went up into heaven, except the one who came down from heaven, the Son of Man whose home is in heaven.' Among human beings, only one – the Son of Man – has direct experience of the heavenly world. He it is who ascends thence, and returns. But how and in what way?

The Serpent

The answer is in verse fourteen 'This Son of Man must be lifted up, as the serpent was lifted up by Moses, in the wilderness, so that everyone who has faith in him, may in him possess eternal life' (vv. 14,15). 'Lifted up' is a word of double meaning, pointing both to exaltation in glory and to lifting up on the Cross. Yet, these are two aspects of the same thing; to St John, the crucifixion of Jesus *is* his glory. The Son of Man is lifted up in this way, in order that those who believe in him may be saved.

Renewal and Redemption

The old emblem of the Serpent is renewed and changed and restored; as those who were bitten in the desert were healed by looking at the brazen serpent, so those who follow Christ are saved by 'looking at' and believing in Jesus. And so they are redeemed and restored, and brought to the true Eden, Paradise regained, in the age to come.

> *This is love, not that we loved God:*
> *but that he loved us and sent his Son.*
> *He is the sacrifice for our sins:*
> *that we might live through him.*
> *If God loves us so much:*
> *we ought to love one another.*
> *(Patterns for Worship)*

Corpus Christi: see p. 206

The First Sunday after Trinity   14 June 1998
The Lesson of Love

'He who is forgiven little, loves little.' Luke 7.47

Forgiveness

Life has many paradoxes; as we go through life we become aware of many odd and surprising things – the miser who scrimped and saved all his days, only to die before he could enjoy any of the fine things and great times he had been looking forward to; or the other character who seemed to care for nothing, lived hand to mouth – then won the lottery. Today's story of Christ, the Pharisee and the woman of the town, has something of the same unexpectedness.

At the House of Simon

Not all Pharisees were opponents of Christ. Jesus had a considerable reputation by now; a much talked about personality, a powerful preacher, maybe even a prophet; Simon has an eye on the main chance, and entertains him to a good meal, no doubt with the local gentry. Somehow, the 'woman of the town' manages to enter the house and join the guests; her presence might have gone unnoticed by the 'righteous', until in a surprising move, she pours out her ointment, weeping with joy, anointing and kissing the Lord's feet. Simon is horrified: 'Not much of a prophet, this Jesus, if he can't tell what sort of sinner this woman is!'

Jesus takes him up, and puts to him the story of the two debtors, and the lender who let them off their repayments. It is the debtor who owes most who has been forgiven, and therefore loves the lender more. Simon, the host, did little to welcome Jesus; in contrast, the woman has been giving care and attention and affection. Surely then, this shows she has already received God's forgiveness; while Simon, 'righteous Pharisee' that he is, cannot begin to comprehend the love of God, and the joys that could be generously showered upon him, if only he would abandon his critical and mean-spirited outlook.

Acceptance

Jesus never classified people; he was interested in them, loved them, as individuals, as persons, each different, each with their own gifts and needs, their failings and successes. And he accepted them as they were. To accept forgiveness we have first to accept our mistakes, our faults, our guilt; then it is possible for us to admit our failures and receive the healing power of genuine forgiveness. Simon was a good man, but his love was cold, formal; are our spiritual lives too easy-going over our faith, and is our love too cold? Today we see something of the mind of Christ. To him, the grand gesture, the ardent passion, the heights of love – and the depths of despair – these are things he understands, welcomes, approves. Lord, inflame our dull hearts!

The First Sunday after Trinity   *Second Sermon*
Christ the Teacher

'How shall we picture the kingdom of God; by what parable shall we describe it?' Mark 4.30

Success

To what was the success of Jesus as a teacher due? He had a note of authority, we are told, which the scribes and Pharisees did not have. Was his success due to this note alone? No – surely there was far more than that to it.

Like all genuine teachers who have learnt how to communicate to those who are being taught, Jesus adapted his teaching, both in method and content, to the intellectual and spiritual capacity and stature of his hearers. Who were his hearers?

First his disciples, of course; then his enemies, anxious to pick holes – but above all the people – 'the multitude', 'the crowd', 'great crowds', 'all crowded in to hear him' – we constantly read.

Parables for the People

Jesus taught the people usually through the medium of parables – attractive stories adapted to drawing attention and readily remembered. The characters are often easily recognized from daily life, in the country, on the farm, in the village or small town. Here today we are shown the lamp, brought in to light the cottage room and put on its stand where its light will shine out best. No-one would put the lamp under a bed or a basket! Be fair with your friends – give them fair shares of wheat or grapes, then in turn they will treat you fairly.

With farms all around, how marvellous it is to see the harvest grow – from the seed being sown, then in secret the sprouts and roots grow out, until it is fully grown and the harvest can take place – straightway when the grain is ripe. Then, the 'Kingdom of God' – we talk about it a lot. But what is it? Why, it is like mustard seed, which grows so quickly; tiny though it is as seed, yet when it grows it soon becomes tall and full of branches, bigger than any other shrub, and shelters the birds of the air. The Kingdom will be like that! We are told that Jesus explained carefully every parable, for the benefit of his disciples, when they too – no doubt – were explaining the meanings to the ordinary people.

A Miracle
When Jesus had finished his teaching the disciples simply put out with him in the boat. A graphic description of the storm, the waves breaking into the boat so that it began to fill; the terror of the disciples contrasts with the calm serenity of Jesus. A lesson of the story is the example of absolute faith and confidence set by Jesus; and at the coming of the calm, the disciples raise the question which is also raised in the mind of the reader: 'Who then is this?' Mark, it would seem, is concerned to tell us that he who could calm the storm was present still with his own, amidst the storms and stress of life. May we take this message to our hearts.

The Second Sunday after Trinity 21 June 1998 In Foreign Territory
'They arrived at the country of the Gerasenes, which is opposite Galilee.'
Luke 8.26

'Legion'
After crossing the lake, Christ and his disciples land on what is pagan (Gentile) territory. They have hardly got onto the beach, it would appear, when a sad case of a maniac appears. As Luke tells us, this unfortunate man is possessed by demons, lives isolated amidst the tombs of the area, has no proper clothing – does he

refuse clothes, tear them off when clothed, or has he some painful skin disease which prevents him from wearing anything? In earlier days, the evangelist tells us, he was kept under guard, even bound and chained; but broke free and ran off into the wilderness.

Somehow, he must have received knowledge of Jesus and his healing power. He recognizes the Lord, and the demon-spokesman (as it were) asks for mercy. His name he gives as 'Legion', which indicates that there are a vast number of other spirits within the victim – as if today the unit would be 'Regiment'. The title he gives to Jesus – 'Son of the Most High God' – has a striking resonance with us today, but would not, the experts tell us, be a Jewish phrase; rather from a Greek religious cult.

The Pigs
The demon asks that he and his companions should not be thrown into the 'Abyss' – the place appointed for the powers of evil according to Jewish mythology – but allowed to enter the herd of pigs, which are quietly feeding nearby. So it is – and the herd rush down a steep bank and are drowned; which seems hard lines on the farmer who owned them! The herdsman spread the news around the countryside, and as ever, crowds come to see what has happened. The man from whom the evil spirits had gone, is now in his right mind, clothed and sitting at the feet of Jesus. He even asks to be allowed to become a follower of the Lord, but this Jesus tactfully puts aside, telling him to go home, and spread the news of what God has done for him, in his neighbourhood.

A Motto for Us
Few of us will have an experience like the unfortunate victim (though indeed our age, while hardly accepting the reality of demons, does have many strange psychological problems). Yet we can show something of a true Christian style when we are asked to help – with service or with money – the many good causes who are working in our own time for the relief of the mentally disturbed, either in our own country or overseas. In our prayers let us remember the needs of all such.

Gadarene Swine
The madman is certain that he is occupied by demons, and equally certain that Jesus can get rid of them. Jesus performs an exorcism, and the evil spirits enter a herd of pigs feeding nearby; at once

the herd rushes headlong down the hillside, and all are drowned in the lake below.

A Lesson for us

This strange event has a lesson for us. How we rush along with the majority! How easily we are seduced into keeping up with the latest fashion, the latest gossip, the latest views on the box, in the papers, in the advertisements.

But what is this 'latest' we are so anxious to catch up with, to hold onto, to be dragged along by? At best it is a fad, thought up by those who want to be known as leaders of fashion. At worst it is what is being subtly – or not so subtly – plugged by manufacturers. Anxious to make a higher profit, or faced with surplus stock, what is easier than to take over a few 'leaders', so that in no time everyone must be wearing or carrying whatever is the 'newest' style or fashion. And worst of all is the drug fashion, fed by crime . . .

Followers

So we come to be followers. And having got into the habit, how difficult to get out of it. 'Stop the World, I want to Get Off' – many would be only too glad to halt the treadmill, slow down the merry-go-round, let up on the drugs or tobacco, and begin to re-charge physically, emotionally, and spiritually.

Stand Back . . .

It takes some effort to make the effort.

But how worth while it is, if we can only step out of the race, stand aside, look at ourselves, attain a better balance.

Otherwise, we may all too truly find ourselves sharing the miserable and futile fate of those pathetic swine.

Father, we pray for the mentally ill, for all who are disturbed and troubled in mind. Be to them light in their darkness, a refuge and strength in fear. Give special skills and tender hearts to all who care for them, and show them how best to help your work of healing; through Jesus Christ our Lord.

(Timothy Dudley-Smith)

Second Sunday after Trinity *Second Sermon* Healing

'Who touched my garments?' Mark 5.20

A Touch of Faith

'Who touched my garments?' asks Jesus.

What a strange question! He was in the midst of a crowd, people were pushed up against him on every side, eager to hear what he said. They wanted just to be near this preacher who had made such a name for himself. Notoriety, the need to be near someone well-known – how often do we see TV pictures of the crowds around some famous figure, pushing, shoving, so anxious to be near. 'Touch?' what a strange question! But, Jesus had a particular touch in mind – the touch of faith – a touch that drew power out of him, and brought healing.

Power

St Mark's story gives the impression that for a moment the Lord was somehow drained of energy – 'power had gone forth from him' (v. 30). How much of a strain must his daily life have been; the constant demands, the drain of psychic forces being used up. No wonder he needed to go away alone, to meet his Father, to 'recharge' if we may use such a term. We too, in our small way, can do something similar – we can go 'on retreat', take a 'quiet day' away – or just in the midst of our busy life, drop into a quiet church for a brief service, or a short time of peace and silence.

Faith

The power of Christ was released by faith. A power strong enough to cure a long-standing mania, strong enough to raise a little girl from her deathbed. On one occasion we are told that Christ would work no miracle because of the lack of faith of the people of the place. Today, the child was raised because of the *father's* faith. Faith creates an opening for the power of God to enter; it opens the door shut fast.

Rejoice!

There are those, who like the mourners in the room with the dead child, refuse to believe Christ's words, and laugh at him. These are they who refuse to accept that our life here – compared with the future that is promised – is like a sleep, a dream, from which we will be awakened by the touch of Christ's hand. Death, they think, is a dead end; but we are to be like Peter, and John, and James. They stayed to witness the power of Christ, and they rejoiced to see it. We too may indeed rejoice to share that vision.

Third Sunday after Trinity   28 June 1998
On the Jerusalem Road

'When the days drew near for him to be received up, he set his face to go to Jerusalem.' Luke 9.51

Moment of Truth

That muscular, tough, uncompromising writer, Ernest Hemingway, deals in his books with some great themes: he writes about youth and death, about love and war, about tenderness beneath brutality, and perhaps above all, about what makes a man. Hemingway's men characters are confronted, in story after story, in one way or another, what the bull-fighters call 'The Moment of Truth'.

That moment when everything unessential, extraneous, and incidental drops away, and there is a great clarity. The issue is seen, in that Moment of Truth, very clearly and sharply – what makes a real man?

Integrity

The answer, lit up in a pure white light, is – his integrity.

A man – to Hemingway – is one who makes a stand, is ready to be counted, come what may, for his beliefs. Perhaps 'beliefs' is too strong a word for some Hemingway characters; but listen to Robert Jordan, hero of *For Whom the Bell Tolls*. At the end of the book he is left, badly wounded, by his comrades to cover their retreat. As Jordan looks along the road where the enemy will soon come, Hemingway puts down his thoughts . . . 'Now, finally at last, there is no problem; however all of it will ever be . . . I have fought for what I believe in . . . a good cause and worth the fighting . . .' His last task is to hold up, even for a short time, the enemy; even though he himself is inevitably to die. He has chosen to make his stand, whatever the consequences – and clearly seeing those consequences.

The Moment of Truth

Does it seem strange, or even blasphemous, to talk about a Hemingway hero and about Jesus Christ, in the same breath?

I hope not. Because we have brought before us in today's reading, the moment of decision for Jesus. His Moment of Truth. That decision was, whether to continue on the road to Jerusalem at the end of which he could clearly see death, or not. 'When the days drew near for him to be received up, he set his face to go to Jerusalem.' From this moment, Jesus began to make it clear to his disciples that he was destined to go to Jerusalem and to suffer death, a cruel death upon the Cross.

Integrity

Here again was the temptation he had been confronted with at the very beginning of his public life – to take the safe way out. Surely God does not expect a man to go on to certain death, for failure, for nothing? Let's be sensible!

'Yet,' says our Lord, 'what will a man gain if he win the whole world and lose his integrity? Get behind me, Satan! My path is God's path, not man's.'

So Jesus took his decision, and as St Luke puts it, 'set his face to forward to Jerusalem' (Luke 9,51).

God help us to be truly human, truly men and women, ready to stand up and be counted, to keep our integrity, to stand by the things we believe in, in the face of opposition, in the face of the soft option, and in the face of hatred, betrayal and even death itself.

Third Sunday after Trinity *Second Sermon*
'Rejection'

'He came to his own country . . . and on the sabbath he began to teach in the synagogue; and many who heard him were astonished . . . And they took offence at him.' Mark 6.1,2,3

Versions

We are given differing versions of the Return of Jesus to Nazareth; that given us by Mark places his return to Nazareth fairly late, after the beginning of the Lord's ministry and preaching, which had led to his being regarded with much awe and reverence – but not in his home town, as we learn from the caustic and angry comments. 'Where did this man get all this? Is not this the carpenter, the son of Mary, with brothers and sisters here with us?' This could be no prophet, but the boy who had grown up in the village, where everyone knew him. Jesus could make no impression; their familiarity with him obscured the great and wonderful message he was trying to bring. He does heal a few sick, but no more 'mighty works' can be accomplished. Mark tells us Jesus was astonished at the local unbelief; though later he did go among the villages, teaching.

Luke

Luke sets the whole event quite early on, after Jesus returns from the forty days in the wilderness, in the power of the Spirit, having defeated the Evil One and rejected temptations. Now his teaching in the local synagogues goes well (ch. 4 v. 15) and coming to Nazareth, he goes, as his custom was, on the Sabbath to the synagogue. His sermon reproaches his hearers and implies an end to the privileges of the old Israel; 'all in the synagogue were filled with wrath' and attempted to throw Jesus headlong from the hill on which the town was built. However, mysteriously he passes through the midst of them unhurt, and goes away.

His listeners disliked the message Christ brought, and would have destroyed the messenger: but if the Lord had not spoken out, he would have been failing in the truth. His words were not in condemnation, so much as pointing to a better way. Such courage is something we all need at certain times, though we run the risk of rejection. Truthful speaking may cost a good deal, yet it is an essential part of our growth and life, in family, in church affairs, in the politics of the country.

Fourth Sunday after Trinity   5 July 1998
Heal the Sick

'When you come into a town ... heal the sick there, and say, "The Kingdom of God has come close to you".' Luke 10.8–9

The Church and the Sick

There has always been a link between Christianity and work among the sick, from our Lord's own lifetime and example down to the present day. The accounts in the Gospels of our Lord's ministry clearly shows how that as well as preaching and talking to individuals about spiritual matters, he gave a great deal of his time to work among the sick; and he instructs his disciples to heal the sick and tell them 'The Kingdom of God has come near you.'

In the Middle Ages, the care of the sick was almost entirely in the hands of monks and nuns; the names of some of the great hospitals – St Bartholomew's, St Mary's, St Thomas's in London, and others elsewhere, remind us of their close links with the Church in their earlier days. The State has taken over most responsibility for the sick in Britain, but the Church – and individual churches in a number of cases – is still closely interested in what is done for the sick, and in research.

Ethical Problems

Our ancestors heard little or nothing about birth control, legal abortion, euthanasia; or the transfer of organs – hearts, livers and so on – from one person usually dead, to restore a living patient. These and other medical matters create many problems of right and wrong; is this operation or transfer really for the patient's good? Is what we are doing, right in the sight of God? The Church has the duty of seeing that if any of these actions or treatments are wanted, they must be used in the right way and with the right motives. If there is doubt, or the motives are wrong, then the Church should be protesting. In particular, the vast spread of Aids in Africa and undeveloped countries is a threat to the whole population of many nations. Here again sexual ethics are of immense importance and need our careful consideration, from a Christian point of view.

Mental Health

Christianity is also concerned with humanity's mental health. Life is so rushed today, that many people feel the strain – travelling to and from work; the effect of certain types of work upon mind as well as body. Today's lowering of moral standards and lack of faith is no help in keeping calm in times of great trouble whether personal or national. At such times, we need something in which to trust, and a hope which is not based on this world only. How much help, not only in difficult times, but in ordinary life, will a firmer faith in God and a greater respect for his laws, give to many people; even restore the inner calm we all need to help us through life.

Spiritual Healing

There has been a great revival – or perhaps discovery might be better – in all the ways of spiritual healing. Many churches offer services of Healing, when not only prayers are said for recovery, but anointing and the laying-on of hands on the sick are practised (we can refer not only to our Lord's example (Mark 6.13), but to such advice as St James gives – The Letter of James, chapter 5, vv. 13–16, is well worth reading for the Apostle's advice.

Such shrines as Walsingham and Lourdes attract enormous pilgrimages, and many ill folk. Even if nothing much is done in the way of physical or mental healing, those who have been come away refreshed, spiritually strengthened, better able to cope with the world and their particular problems.

Today

The work of caring for the sick, which long ago was chiefly the responsibility of the Church, has now passed to other hands. Keep in mind, however, that the Church is still concerned with the sick, in at least two ways. At home and abroad organizations like Christian Aid and other charities, help the poor and the under-privileged in a number of ways, including the prevention of, and the relief of, sickness of so many kinds. In our parishes, the Church still offers to the sick who will accept her care, the ministry of visitation and of prayer. In doing all these things surely the Church is following the example and the commands of her Master, the Lord Jesus.

Fourth Sunday after Trinity   *Second Sermon*
Mission Journeys

'Jesus called to him the Twelve, and began to send them out two by two.'
Mark 6.7

Urgency!

A note of urgency is revealed here; the disciples are to take nothing with them except a staff. No food, no money, no bag; they are to wear sandals, but not to have two tunics. The missionaries are to be like an invading army, that is, to live off the countryside, as one commentator puts it. Nothing is said about the message they were to deliver, but it must presumably have related to the near approach of the Kingdom. A warning of wrath to come, we may presume to think. Incidentally, it was this passage of the Scriptures – the 'Mission Charge' as it has been called – that inspired Francis of Assisi to embrace 'My Lady Poverty' and begin his life of preaching and prayer.

Refused!

It will be the worse for any places that refuse to offer hospitality, and equally refuse to hear the message – when the disciples leave, they are to 'shake off the dust that is on your feet, for a testimony against them' (v. 11). This is said to have been the practice of the earliest Christian missionaries (Peake). The action is symbolic, indicating that the place is to be regarded as heathen, but is not to be taken as an acted curse, but as a testimony to provoke thought and repentance. It seems that the mission was reasonably success-ful (v. 13) (Note the reference to anointing with oil in the healing of the sick – compare with James, 5.13–16, as quoted in first sermon.)

A Note:-   Martyrdom of John Baptist

Mark 6.13–29

This is the story of King Herod and the Death of John Baptist. The scholars say that there may well be a solid core of historical fact, since the historian Josephus claims that Herod put John to death, lest his influence over the people should lead to a rebellion. (The

influence of Jesus must have seemed at least as dangerous.)
Herod's rejection of his first wife, in favour of Herodias, led to a
disastrous war with her father Aretas, King of Arabia. Many
people interpreted this as a divine retribution on Herod for the
death of John. The scholars say that there may well be historical
fact in John's rebuke of Herod, and Herod's subsequent hostility.
Mark is certainly faithfully correct to the character of Herod
(Peake).

The Fifth Sunday after Trinity   12 July 1998 'Who is my Neighbour?'

*'But he, desiring to justify himself, said to Jesus, "And who is my
neighbour?"' Luke 10.29*

A Narrow View

The lawyer, quite rightly, quotes the Old Testament in reply to
Christ's turning back of his own question upon him.

To 'love your neighbour' was not a new idea that Christ was
introducing; it was a precept based upon the ancient law set out
in Deuteronomy and Leviticus. But, note that the Old Testament
limits deeds of mercy and kindness to fellow Jews. It is true that
other people are not expressly excluded, but the idea of helping
anyone – anyone at all, in need – scarcely occurs. So it is that the
lawyer is going right to the heart of the question by asking, 'And
who is my neighbour?' Perhaps he already sensed that the answer
of Christ would be different from the usual and standard; maybe
he hoped to trick Jesus on a point of law.

Christ's Answer

In his answer, Jesus widened the circle to its utmost limit. His
story displays a Jew who has been waylaid and robbed, then
helped by one who was – by tradition – an enemy. The Samaritans,
so close to the Jews in so many ways, were yet bitter opponents.
How often is it, that our sharpest criticism, our deepest dislike, is
against those who are so nearly like us, but differ on some small
but vital point. How true it is of religion and politics!

The two men who walked past the bleeding body, were a Priest
and a Levite. Both may well have been on their respective ways

to the Temple, where they would have their sacred duties to perform. The man on the roadside might be dead – to handle him would make themselves religiously unclean, impure; even if they touched blood, that would likewise make it impossible to carry out their rites; God would be without his proper honours. For ordained clergy, such a course was unthinkable; so they go on their way, carefully avoiding even their robes touching the unfortunate fellow – probably saying a prayer, of course, for his soul.

The Samaritan

Now, the man who did help the injured traveller was a Samaritan; the Samaritans differed from the Jews on numerous doctrinal points; from the Jewish point of view, all that lot were disgusting heretics. (Who knows what they might do!) And of course, the Samaritan ran considerable risk himself – he might become another victim of the robbers, who could still be lurking nearby, in the bushes and trees.

To be followers of Jesus, we need to have courage in a variety of ways. Sometimes we may need physical courage, but far more often we need moral courage. We need courage to resist temptation, or to answer the call of duty, or to continue what we have begun. We need courage also, not to be swayed by prejudice, nor led by popular opinion, to the neglect of a demand upon our humanity.

Prejudice

The crowd who stood around Jesus, and heard him tell his story of the Good Samaritan, were without doubt more struck than we are, by the fact that the rescuer was a Samaritan, and the man he rescued was a Jew. Before he helped the injured man, the Samaritan had to break down the prejudice in his heart – help a Jew! He probably found this harder to do, than to overcome his fear of the robbers.

The smart, smooth lawyer must have been shattered to have to admit that a Samaritan could be a human being, just like him. Instead of tricking Jesus with his clever questions, he has to admit that only the Samaritan could be the 'neighbour', and endure the infuriating request to 'Go and do likewise'.

Do we ignore or distrust or dislike, our culturally different fellow-travellers on life's road? God's commandment is simple: love one another as he loves us.

Set us free, O Lord God,
from the bondage of prejudice and fear;
that in your service we may find our true freedom,
and in your will our true peace;
through Jesus Christ our Lord.

(PHG 106)

Fifth Sunday after Trinity   *Second Sermon*
Discipline

'You leave the commandment of God, and hold fast to the tradition of men.' Mark 7.8

The Commandments

The Commandments of God were brought down from Mount Sinai, the holy mountain, by the great leader of the Hebrews, the man Moses. On that mountain God spoke to his people through Moses; and Moses recorded the words he heard on stone tablets, which he carried to the tribes of Israel, down through dense clouds of smoke and steam, lit by flashes of fire and accompanied by deep rumblings and thunderings and lightning.

We in our time would recognize a volcanic peak, with its associated effects when in eruption; for the people of Israel it was indeed a display of the strength and majesty of God, and a warning against rebellion or disobedience against his will. The Commandments were a vital element in leading the people from animism and superstition, to the religion of the One God, a great, good and personal Father who cared deeply for them, and had a great future they were to fulfil. Obedience therefore was an essential part of the Hebrew religion; and at the heart was the keeping of the Commandments. They are a code of behaviour of vast importance, setting a standard which in many ways has still to be reached by all too many of us; they are a discipline which we should all respect and obey.

Additions and Alterations

In the course of time over centuries, and remembering the wanderings and persecutions the Hebrew folk have had to endure, it is not surprising that many additions were made. Jesus points to some of these, and to alterations; too often against the spirit of the commandments, and preferring inferior ideas and even easy ways round the discipline of the Word of God, as Jesus points out.

The late Lord Mountbatten spoke wise words about discipline. He said that discipline is not merely a question of 'touching your cap' but a recognition of ability; and went on to say – what we all know too well today – that 'discipline' has almost become a dirty word to too many of us. He explained that 'discipline' comes from the Latin 'to learn' and means teaching and instructing disciples.

Discipline

Why is there such a lack of discipline today? Why are so many, especially the young, unable to control themselves? Because there has been a lack of discipline, a lack of teaching by parents and schools of sanctions – religious, moral and legal. Crime is vastly increased and is punished less severely; immorality is disregarded simply because our society has no longer any fixed moral standards. Kids will not respect parents who show no respect themselves. For too many, morality has become a meaningless word, replaced by 'I do as I please because I recognize no one more important than myself to please; and I do what I do for kicks'.

The best we can do is, to show by word and example that the law of God is still to be respected and obeyed, in the Ten Commandments and in the example of Jesus and his teaching. 'Discipleship' is closely connected with 'discipline'; and he said, clearly and simply, 'Learn of me . . . Follow me' (Matt. 11.29).

Sixth Sunday after Trinity   19 July 1998
Mary and Martha

'One thing is needful.' Luke 10.42

What things do matter?

It must have been a blessed relief for the Lord; to be received on his own into a house, given some peace and quiet. No crowds pressing around; no demands for healing, or prayers, or settling of arguments; no smart alecs trying to show off how clever they were – like that lawyer this morning (Luke 10.25–37). And to be honest, quite a relief not to have the apostles themselves – good though they were, but sometimes such fuss-pots! and full of questions too.

Hospitality offered by this pleasant lady of the house, Martha; a chance to sit down in the coolness and shade, and enjoy a time to relax. The lady of the house is busy and rather harassed by coping with the domestic strains of a guest; her sister Mary comes and sits at the feet of Jesus, and is a ready listener to what he has to tell her. Martha, bustling in and out of the kitchen, peeling the vegetables, stirring the soup, is just a little irritated. 'Lord, do you not care that my sister has left me alone to get everything ready? Please tell her to give me a hand!' Jesus does seem to reply rather harshly; does he condemn Martha's service? Surely not; just earlier he has been praising the unselfish service of the Samaritan, as an example for neighbourliness. What Jesus really intends, we may say, is a gentle hint to Martha – who we have been told, 'is distracted with much serving' – 'Not to worry and fret about too many things; one thing at a time is all we can manage!' To serve, and become distracted by one's serving, can mean losing touch with 'the better part'. We need to be inspired and nourished spiritually, sitting at the feet of Jesus, so that we can be guided by his words, for our practicalities. We all need to be both Martyrs and Marthas!

(A passage from *Jesus Caritas*, the magazine of the 'Little Sisters of Jesus' who work in great difficulties in the most desperately poor and deprived areas of South America, Africa, the USA: 'Doubts are sometimes expressed over the difficulties of our contemplative dimension; some suspect it as an evasion and flight from the immediate demands of neighbourly charity and care . . . Why see things as contrary rather than complementary? Nearness to Jesus cannot separate us from our suffering brothers and sisters, nor will his love make us less likely to become the "salt of the earth" to share with others . . .')

Sixth Sunday after Trinity *Second Sermon*
Difficulties

'When slandered, we try to conciliate.' 1 Corinthians 4.12

Problems among the Flock

Corinth lay on the criss-cross of trade routes between east and west; its two seaports were notorious, its population was a confused mix of Greeks, Romans, Jews and others, and its very name implied the dissolute life. The Christian faith had been introduced, but differing parties had arisen, not helped by the rivalry of the leaders. Apollos, eloquent bible student, captivated many among the Jews, who contrasted the poor presence and feeble diction of Paul (2 Cor. 10.10). Other converts claimed to belong to Cephas (Peter) and there may even have been a 'Christ' party, intending to go back behind all parties to Jesus.

Disputes

In the disputes, Paul contrasts his converts' fanciful bliss and boasts, with the actuality of the conditions of himself and Apollos. There is no real ground for the converts' self-esteem – Do they really think they are filled, and rich, with heavenly blessing? Do they imagine they are reigning royally, and offering to share their powers with Paul? Untrue! for any gifts they have, have been from God, through Paul's efforts and others. The converts' hypothetical spiritual wealth and 'royal status' in the Kingdom, Paul contrasts with the actual life and lot of the apostles – like doomed gladiators, 'sentenced to death', displayed before the world, before an audience of angels and humans!

The Contrast

Paul puts forward his style of life – no honour, nor praise, but hunger and thirst; ill-clad, knocked about, no home to go to; scratching a living by working with their hands. (Do we remember Paul's craft of tent-making?) Life as it really is – returning blessing for curses; enduring gamely when persecuted; slandered, but showing good intentions; always battling for the truth. This is the real life of an apostle – treated as rubbish and refuse. (It is possible the words used here may carry the sense of 'human sacrifice', the scholars tell us. Is Paul perhaps half-prepared for an attempt at assassination as described in Acts 23?)

Problems
We get here a glimpse of the problems and difficulties the early Christians had to face; even such a powerful figure as Paul, had a hard battle against the spirit of faction that had developed in the church at Corinth. Let us work and pray for unity and fellowship in our churches today; and for tolerance and the spirit of understanding to work in our hearts.

The Seventh Sunday after Trinity 26 July 1998 Prayer
'Lord, teach us to pray.' Luke 11.1

The Family Prayer
What is prayer? Perhaps the best definition comes from St Augustine; it is simple – like the Lord's Prayer itself, which we have just heard – but deceptively simple. St Augustine's definition is:

> *'Prayer is the raising of the heart and mind to God.'*

Jesus has given us a picture of a very 'religious' person – that Pharisee who 'stood and prayed thus with himself' – something that, alas, many of us will spend too much time doing. Not only is it a waste of time, it will lead in the end to the destruction of the soul. 'He that loveth his life shall lose it.' We get eaten up with self-pity, self-flattering, self-justification — and self-love. How can we be of use to the family of God when we are like that?

Useful Prayer
We become useful to the family of God only when, and only in proportion as, we turn our self-centred soliloquies into a dialogue, with – instead of ourselves – at the centre we place Our Father. 'I will arise and go to my Father', and in place of ourselves and our complaints we put 'Hallowed be thy Name' – 'Thy Kingdom come' – 'Not my will but thine be done.'

Remember that our Lord knows our human needs well; how

144

lovingly he comes to the aid of our weakness, our constant distractions, our anxieties, our fears. Because he knows our world of talk, in which we so often set off on tangents, lose our way, get confused, become self-centred in a fog of theories, opinions, words – he showed a way to find a personal focus, not only of the mind, but also of our senses and our heart.

'Father, not my will but thine'

The whole approach to God, according to Jesus, is that of sons and daughters to their father, not of subjects to their king. Our Father's dwelling should be seen as a home with the entrance wide open, not as a palace carefully guarded. 'Give us . . . Forgive us . . . Lead us . . . Deliver us . . .' The scholars tell us that in Aramaic, the common language of the Holy Land in the time of Jesus, petitions might rather be affirmations – 'You will give us . . . You will forgive us . . . You lead us . . . You deliver us' – not so much petitionary prayer as affirmatory prayer. 'Your Father knows your needs before you ask!' If God is your Father, how much more will he grant the petitions of his children!

Seventh Sunday after Trinity *Second Sermon* **Temptation**

'God keeps faith, and he will not allow you to be tested above your powers, but when the test comes he will at the same time provide a way out, by enabling you to sustain it.' 1 Cor. 10.3

Trials

Temptation is a very real thing; but it is not sin. Yes, it may lead to sin; but it need not do so. We need to remember that we would not be truly personal human beings if the power of choice was not ours – and God-given. Temptation may lead to a wrong choice; but it may equally lead to the right and good choice. Temptation can lead to greater strength. If it is not resisted it may lead to further, and still further, weakness. Oscar Wilde (in *The Picture of Dorian Gray*) gives a warning hidden behind superficial cynicism: 'The only way to get rid of a temptation is to yield to it.'

It may be that there was something of this gloomy outlook in the minds of his readers when St Paul reminds them that temptations are not superhuman. They are such as we mortals have resisted, and will be called upon to resist. In all this God is faithful to himself and to us. He has called us, and he is ready to help and protect: 'The Lord is well able to rescue the righteous out of trials' (2 Peter 2.9). He will always provide a way out, a means to overcome the allurings of evil.

Assurance

There is assurance in St Paul's words. God allows us to be tried and tested, with a view to strengthening us; when we are being tested he shows us how to overcome the claims of evil. Life is a thoroughfare, and we can find the exit just as we found the entrance.

God does not force his help upon us, yet it is always available. Nothing will befall us that we shall not be able either to baffle or to defeat – so long as we have God's strength available and call upon him in our need.

> *O Lord Christ,*
> *before whose judgement seat we must all appear:*
> *keep us steadfast and faithful in your service,*
> *and enable us so to judge ourselves in this life,*
> *that we may not be condemned*
> *in the day of your appearing;*
> *for your tender mercies' sake.*
>
> *William Bright (PHG)*

Eighth Sunday after Trinity   2 August 1998   Self-satisfaction

'Take your ease, eat, drink and be merry!' Luke 12.19

A Story

In old story books, you may read the account of a certain knight, who asked – no, demanded – a really decent reward for some extra important service that he had done for the king. What it was that the knight actually did, is not specified, but it must have been something valuable and it must have been difficult. What the knight thought he ought to get for his efforts, was a nice decent-sized manor, somewhere pleasant and fertile of course. The king, unfortunately, had nothing available, and did not want to upset any well-to-do supporter by confiscating *his* manor and handing it over to the new man.

So, in the end, the king took the fellow out to some fairly wild area, and told him that he could have as much land for his manor, as he could run round in a day. Out in the country, the king and the court were there to applaud, and the man set off at a great pace, making as wide a sweep as possible to take in plenty of land. Well, he ran so hard that towards the end he had a heart-attack and died. So, all he actually got was a six-foot hole in the ground.

That story has some echoes of the vivid parable that Jesus tells, in today's Gospel. It is a parable about a rich man who set his mind on getting as much in the way of wealth as possible. His barns were not big enough to hold all his goods and his crops as they increased, so he decided to build bigger ones; and then he could sit back and enjoy life knowing he had enough in stock to keep him comfortably for years ahead; but he was completely forgetting the purpose of his life, and his ultimate destiny.

Choice

We have freedom to make our own choices in this life of ours. We can choose what we prefer in so many directions and so many areas. This freedom or self-determination is ordinarily, and indeed rightly, attributed to every normal human being. We are entitled, we say, to make up our minds for ourselves and to do as we think fit. But as soon as we have said this, doubts do creep in.

We can't buy, say, new curtains if we haven't got the money because we are unemployed or underpaid. And then, what about people who not only have no curtains, but no room to live in? No house, no shelter even.

So our choices are limited by all sorts of considerations external to us; also by our upbringing, heredity, and other factors. And how many of the things we choose are just for our own self-satisfaction, careless of any reference to our faith or our God. We cannot live by bread alone, said Jesus; that is, we must keep the vision of God in the world, and not let him be blocked out, by the worship of material goods for themselves alone.

Eighth Sunday after Trinity   *Second Sermon*
Spiritual Gifts

'Make love your aim, and earnestly desire the spiritual gifts, especially that you may prophesy.' 1 Cor. 14.1

Charismatic

Charisma in the Greek, means 'gift' or 'gift of grace.' In the Early Church speaking in 'tongues' and prophecy, were both taken as signs of God's Spirit being present, and of his Kingdom having arrived. Paul in today's lesson writes about the different kinds of gifts which the Holy Spirit imparts to those who are baptized. St Paul clearly prefers 'spiritual gifts' (Gal. 5.22 f.) or the 'greater gifts' (1 Cor. 12.31) that is, faith, hope and love, to the more 'showy' gifts such as 'speaking with tongues'. However, he certainly enjoyed the gift of tongues, but he wanted to limit its use in public assembly, and maintained that prophecy was a more important gift. 'One who speaks in a tongue speaks not to men, but to God; for no one understands him, but he utters mysteries in the Spirit. On the other hand, he who prophesies speaks to man for their upbuilding, their encouragement and their consolation' (vv. 1,2,3). Certainly it seems that the Christian prophets were inspired preachers, proclaiming God's will, and warning of the results of failure to follow that will.

Interpretation

Anyone who speaks in tongues ought to pray for the gift of interpretation; there is little use unless the glossalia is interpreted that the Church may be built up or edified. If St Paul arrives exercising his glossalia, what profit would it bring unless he made it into revelation, knowledge, prophecy or teaching? So a Christian, to be understood, must speak intelligibly or else – talk to the wind.

Both understanding and spirit have their place in singing and in praying; but if a blessing is given 'in the Spirit' how will the uninitiated be able to say 'Amen', if not understanding what has been said? This would be confusing for interested visitors – perhaps members of a family where one person is already involved with the church – who have come along to see, and to take an experimental tasting of what goes on, to see how they liked it, and whether it was of any use or indeed interest.

Today
There has been a considerable revival of the speaking in tongues in our own time, and indeed in the variety and agility of the prayers used and welcomed in every activity, mental and physical. 'So we prayed about it for a while.' 'We prayed it over.' 'We prayed it through.' 'We instantly called a prayer meeting.' Dr Carey's book *The Church in the Market Place* is full of praying things through, and he explains how prayer kept the projects going, how bewilderment turned to praise, how despondency was overcome ... The church in Durham is now large, warm and rich with facilities. (*The Church Hesitant*, Ysenda Graham, 1993.)

The Ninth Sunday after Trinity 9 August 1998 The Coming of the Son of Man

'Blessed are those servants whom the master finds awake when he comes.'
Luke 12.40

Preparation
The warnings in the previous chapter – 'Why be anxious, O men of little faith! Do not be anxious about small things – food, clothes, the needs of life – Seek God's kingdom and all these things shall be yours as well' – are swept up in the tremendous promise – Jesus tells his 'little flock' that it is the loving pleasure of the Father to give them the kingdom. With this assurance, by all means go ahead, sell what you have, and give alms – so you will provide yourselves with unfailing treasures in heaven.

Readiness
We are to be ready like servants waiting for their master, as he returns from the marriage feast – that is, the heavenly banquet; for if they are awake and ready, he himself will minister to them. Servants have to be vigilant, and their master's reward will depend on how he finds them when he arrives. They are left to administer Christ's household, and when the glorified Son of Man arrives and they are found faithful, they will be rewarded. For the time of the arrival will be unexpected, and they must be continuously alert.

The Kingdom

Luke sees the effect of Jesus coming on earth amongst men and women as joy, gladness praise and thanksgiving. He leaves no doubt of the way he conceived the difference Jesus made to human experience. Faith in Christ was doing far more for people, for human souls, in the bemused, decaying and disintegrating society of the time than any Mystery-Cult, philosophy – Greek or Roman, or political revolution could do. Life, Luke tells us, gains meaning, value, zest and purpose in Jesus. From Luke we learn to find in Christ an invigorating, liberating, joyous life-enhancing zest and drive, that would bring the world to the feet of the Lord.

For the full consummation and power of the Kingdom, is still to come; and we wait for, pray for, and seek its arrival. In and through the Church, the Kingdom has begun to come, and is indeed coming to many; and may yet come in power in the world, allowing its blessings to comfort and enrich the lives around it.

> Eternal Giver of love and life,
> your Son Jesus Christ has sent us into all the world
> to preach the gospel of his kingdom;
> confirm us in this mission,
> and help us to live the good news we proclaim,
> through Jesus Christ our Lord.
>
> *(Patterns for Worship 52.26)*

Ninth Sunday after Trinity *Second Sermon* Not Yes and No, but always Yes!

'The Son of God, Jesus Christ, whom we preached among you, was not Yes and No; but in him it is always Yes.' 2 Cor. 1.19

The Divine Answer 'Yes'

In Asia Paul had suffered a crushing experience – perhaps it is what is referred to in 1 Corinthians 15.32 'I fought with beasts at Ephesus'? or perhaps the riots mentioned in Acts 19? Whatever it was, Paul was so overwhelmed that he was expected to die (2 Cor. 1.8–11) but he recovered. God rescues still, and Paul asks for the prayers of the converts that he can still rely on his deliverance, and that many may be made thankful for the answer to this prayer.

Paul had altered his plans; his letters were written straightforwardly for all to understand. They show, like his life, that the converts have him as their basis for any boasting, if such there is to be! He has not been 'fickle' in any real sense, by altering his plans; he was in fact hoping to see them again.

He makes a comment on the nature of the Son of God – Christ is the affirmative answer – 'Yes' – to all God's promises. Paul believes in a God who carries out his promises, so how can he be anything but sincere?

When the church answers 'Yes', 'Amen', 'So be it', it is endorsing the truth of the preaching.

Paul and his converts were together made over to God through Christ, consecrated, marked with his seal in baptism, as he puts it (v. 22) a pledge (guarantee) of the blessing to come; the Spirit being the 'anticipation of the end in the present'.

The Tenth Sunday after Trinity   16 August 1998   The Fire of Love

'I am come to cast fire upon the earth; and would that it were already kindled!' Luke 12.49

Kindled and Ready?

Jesus said, 'I am come to cast fire upon the earth; and would that it were already kindled!' Is that fire kindled in us? Is there in us the fire of Christ, ready to flame out at the prompting of the Spirit?

In the midst of our regular, commonplace, ordinary life, there comes to us, every now and then, impulses telling us to break away from our ordinary habits and customs, to disregard appearances, to yield to the impulses of the Spirit of Christ, disregard the opinions of the world – and the opinions of our neighbours! Dare we ever make that venture?

Dare we risk anything for loyalty to the voice that speaks within us? Dare we rise to the standard to which we are called? The call is the same call that the early disciples heard by the lakeside – 'Follow me!'

Taking Risks

It is in our devotion to love that we are called to show our mettle. It is in our devotion to love that we are called to run a risk, to make our venture. Life is full of opportunities to show that love, which is the mark of Christ, in ordinary life. And we neglect them – sometimes over and over again.

Why? Because we are afraid of disturbing the comfortable relations between ourselves and our world. We are tied and bound by the customs of our own life and the customs of the society to which we belong; we are afraid of the unknown, of anything that will break up the comfort of our peace.

The unknown and dangerous force is the force of the Divine Love; struggling to make itself felt as a living Power within us. It is only by running the risk of losing, that we can gain a victory. It is only by making a venture, that we can win the prize.

True Life

Religion is not a department of life – it is Life itself! And Life is really one thing: fellowship of spirit with spirit, of humanity with God, of one human being with another.

Here is the great adventure, the great true romance of life – to follow up in every form and degree of human fellowship, and in all our social life, the revelations of the possibilities of love – revelations, all of them, of that Divine Love which calls us 'at the lakeside' – the Divine Love, whose fire is kindled in the human soul.

Tenth Sunday after Trinity *Second Sermon*
Human Speech

'You who are so rich in everything – in faith, speech, knowledge, and zeal of every kind.' 2 Cor. 8.7

A Great Gift from God

One of the greatest gifts which God has given the human race is – the ability to talk to one another. There are a number – not very many – of attributes which make humanity unique among the living creatures in our world. One is speech. Birds and animals have some power of communication with others of their own kind, but only to a very limited extent, and by sound and signs, not words. Human beings can exchange ideas of the most complex nature.

Think how much the ability to talk – once humans discovered how to do it, helped our race to rise above the wild beast level, and then by slow degrees, from the savage to the civilized. Speech enabled the discoverers of wonderful things; like fire, to pass on their discoveries to others, who in turn spread them still further.

Increased Usefulness

From time to time developments in human knowledge have greatly increased the usefulness of speech. The arts of reading and writing, putting down sounds on clay or stone or papyrus or paper, has done most of all to make extensions of speech. Knowledge can be sent to distant countries, or can be kept for future generations long after the authors are dead. Radio and television have made it possible for one human being to communicate with one or thousands – perhaps on the other side of the world – all at once.

Misuse of Gifts

There is another side – while all God's gifts to us are meant to be well used, this is not always so of speech and communication, as the Bible reminds us. The Book of Proverbs, for instance, contains much about wrong and foolish talk, and the sin of lying. St James, in his short but pointed Epistle towards the end of the Bible, has sharp things to say about 'the tongue' – the tongue is like a fire, which can soon spread and cause vast destruction if misused. Spiteful talk and malicious gossip can hurt, whether on a village scale or through radio and TV on country-wide, or even international, scale.

Good Use

On the other hand, we can use our abilities to express sympathy, to cheer and encourage; we can spread the truth against lies or mistakes. We can speak up, and not keep quiet as the easy way out. And of course we can use our abilities in teaching and instruction; and in spreading friendship amongst the lonely or old. May our words, as well as deeds, advance Christ's kingdom on earth.

The Eleventh Sunday after Trinity   23 August 1998   Bound and Loosed

'Ought not this woman, a daughter of Abraham whom Satan bound for eighteen years, be loosed from this bond on the sabbath day?' Luke 13.16

The Woman with a Spirit of Infirmity

Israel's repentance in face of the crisis of the Kingdom, may be seen chiefly in respect of those treated as outcasts or in bondage. The woman in the synagogue is 'bound', with the implication (v. 16) that a daughter of Abraham is being treated as an outcast.

She is bent over and unable to raise herself; condemned for eighteen years to stumble through life with head down, she is released by Christ, lifted up, and set walking upright in the world, to look the rest of society in the face. So, Luke implies, Jesus has done for all women; and so, as we know, he has done for women in every land, and of every generation.

'Praise God!'

She praised God for her relief, and is at once condemned by the ruler of the synagogue; clearly an opponent of women taking any part in public worship! Perhaps he is still bound by the prejudices based upon the story of Eve; at any rate, 'all Jesus' adversaries are 'put to shame' (v. 17) and everyone 'rejoiced at all the glorious things that were done by him'.

Luke sees in the person and the teachings of Jesus, a fairness and a tenderness, a dignity and opportunity, given to women which contrasts strongly with the treatment and thinking of Jews and pagans. Indeed, here are to be seen lessons which might well be taken to heart in our own day and circumstances. The dawning of the Kingdom of God brings with it a new era in all respects, and in all human affairs and relationships.

Narrow Legalism

Israel's response in face of the crisis of the Kingdom will be shown chiefly in respect of the treatment of those in bondage and the outcasts. The rulers of Israel are blind to such needs and opportunities, because of their narrow legalism, which prevents them from seeing the significance of the words and works of Jesus. The ordinary people, however, rejoice.

Grant us your light, O Lord,
that the darkness of our hearts being done away,
we may be brought at the last
to the light which is Christ.

Ven. Bede (PHG 49)

Eleventh Sunday after Trinity *Second Sermon* 'God loves a cheerful giver'

2 *Cor.* 9.7

The True Spirit of Giving

Paul may write that it is 'superfluous' for him to write more about the touchy subject of giving; but he does in fact carry on doing so for some length! We would all agree that there should be no compulsion on the part of whoever is asking for the gifts, and equally there should be no grudging on the part of the giver. God loves a cheerful giver, and can bless us with more than enough, both to meet our own needs and to allow for gifts for the benefit of others. The charity – or righteousness (as often the benevolence of God is named in late Judaism) 'endures for ever' – that is, is a constant aspect of the love and mercy of God, as noted in Psalm 112.9.

Thanks to God

God will supply those who will give; and to God we should give our thanks for the donations. Contributions of this kind will give rise to praise for the effects of the Gospel, as well as for themselves. The poorer members of the Christian community will have their needs fulfilled, and in return will give overflowing thanks to God. Christians in Jerusalem will be attracted to the converts and will certainly include them in their prayers. There will be, in fact, an increase in mutual love, understanding, and concern all round, through the grace of God.

So let us thank God for his gift past all expression, that is, the Lord Jesus Christ the example and self-embodiment of the self-giving of God, the source of all our Christian giving.

Gifts and Giving
When we receive God's bounty, we should be bountiful in our thanks to him; whether in money, in goods or in service is for us to decide, depending on how we have been blessed. Thanks for bountifulness should be showed not only by our lips, but also by our lives. The bountiful person is never a selfish person; we should recognize that God's gifts to us – which enable us to earn our living, and to make the best we can of the life and opportunities we perceive and make proper use of – these gifts are our capital, as it were, and God's gifts should be acknowledged. God should first of all receive back his own proportion, and when that has been given back to him, he sanctifies all that remains.

> *May Christ the Lord*
> *draw us to humility and worship,*
> *and give us the will each day*
> *to live in life eternal.*
> *(Patterns for Worship)*

Twelfth Sunday after Trinity 30 August 1998 'Places of Honour'

'Every one who exalts himself will be humbled; and he who humbles himself will be exalted!' Luke 14.11

Top of the Table
In one of his books, the philosopher Lord Bertrand Russell claimed that our lives are controlled by one single urge – to gain power for ourselves over others. Man's material needs can be satisfied, but his longing for power is insatiable. Jesus, however, takes a different point of view.

'Don't take the top seat at a function' the Lord tells us. The pushy powerful person loves to be in the limelight; he is going to sit in the place of honour at a feast. so he shoves everyone else aside. But he is not great in God's eyes; in fact he takes a very low place in God's estimation. The Pharisees 'religiously' arranged their guests; Jesus, the Gospel tells us, seems to use such invitations to take them to task – he reverses everything they regard as 'correct' and tells them who they should really be entertaining – 'the poor, the maimed, the lame, the blind'.

Power of Wealth

The power of wealth to assist others is frequently insisted on by Jesus. The giving of alms, for example – 'Sell all that you have and distribute to the poor, and you will have treasure in heaven' (18.22) and 'Sell your possessions, and give alms; provide yourselves with purses that do not grow old, with a treasure in the heavens that does not fail, where no thief approaches and no moth destroys' (12.33). Do good, expecting nothing in return. 'As you wish that men would do to you, do so to them' (6.31).

Rules

Jesus attacks any establishment which believes that the way to God can be planned according to human rules and ideas. How do our Christian communities come out of this approach? Jesus tells us that nothing can be further from the truth. Yet, we still fuss over who can be allowed to take a place at the Lord's Table! When Jesus expounded his belief in a parable about eating bread in the kingdom of God, he gave his view on who would be suitable table companions (14.15–24) with him. Can we really still hold back from admitting those, who we think are not 'proper', for this or that reason of man's devising?

Real Treasure

Both wealth and poverty were, for Jesus, among the accidents, not the essentials, of life; humanity's real treasure 'the pearl of great price' is to live under God's rule. Detachment – the ability to be rich without loving money, or growing proud, or to be poor without anxiety or envy – here is the way towards contentment.

Twelfth Sunday after Trinity   *Second Sermon*   The Testimony of John the Baptist

John 3.22–36

Jesus and John Baptist

In this passage from the Gospel, John the Evangelist places Jesus and John Baptist as both pursuing their calls and their work at the same time; both are baptizing, and John is not imprisoned as yet.

John's disciples are told what they already know; that is, that Jesus is more successful than John – 'All are going to him!' This comment does not rouse in John any irritation or annoyance; he accepts – as he has said before – that he is the Herald, the Precursor, the one sent ahead. Now that the Christ has come, he must recede into insignificance. This is how it must be. In a wedding, the best man has a part to play; but in no way does he compare in importance with the bridegroom.

The difference between John and Jesus is, of course, that the former is a man – commissioned, indeed by God, but no more than a man; but Jesus is the Son of God. The following verses are thought by the scholars to come from a different hand; some trace an Aramaic original. The theme is that Father and Son are one through the Father's love, and the Son shares the Father's authority. The climax is in v. 36; belief in the Son is of ultimate significance – 'eternal life' or the 'wrath of God'.

This indeed might be taken to be the message of John in its most concentrated and clearest form; and it is here being pressed upon the readers. The Baptist cannot be understood except as the one who comes before the Lord, to prepare the way of the Lord. As a Nazarite, perhaps an Essene, he was taught to see the world as a terminally ill case, dependent upon the mercy of God to redeem it. That redemption, for John's thinking, was inseparably associated with the promised Messiah; and that Messiah, he had come to believe, was in the person of Jesus of Nazareth. He, John, had come also to believe that he was the Precursor, the one who prepares the way, for the Hope of Israel.

> *Almighty and everlasting God,*
> *whose servant and prophet John Baptist,*
> *bore witness to the truth as a burning and shining lamp,*
> *lead us to bear witness to your Son,*
> *who is the eternal Light and Truth,*
> *and lives and reigns with you and the Holy Spirit,*
> *now and for ever.*

(PHG 42)

The Thirteenth Sunday after Trinity
6 September 1998   Think before you Act
'This man began to build, and was not able to finish!' Luke 14.30

Crowds
Jesus had become well-known as a striking and impressive preacher; so much so, that as St Luke tells us, 'Great multitudes accompanied him' (14.25). What did he mean by his very powerful opening – 'If anyone comes to me and does not hate his own father and mother and wife and children and brothers and sisters, yes, and even his own life'? This was Jesus' opening, according to the evangelist, to the crowds. Was it not directed at the people who had come out for an afternoon, and said, 'Let's go and hear that new preacher – he's a real fire and brimstone man, uncle says – he listened to him yesterday and was really shocked!' May it not be that Jesus was becoming tired of crowds, followers who merely wanted a thrill, as it were, and had no real interest, and certainly no desire, to understand what he was saying.

Tough Talk
When idle folk heard what he was saying, we can imagine that they were 'turned off' when they heard such tough demands put before them. *Hate* your own family? *Renounce* all that you have? But those with a deeper insight, those who were indeed looking for a new life, a new way of living, a complete change – these might have been shocked, yes, at first – but on thinking what they had heard over, the real message of Christ would come through. He is telling them that indeed there may be suffering, pain, trouble – even death – but you will be with me!

Do you want to make something of your life? Do you want to really serve your fellow human beings? Do you want to truly help to improve this world, this country we live in? Above all, do you believe in a God of love, of power for good, who cares for each individual living soul? This is my Father – and your God and Father.

Christ
The tremendous personality of Our Lord; his love, his spiritual power, his wondrous character, his deeply religious nature – if down the ages, what is recorded in the New Testament is powerful

enough to draw men and women to his service, prepared to give all – including their lives – what effect must the living Lord have had in Palestine two thousand years ago?

He does not expect every follower to give away everything he possesses; but he expects love to dominate everything done. We must give whole-hearted service; whatever the cost may be in self-sacrifice. We cannot take up his demands without deepening our faith, increasing our love, putting aside our own demands; but when we do, our eyes are opened to a wonderful world, and we have beside us the most wonderful Person we – or anyone – has ever known or will know.

Thirteenth Sunday after Trinity *Second Sermon* The Witness to Christ

'The testimony which I have is greater than that of John; there is enough to testify that the Father has sent me, in the works my Father has given me to do and to finish – these very works which I am doing.' John 5.36

What do you think of Christ?

Plenty of people are ready to admire Christ, and believe – no doubt – that if more people followed his teaching, the world would be a better place. What they lack is a real and vital belief in the divinity of Christ, in the divine grace and power that can make possible the impossible, can triumph where there was nothing but failure.

What do you think of Christ? The only real answer can be that he is the divine Son of God.

The Witness of John

Jesus speaks of the testimony of John the Baptist. He was the lamp which bears a borrowed light, burning and shining – there was a warmth about John; but he pointed to Christ: 'Among you stands one whom you do not know, but he is the One who is to come after me' (John 1.26,27).

There was an exciting quality about the teaching of John, and for a time the Jews enjoyed it and were excited by it. Well, there are always some people like that, who look for excitement and enjoy the preacher's style and material – so long as it doesn't involve a change in their lives and conduct. 'You were willing to exult in his light.'

The Witness of the Works

Jesus then points to the witness of his works, 'these very works which I am doing', as witnessing to the power of God at work through him. When John was in prison, he sent to Jesus, asking if he was the Christ, or must they look for another? For answer, Jesus, told the messengers to tell John what they had seen – 'The blind recover their sight, the lame walk, the lepers are made clean. The deaf hear, the dead are raised to life – most astonishing of all, the poor have the Gospel preached to them' (Luke 7.22). The power of God is seen in the works that Jesus performed. The fact that we respond to Jesus, that there is in him that which attracts and draws us – is a sign of the God within us.

God witnesses to Christ in the scriptures; the scriptures point to Christ, and they find their meaning in him. The Jews searched the scriptures (v. 39) but they did so in a wrong way; using the scriptures not to listen to God, but to find arguments to support their own position and beliefs, and not for God. 'I know that you have no love of God in you' (v. 42). The standard that matters is that of God, for it is by this that we shall be judged. Jesus was not seeking his own honour: 'I do not look to men for honour.' What he did, was for love of us, to save us. 'You refuse to come to me, that you may have life' (v. 40). The Jews had no welcome for Jesus, but were only too ready to believe in some impostor, some self-accredited Messiah (v. 43). Their own condemnation – who say they believe in Moses – comes from Moses, for he pointed to Christ, as the One who was to come.

Fourteenth Sunday after Trinity   13 September 1998   Losing and Finding

'Rejoice with me, for I have found my sheep which was lost!' Luke 15.1–10

The Call of Jesus

Let us try to see Jesus for a moment. Visualize him, standing perhaps on the beach at Galilee, the blue sky above and the green hills behind, the little waves rippling at his feet. Or imagine him sitting on a bench outside a hostelry (just an ordinary house but with a leafy branch over the door) talking with some of the men of the place; enjoying a drink and a joke, having a laugh; and in turn telling a tale or two himself. The snooty clerics pass by, muttering – 'disgusting!'

So Jesus tells the shepherds and the farmers a story or two, with a message tucked inside each of them. Just as pointed for us today as for them far away and long ago.

The Individual

Notice the care for the individual looker or seeker, that Christ mentions twice in our gospel story today.

The shepherd who goes off into the wilderness, the countryside, at the end of the day, to seek everywhere for his one lost sheep. And the housewife, sweeping and seeking everywhere in the little house for that one lost coin. Was it from her well-worn purse, or was it from her single piece of jewellery, her marriage necklace? Whichever it was, she is so pleased when she finds it!

Do we put that care and that effort into our attempts to reach out and make friendly contact with others, to reach out to that someone who may be lost? Do we welcome someone who is a stranger at our service? A smile and a word of welcome for you – what an effect that simple action can have! And don't think you have to leave everything to the clergy or to the churchwardens – they have enough already. Try it yourself; throw aside your shyness, make the effort; once you have tried it, it's surprising how easy a habit it becomes. But – it must be genuine, not forced.

Our Care

Then, away from church, in our work, at our office or factory or shop, with the folk we meet in our daily lives – with our family and neighbours and friends – How do we show the Love of Christ to them? How much do we attempt to reflect something of the mind and attitude of our Lord and Master, Jesus Christ, into their hearts and minds? Our mission is not a question of preaching at people; it is a question of openness, of sympathetic understanding, a certain sensitivity also, and above all, our being ready to listen.

It is a forgetting, or at least a laying on one side, of our own worries and problems even if only for a little while – and of opening ourselves to others.

The Body of Christ (at the Eucharist)
In a little while we will be saying 'We are the Body of Christ' at the Peace. We will clasp hands together as a symbol of fellowship, and of the task we share in common – clergy and layfolk working together with a common aim. 'We are the Body of Christ,' we say. What a claim, and also what a responsibility! Because – Christ has no body now on earth – but ours. No hands – but ours. No feet – but ours. Ours are the eyes through which Christ's compassion looks out upon the world. Ours are the feet with which he is to go about doing good. Ours are the hands with which he is to bless men and women now.

We are all he has. Sometimes we may think we are not much, but – we are all he has.

Fourteenth Sunday after Trinity *Second Sermon* **Bread from Heaven**
'My flesh is food indeed, and my blood is drink indeed. He who eats my flesh and drinks my blood abides in me, and I in him.' John 6.55,56

The Eucharist
The Eucharist – that is, 'The Thanksgiving', which is what the Greek word means – has been the centre of Christian life and worship almost everywhere and at almost every time. Sometimes, it is true, there have been relapses towards primitive conceptions, sometimes there has been corruption, or slackness, or conflicts of theories; there have been sometimes bewildering divergences of practice.

And yet, and yet – in spite of all this, the Christian can still find the same essential source of worship, of refreshment and of spiritual life; the same access to the Love of God, and the same invitation to offering and communion, in the oblation and hallowing of the bread and the wine.

Symbols of Life

In this service we take bread and take wine. What are they? They are the perfect symbols of the work and life of humanity. Before there can be bread, the land must be ploughed, the seed sown, the harvest gathered in, the corn threshed, the flour baked. And before all that, there must be the gift of God in the life of the seed, the nourishment provided by the soil, the rain, the sun.

Bread then, is an example of God's gifts made available to humanity by human labour for the satisfaction of our human needs.

The same is true of wine; the planting and cultivation of the vine, the gathering of the grapes, the pressing in the vats, the maturing of the juice into wine; all dependent not merely on man's labour and skill, but on the natural world of soil and sun and rain.

Co-operation with God

In the production of bread and wine, we humans co-operate with God. The farmer who cares for his land but neglects his prayers, is – as a farmer – co-operating with God. And the farmer who says his prayers but neglects his land and its needs, is failing, as a farmer, to co-operate with God.

'It is a mistake we often make, to imagine that God is only – or even chiefly – concerned with religion', said the great Archbishop William Temple. But of course the truly Christian farmer cares for both land and prayers together.

Offering to God

We take the bread and the wine – symbols of humanity's industrial and commercial life – and offer them back to God. Then, because we have offered them to him, he gives them back to us; not merely as food, necessary though that is for our animal or material side, but also as the means of nourishing our spiritual life. He makes us, through this sacrament, agents of his purpose, limbs of a body which is to do his will in the world, and sharers of his life.

And, as we share God's own life, so we share the lives of other human beings, in true and real fellowship.

Two fine prayers are often said at the presenting of the bread and the wine in the Communion service. They are full of teaching and we may care to use them ourselves privately, if they are not said aloud.

Blessed are you, Lord, God of all creation.
Through your goodness we have this bread to offer,
which earth has given and human hands have made.
It will become for us the Bread of Life:
> *Blessed be God for ever.*

Blessed are you, Lord, God of all creation.
Through your goodness we have this wine to offer,
fruit of the vine and work of human hands.
It will become the Cup of our Salvation.
> *Blessed be God for ever.*

The Fifteenth Sunday after Trinity
20 September 1998   God and Mammon

'The master commended the dishonest steward for his prudence.' Luke
16.8

A Sharp Operator

In Palestine of old, it was a common practice for country estates
to be run by stewards, in the place of the absentee owners. The
story Jesus tells today is about one such steward, and his somewhat tricksy goings-on.

This steward had been caught out in doing deals on the side
for cash. Now, the owner had found out, and was in process of
sacking him. So what was the steward to do? He had been
enriching himself by lending at high interest, money taken from
the profits of the estate. In strict Jewish Law, this was a crime and
the sin of usury; but there were ways round, enabling the steward
to keep just on the right side of the Law.

Profit!

So, if the debtors were not in arrears of rent, but borrowers of cash,
the situation is intelligible. The difference between a thousand and
eight hundred bushels of wheat represents interest at 25% (not an
unusual rate, we are told) while the difference between one thousand and five hundred gallons of oil represents interest at 100%
– which sounds high, but is paralleled in antiquity. This interest

is what the steward had hoped to snatch as personal profit; the rest represents what had to be paid to the owner.

Approbation
Being found out, and in imminent threat of dismissal to poverty, the steward thinks quickly. He will forgo the profit he had visualized, liquidate the original agreements 'on the side', and replace them with bare statements of the amount of the original loans. Thus he earns the gratitude of the debtors and can look to their future help. He is also back in the 'good books' of the authorities, for to ease or remit the payment of loans was regarded by the religious hierarchy as a meritorious act.

Again, as the steward has abandoned his plans for quick profit, the owner recovers his capital intact; pleased, he commends his steward for this piece of sharp thinking – and very probably keeps him in his employment after all.

Comment
Jesus comments that the steward – crook though he may have been – offers us a good example of radical and rapid action in the face of a crisis. Good pious people are rarely sharp enough when dealing with financial matters; 'Sons of Light' they may be, but they should give some more attention to making friends with the rich, and using their experience and their fortunes to help the needs of the Church. So it may be that we all may meet happily in the 'eternal habitations'!

Trust
The next group of sayings simply commend trustworthiness, and warn against greed. If we are not considerate of the needs and rights of others, we need not look surprised if our own needs and rights are not cared for. Again, we cannot serve two differing causes – we will either do all we can for the one, and let the other fall to the ground, or the reverse. We have to make our choice and stick with it when made. And let us be warned and not take the sharp practice of the dishonest steward as our example in our lives. Astute as he was, he had to learn the hard way that trying to be too clever led to disaster in the end.

Fifteenth Sunday after Trinity *Second*
Sermon **Jesus at the Temple**
'How is it that this untrained man has such learning?' John 7.14–36

His Teaching

Jesus went up to Jerusalem for the Feast of Tabernacles; not at the beginning, but towards the middle of the celebration. He taught publicly in the Temple; telling his listeners that he was proclaiming the divine gift of learning, something which they have misunderstood. He makes it clear he is not some prodigy of self-taught learning, trying to make a name as a teacher. His teaching is not his own but God's – as can be recognized by anyone who seriously tries to do God's will, and be obedient to God.

The very fact that Jesus does not seek notoriety for himself, but seeks the glory of the Father who sent him, is his authentication. In response he carries the attack into the enemy's camp – Moses gave them the Law, but they do not keep the Law. They are trying to kill Jesus – why?

The Sabbath

It appears that the dreadful sin is – curing a man on the Sabbath! This was the man who had been lying at the edge of the pool of Bethesda (5.2–9) – for thirty-eight years! It is Jesus' healing on the Sabbath which arouses powerful opposition; breaking the Sabbath is an offence against the basic principles of the Jewish faith!

On the other hand, there were certain exceptions – the case of the boys born on the Sabbath day who were circumcised on the following Sabbath (the 'eighth day' as the Law demands. (If this act is right, surely even more so is an act giving 'health to a whole body?' Why then be angry?

We get here an indication of the fierceness of the opposition. While the crowds – divided between friendly applause and hostile criticism – are very much in evidence, the friendly voices are fainter, the hostile ones are loud. Questions are asked about his early education and his authority to teach. Surprise is expressed that the Sanhedrin did not arrest him earlier (John 7.26,30,32). But no one ventures to touch him, daring though his words seem to be.

Where does he come from?

A strange argument is now put forward – scornful remarks are made about Jesus' origin, which is by no means as mysterious as that of the Messiah should be. The Messiah should appear, an unknown, from some secret recess; not like Jesus, whose village origin is well known. 'How foolish!' Where he came from was irrelevant; what mattered was that he truly and really 'came from God' (v. 29). 'Can it be that the authorities really know that this is the Christ?' (v. 26). The Pharisees and chief priests sent officers to arrest him (v. 32); 'I shall be with you a little longer, and then I go to him who sent me; where I am you cannot come'.

'Coming from God' implied that he would soon 'go to God' – his hearers are baffled; 'What does he mean?' Was he going to leave Palestine perhaps? 'Would he go off to the Dispersion' (the scattering of Jews among the Gentiles)? 'Would he teach the Greeks?'

Prophetic!

After his departure to the Father, the Gospel will indeed be taken to the Greeks – and they, unlike the Jews, will accept it. Here we see a certain prophetic truth – a great deal of the ultimate purpose of Jesus' life and work was indeed to 'teach the Greeks' from whom the rest of the world received the Gospels and indeed the whole New Testament. Thanks be to God!

The Sixteenth Sunday after Trinity
27 September 1998   God's Judgement

'Now he is comforted, and you are in anguish.' Luke 16.25

The Rich – and the Poor

Jesus paints a striking picture in this parable, using strong colours and dark shadows. It is a warning that we should set our sights on things above, rather than the enjoyment of the good things of this life.

The first picture is one of strong contrasts. We see the rich man in all his glory, surrounded by delights and pleasures, while at his very gate lies this pathetic figure, full of disease and racked by sores.

Who is the happier – the rich man without God, or the poor man with God? But this is not the question posed by Christ. Nothing is said about any kind of moral judgement between Lazarus and the rich man; one is very rich, one is very poor – that is all.

Life after Death
In the next scene, the second picture of the series, close together the two men lived and close together they died. But their fates are very different. Jesus takes the scene from contemporary Jewish folklore; he is describing in his parable what was (and probably still is, and not only in Palestine) the typical beliefs of the average person. Death is followed at once by judgement, and the soul goes at once to hell or heaven. Equally simply, the destination is decided not on whether, during life, behaviour had been 'good' or 'bad' – but whether rich or poor; and afterlife brings the appropriate pains or pleasures. This is a typical pronouncement from Jesus (which must have been highly popular with the ordinary folk who had heard him preach – 'Blessed are you who are in need' but 'Alas for you who are rich!' – Luke 6.20,24).

Can Nothing be Done?
The Rich Man is at least thinking not only of himself – he has in mind his five brothers – can they not be warned? Can Lazarus be sent to warn them, so that they may escape this place of torment?

What had the rich man done in life? No doubt he thought of himself as a decent enough fellow; no doubt also a moderate and well-intentioned follower of the religion of Israel, within limits, of course. He did not take in what was being plainly preached, anymore than his brothers. 'Moses and the prophets?' Listened to, but not heard – what is needed is a shock. What if someone was raised from the dead, would they not repent then?

Hopeless . . .
'If they will not listen to Moses, nor the prophets, they would not be convinced if someone should rise from the dead!' is the blunt answer. Was Jesus talking about another Lazarus, the brother of Mary and Martha, who indeed returned from the dead? or was he thinking ahead about his own resurrection – which at first was received with incredulity and even mockery (Acts 17.32).

We cannot take shelter in the excuses of the Rich Man for not believing – for we have our Easter, and we believe in One who is risen from the dead. Do we hear him, try our best to shape our lives to his directions, live in his Spirit, above all grow in his love – or not?

Sixteenth Sunday after Trinity *Second Sermon* Abraham's Children

'You will know the truth, and the truth will make you free.' John 8.32

True Freedom

Even the Temple police were attracted by Jesus; when ordered to arrest him (John 7.45) the reply they gave to the chief priests and Pharisees is striking: 'No man ever spoke like this man!' (John 7.45,46). There were indeed Jews who took Jesus very seriously (John 8.30) and to them he gave what should be words of great comfort – 'If you continue in my word, you are truly my disciples, and you will know the truth, and the truth will make you free' (John 8.31,32). Their query (v. 33) seems to stem from some doubt as to whether their Jewishness is being denigrated, as descendants of Abraham. Jesus states that those enjoying complete freedom in the political sense, may yet be slaves of sin; and true freedom comes by obedience to the word of Jesus. This is upsetting; they know *they* are children of God, and insinuate that Jesus' own claims are untrue.

Insultingly, they suggest Jesus is no true Jew, but a Samaritan. This is indeed a studied insult – they are identifying him with their bitterest enemies, and in addition suppose that he must be mad, 'possessed' by a demon.

Of course, Jesus is not mad, but he is certainly unusual in that he seeks not his own glory, but God's (v. 54). The offer of eternal life pushes the opponents further. 'Who do you claim to be?' The Jews' error was not that they did not recognize Jesus for what he was, but that they did not 'know God'. Jesus makes his reply in terms of Rabbinic teaching, which was that Abraham had seen the day of the Messiah, and rejoiced. The crowd prefer to take this as a blasphemous claim on the part of Jesus that he was alive many centuries ago. John, writing this gospel, put 'In the beginning was the Word, and the Word was with God' and thus 'Before Abraham was, I am' is meaningful and true. 'The crowd take up stones to throw at the Lord ... Mysteriously, Jesus is not to be seen; but left the temple' (v. 59).

The Seventeenth Sunday after Trinity
4 October 1998 **The Faith of a Servant**

The Apostles said to the Lord, 'Increase our faith!' Luke 17.5

Coming Event

The little band of Jesus and his companions are on the road again now, a journey which is gradually coming into their minds as being more than another evangelistic endeavour. Here is something of very grave importance; it has already been marked by the Transfiguration, which in its awesome happenings has foreshadowed – or perhaps illuminated – a fearful and wonderful event which is going to take place when they reach Jerusalem. A triumph? perhaps – or a disaster? Either way, their nerves are constantly being stretched and the atmosphere is tense.

'Increase our Faith'

No wonder then, that they ask the Lord for an increase of faith; they need a boost for the future, to help them to cope with whatever is coming. Faith and trust, together with their love and admiration of Jesus, need to be given a boost. The Lord takes the opportunity to compare faith to a mustard seed – tiny, but when it is planted and watered and grows, as in Mark 4, verse 31 – 'when it is sown it grows up and becomes the greatest of all shrubs, and puts forth large branches, so that the birds of the air can make nests in its shade.'

Jesus recalls this image – with the even more striking miracle of another tree, the sycamore, being rooted up and flying into the sea!

And Service . . .
Everyone understood the relationship of master and servant; and by calling oneself 'Servant of God' this little parable comes to life. The relationship between God and man has obvious parallels with the master and servant (or more correctly, 'slave'). This farmer is a small-holder in our terms; his one slave works the fields and cares for the sheep, prepares the food and serves it. The farmer is under no obligation to put the slave's comfort before his own. He doesn't thank the slave for doing what is commanded. No more should you expect thanks from God for doing what we are ordered to do; rather, say 'We are unworthy servants, and have only done what is our duty.'

Christ's Words
'Christ's words – and this is what makes them the Good News – persuade us that there is a purpose which can order our unruly desires without cramping them, and that our infinite longings point to our most intimate reality. They call us into acceptance of ever-shifting and changing human relationships, of unreserved committal to the creative experience of love, friendship and companionship, into our true life . . . But Jesus did not only demand commital; he committed himself, without reserve, to his friends; although he knew they would betray him. He loved them to the end; and that is our hope.' (Werner Pelz, *God is No More*)

Seventeenth Sunday after Trinity *Second Sermon* **The Light of the World**
'I am the light of the world.' John 9.3

A Dilemma
The situation of Jesus and his disciples is gloomy in the extreme; a huge and black shadow may be said to be hanging over the small band. The authorities have begun to show their hand with increasing hostility, witness the arguments at the Temple over the claims of Jesus. Stoning would have been the next step, if Jesus had not hidden himself, and slipped away.

Safe for the time being, Jesus halts at the pitiful spectacle of a blind beggar who no doubt hopes for charity from worshippers as they leave the Temple. The query from the disciples is based on the idea that disease or suffering must be due to sin. Jesus rejects this, and points to the opportunity offered for making manifest the intentions of God, health and light – and he claims again what has become perhaps the best-known of his titles, 'The Light of the World'. The man's eyes are anointed, and after the washing, as instructed, he sees; but interrogated by the Pharisees, their examination becomes, as it were, a trial of Jesus. However, they are caught on the horns of a dilemma. As Jesus has performed 'work' on the Sabbath it is not possible to accept him as 'from God' – but the dilemma is, how could a 'sinner' perform such a work?

A Marvel!

In his blunt forthright way, the beggar stands up for Christ – 'Why, here is a marvel! You do not know where he comes from, yet he opened my eyes ... If this man were not from God, he could do nothing!' Furious, the Pharisees reply, 'You were born in utter sin, and you presume to instruct us?!' and cast him out – excommunicate, as we would say.

Jesus heard about this, we are told, and sought out the man. Jesus asks if the 'excommunication' has been handed out for belief in the 'Son of Man'? Who is he, asks the beggar. Jesus reveals his identity, and is worshipped. No doubt, St John is intending us to see here the spiritual counterpart to the physical cure already performed. The man has believed in the light, and has become a son of light (ch. 12.36). Contrary-wise, the Pharisees ask 'Are we also blind?' The reply is: 'If you were blind, you would have no guilt; but you claim to see apart from the light of Christ, and so remain guilty' (9.41).

> Jesus, light of the world
> we worship and adore you.
> Your life is the light that shines in the dark
> a light that darkness cannot overpower.

> Jesus, light of the world,
> we worship and adore you.
> You came to your own, and they did not accept you.
> But to all who accept you
> You give power to become children of God.

Jesus, light of the world,
we worship and adore you.

(Patterns for Worship 65.2)

The Eighteenth Sunday after Trinity
11 October 1998   The Gift of Faith

'Rise and go your way; your faith has made you well.' Luke 17.19

The Ten Lepers

The healing work of Jesus is bestowed upon all the lepers alike;
but only the Samaritan responds. So it is that the Samaritan, the
one non-Jew, the outcast (in Jewish eyes) comes back, praises God
and thanks Jesus, and is praised for his attitude. 'Made you well'
is the same phrase as 'has saved you'. The same description is
used for healing, as for forgiveness.

A Samaritan

The leper who came back to Christ was an outcast in two degrees;
firstly, he was a Samaritan, whose worship of God – the same
God, would be claimed, as worshipped by the Jews – was, in
certain respects, more in accordance with the genuine, early
Hebrew faith and practice than that of the current time. Of course
this was strongly denied by the Pharisees, the scribes and the
lawyers of the Jerusalem religion. The mutual hatred of Jews and
Samaritans began in the days of the kingdom; it got worse after
the Exile, and reached its climax in the time of Alexander the
Great, when the Samaritans built a temple on Mount Gerizim.
From Nehemiah onwards a spirit of separateness prevailed, and
the Samaritans lost once and for all, the leadership in Palestine.

A Leper

Secondarily, of course, the man had contracted the dreadful disease of leprosy. Contagious, disfiguring, liable to cause the wither-
ing and rotting away of parts of the body – face and hands and
feet; today although still dangerous, it can be treated and pre-

vented from spreading. In olden days there was no hope of cure, and therefore sufferers had to keep – or be kept – away from contact with others – sometimes by badges or clothing of a distinctive nature, more often by threats, violence and brutality, and complete segregation.

The Word of Healing
For us, let the external healing point us to a lesson; let us try to realize what Christ can do for us today, by merely his words. We can experience his power in the reading and preaching of the Word of God; in the sacraments and in our prayers, as well as in the prayers of others. Let us remember that the sick are in some respects an image of the suffering Christ; unable to move, racked by pain, uncertain of their future. We should also remember those who – like the lepers, but in our own time – are outcasts of society; to be seen lying under arches, on pavements, in doorways; lonely and forgotten perhaps in some housing estate. Can we act in our small way as Christ towards such people?

Eighteenth Sunday after Trinity *Second Sermon* The Command of Love
'This is my commandment to you: love one another.' John 15.17

Love One Another
In this chapter the love of Christ for his followers, and the mutual love of his disciples for each other, is given real prominence. 'This is my commandment; love one another, as I have loved you. There is no greater love than this, that a man should lay down his life for his friends' (vv. 12,13). The great archbishop, Temple, comments: 'That the mutual love of Christians, reproducing their Lord's love for them, is to be measured by his death is now made perfectly clear.'

It may be said that faith in Christ, love for one another, and a loving effort and care for the world's salvation, are three of the essential 'notes' of the Christian discipleship. If we have a true faith in the Lord, and a confident trust in him, we shall be not only offering him our adoring love, but also our willing obedience.

Mutual Love

Christ's command of love, is not one of general philanthropy whenever and wherever, but it is a demand of sincere affection towards our brothers and sisters. Whatever differences there may be between Christians of a social character, that is of tastes and habits, interests and education, they are bound together with ties that are so strong that no force can separate them.

Motive of Love

This mutual love has its source, and is sustained, in and by Christ's love for his people. 'As I have loved you' are the words by which our Lord refers all duty and virtue to himself. For each one of us, as believers, Christ is the Master in all behaviour and conduct, and the spiritual power which empowers it. Remember, he loved and loves still, here and now, this world with a love in which he identifies his people with himself; and we are to show our devotion to him by loving humanity – in all its shapes, forms, colours – as himself. Christ alone is the perfect example; he loved his people with a constant, patient and forbearing love of immense depth, enormous width and eternal strength.

Evidence

The love we show to our brethren in Christ and to others, is the test which our Lord has chosen. It is a proof to a believer: 'We for our part have crossed over from death to life; this we know, because we love our brothers' (1 John 3.14). Here is proof, recognizable by our brethren. Love is a means of recognition. It is the language which tells us we have met a fellow Christian. And it is also an argument, and an example, for the convincing of the world, and the bringing of all humanity to Christ's pierced feet, in love and trust.

The Nineteenth Sunday after Trinity
18 October 1998   Pray Continually

'Now will not God see justice done to his chosen, who cry to him day and night, even when he delays to help them? I promise you, he will see justice done to them, and done speedily.' Luke 18.8

Nagging at God?

This parable must seem confusing at first hearing! Can Jesus really mean that if we pester God enough, keep nagging away, our prayer will be answered? We should consider the circumstances in which Jesus first told this parable. Firstly, the judge is not the kind of judge we are used to; in our legal system, your complaint *will* be heard – it may take time, it will almost certainly cost money (unless you are lucky and get Legal Aid) – but when you get to court you cannot imagine the judge simply refusing to listen!

A judge in Jesus' time was a paid official appointed by the occupying Power, that is, the Romans, to deal with 'civil' cases according to local rules and customs. (Criminal cases were dealt with by the occupying Power itself, as in the case of Jesus.)

Bribes

Now these local men were often heavily influenced by money, or political pressure, and if you were poor, and without rich or important relatives for friends, you stood precious chance of your case being heard for ages.

Shocking? Well, here in England it is not so long ago that a very senior judge, Sir Thomas More – later to be *Saint* Thomas More – had a great reputation for fair treatment and justice because, unlike other judges, he would take only *small* bribes! And we can think of cases – like the one-time famous Tichbourne trial, where all the money and wealth were swallowed up by the lawyers before the trial came to its conclusion.

Persistence

Now Jesus is not likening God to this rotten judge; but he is contrasting God with him. 'If,' says the Lord, 'an unjust and corrupt judge can be worried and worn down by a persistent woman to deal with her needs, how much more will God, your loving Father, give you what you most need and are asking for!' And if this is the Kingdom – 'Thy kingdom come' – yes, it will come – but will his people be found faithful? There is the question! Do we really *want* God's Kingdom?

Nineteenth Sunday after Trinity   *Second Sermon*   Keeping On

'I have said all this to keep you from falling away.' John 16.1

Persecution ahead ...

The disciples are warned by Jesus of the times ahead. There is the probability or rather, the certainty – of persecution. And not merely excommunication, but with perverted loyalty and enthusiasm for what is the wrong cause, followers of Christ will be killed.

This was not part of the Lord's teaching in earlier days because of his presence with them; but now he is going away. Where to? No one has asked this, but he is going to the Father, and they will see him no more. Immediately their hearts are filled with grief; the Lord comforts them with the promise of the Holy Spirit – or Counsellor – and he will convince the world of sin, of righteousness, and of judgement. Of sin, since the world will not believe in Jesus – and therefore he will be taken away; of mistaken and wrong ideas about righteousness and judgement. When the Spirit comes, he will guide them into all truth (v. 13).

In other words, Christ is preparing the minds and spirits of his disciples for the tragic times ahead – when he will have been killed, and they will be attacked on all sides as heretics, as wrongheaded, and excommunicate.

Disciples

We are his disciples; as disciples we must be aware that the Messiah, the one sent from God, of God himself, was destined to suffer and die for this world. We are to carry his message and live by his instructions, and above all proclaim the Kingdom that is to come. With the power of the Holy Spirit upon us, to direct our lives, we are to love and serve God, and above all spread the message of the life and teaching of Jesus.

The Last Sunday after Trinity   25 October 1998   Be Watchful

'How lovely is your dwelling place, O Lord of hosts!' Ps 84.1

The Promised Saviour

The Coming of the Messiah was a constant thought in the minds of pious Jews; they looked hopefully for the Day when the Saviour, promised by God in the Bible, would restore the kingdom of Israel, would drive out the oppressors (the Romans) and set God's own people free. Many ideas were current; one was that the Saviour would suddenly descend from heaven by a miracle, and probably arrive in this very courtyard of the Temple. This popular superstition was the background to one of the 'Temptations in the Wilderness' that our Lord went through (Matthew 4.5–7) but he did not follow the Tempter's voice; but he did visit the Temple on several occasions, as recorded by John; and John places the drastic action of 'Cleansing the Temple' near the beginning of his gospel, rather than towards the end.

Sacrifices for Sale

The visitors who came to the Temple from far and away would naturally wish to offer sacrifice at this holy place, and would buy their chosen animals on the spot. Even locals would find it easier than bringing their own. Also, foreigners would want to change their money into Jewish coinage, as all gifts to the Temple and all payments, had to be in the Jewish money. In no time a flourishing cattle market had been established, and there would be tables with men ready to change money sitting ready at them. As time went on, these activities invaded the courtyards, and destroyed any pious calm with unseemly uproar, not to mention shady practices of various kinds.

Chaos!

Jesus, John tells us, made a whip of small cords; his action in the market was not a mere gesture but an effective driving-out of animals from the sacred precincts, a chaos among the money-changers, and finally an ordering-out of the dealers in pigeons together with their cages of birds. 'You shall not turn my Father's house into a market!' Protests came from the Jews: 'What sign have you to show us for doing this?' – 'Destroy this temple and in three days I will raise it up' – but the temple he spoke of was his body; that body where God and man are united – and insofar as the Church is the Body of Christ, it is indeed the new Temple.

No Short Cuts
A lesson for us may well be that we should always be on our guard against what appear to be short cuts in life. Not all are wrong, of course – let us save time and be economical when possible – but some should be avoided. Ways to make easy money – vast overpayments or investments have cost our Church dearly in the recent past; ways to make easy money or winning cheap popularity, may well be sinful or lead us into sin. The popularity of gambling – especially the sheer chance of the Lottery may not be absolutely condemned; but can certainly bring problems and dangers. But if short cuts are wrong, so is inaction. Long before Jesus made his protest, the temple authorities should have cut out the festering sores right there; and it was a sad lack of genuine devotion and care that allowed all that noisy, riotous market to develop on sacred ground. Let us learn from all this to be watchful and careful, not closing our eyes to what is wrong, but showing clearly by our protests that we are on the side of what is right and good.

Last Sunday after Trinity *Second Sermon* **A Letter from St Paul**
'Take your share of hardship, like a good soldier of Christ Jesus.'
2 Timothy 2.3

The Office of Bishop
The Apostle is writing to a young minister, called – probably quite recently – to a position of authority. St Paul, in his first letter, gives his directions about the 'noble task' of the office of bishop (3.1 etc) and how to behave when so chosen.

In later days, St John, according to tradition, lived at Ephesus and acted as its bishop; for the present it is Timothy. To him, the aged St Paul sends his two letters of advice and encouragement. It was a difficult position that Timothy had to occupy, and he needed all the guidance and support the Apostle could give. In this chapter the main subject is battling against enemies.

'Take your share of suffering . . .'
The main subject is that of battling against enemies; the words translated contain the idea of suffering together. Timothy is called to a fellowship in endurance with Paul, with the Ephesian Christians, and with all Christians. The idea suggests the enduring together in fellowship, the standing shoulder to shoulder in the ranks, strong and steady in a discipline like that of the army. This brotherly – and sisterly – fellowship in the Holy Spirit, this disciplined co-operation in good works of every kind, sharing one another's difficulties, and bearing one another's burdens, is an essential aspect of the Church, and one that we should all be helping with, maintaining, and strengthening.

'Together'
From St Paul's call to Timothy we learn – what we already should know – that if we want fellowship with Christ, we must be his fellow labourers and fellow sufferers, and must be having fellowship with one another, whatever names or titles or descriptions we use or have inherited. We must remember that Christ lives on in the Church. Christ is his Church; his life animates it and all its members. In his Mystical Body we share his life, irrespective of class or sex, wealth or colour or nationality. The rich, the poor, the yellow, the brown, the black and the white are all equal at the Table of the Lord. This is the doctrine which will bridge the gap between colour and class, between one culture and another, in a union of love.

The Third Sunday before Advent
8 November 1998   'All live to God'
Luke 20.27–38

Questions and answers
Here is Jesus, as so often, faced with 'enquiries' which on the surface are respectful questions, asking for the solution of some problem to do with the faith, or with correct behaviour, or over

some indistinct passage of the Holy Scriptures; but which the questioners hope will prove to trip him up.

Today the enquiry comes from a group of 'Sadducees'. Who were they? Not an official body like the priests, but the party – priestly and aristocratic – to which the high-priestly families belonged, and which adhered to the written Law, the Torah, alone. They denied the beliefs of the Pharisees about a future life, and about angels and demons; all this was rejected as 'modernism'. The only answer to the question of 'eternal life' in early Israelite faith, was life through the offspring. 'Raise up offspring' equals 'resurrect'. Hence the Sadducees take the extreme case of a levirate marriage based on Deuteronomy 25.5,6 but going into the ridiculous possibility of no less than seven brothers taking the same woman, and still without producing any child, all died. Whose wife would she be in the resurrection?

Jesus treats the whole question as foolishly irrelevant, and the ideas put forward as crude and pointless. Marriage and children are events of this life; in the life to come such matters will have no place. Immortal and equal to the angels, the inhabitants of heaven will neither marry nor be given in marriage (v. 35). So the whole exercise becomes nonsense. As to a resurrection, Jesus quotes to his hearers the passage where Moses speaks to God at the burning bush, and is told that God is the God of the patriarchs, all living in the heavenly places; God is no God of the dead but a God of the living.

So effective is the response that the Lord gives, that some of the scribes who have been present, supporters though they are of the regime of Pharisees and Sadducees, are moved to express their admiration (20.39).

Third Sunday before Advent   *Second Sermon*   Remembrance Sunday

'Who shall separate us from the love of Christ? Shall tribulation, or distress, or persecution, or nakedness, or peril, or sword? As it is written: "For thy sake we are being killed all the day long; We are regarded as sheep to be slaughtered." No, in all these things we are more than conquerors, through him who loves us. For I am sure that neither death nor life, nor angels, nor principalities, nor things present, nor things to

come, nor powers, nor height, nor depth, nor anything else in all creation,
will be able to separate us from the love of God in Christ Jesus our Lord.'
Romans 8.35–39

(see also p. 230)

Remembrance
What does 'Remembrance Sunday' mean to you?

For some, the younger people, to whom the Second World War, Korea, Vietnam, are all far-away events in history, today cannot be a remembrance of old wars, or the dead, or the horrors. The Falklands Campaign is something they may know about, as is the Gulf War, and so today may be made memorable by the scenes they saw on TV, by the news and the stories sent back. They know something of Bosnia, of the horrors of central Africa, of the warfare that seems endemic in so many places. All these are made real and memorable by the scenes we see on TV, the news we read in the papers, the stories sent back by the Red Cross, the UN, the harried refugees, the appeals for help.

For some of us, today is different, a very personal day – remembering someone who died, a son, a father, a fiancé; the family killed in the blitz, or the relatives lost in the camps, the prisons, the gas chambers.

A Remembrance Day indeed
Some older folk may see behind one loved person's death, a whole generation lost; that lost generation cut down in Flanders mud. A cruel blow which ended a world.

And surely we can all see the tragedies, the cruel absurdity and pathos, of events too big for men to control. The horror and wickedness of dark passions, hatred, envy, murder, let loose and still loose now in our world today. Despite bravery and sacrifice, grim endurance, despair sometimes beyond belief, destruction and sorrow, here we are, facing the same trials and disasters, cruelties and mistakes. Do we never learn? Do we never really Remember? Yet there are still, in our thinking today, two threads to pick out and consider if we will.

Obedience – and Redemption
Obedience is the call and the response. We may be called by the mere drive and pressure of events; our response may be incredulety, unworthiness, or even attempted evasion. But a response

there is, and therefore an obedience. And from an obedience will come a redemption.

It may not be, probably will not be, any ultimate redemption; but it will be a deliverance from *this* situation here and now, from *this* present peril, from *this* impending cruel slavery or *this* terrible and brutal captivity.

Thank God for those who have the call and obey it in action of whatever kind; thank God for the redemption they have brought.

So here then is our Remembrance Day. And we know, as we come here to make the commemoration of Christ's sacrificial obedience to his call, that brought our deliverance, that no effort of obedience, no action of duty or of love is in vain. For all is taken up into his greater obedience, and all our small redemptions are united into his great Redemption, the Lord who is the Redeemer of all humanity.

The Second Sunday before Advent
15 November 1998   Take Heed!

'Take heed that you are not led astray; for many will come in my name, saying, "I am he", and "The time is at hand!"' Luke 21.8

Destruction

A picture of the end of the world is given to us in today's gospel. The Lord himself sets out a grim picture of how things will go: wars and tumults are to happen all over the world – frightening pictures indeed. Perhaps even worse, there will be famines, pestilences, earthquakes; even 'great signs in heaven'.

Perhaps we might look back to the remarkable comet that appeared in our skies not long ago; some pathetic and all too easily talked and persuaded people, were led into believing that here was indeed – if not the actual end of the world, at least a chance to achieve another life in another planet. We know what happened – they all committed suicide in the tidiest way, and their properties and money went into the hands of the wicked men who had led them. Do not let us follow those sad and corrupted folk.

Family Hatred and Betrayal

There has been too much of family members betraying each other, in Nazi Germany and Communist Russia, for those who have been through such events not to shudder and weep at the prospect – now or in the distant future – of similar – all too similar – events taking place once again. It has been hard enough to witness on our screens the horrors of Africa all too recently.

We are indeed promised that, even when delivered up into the brutality of the authorities by the betrayal of brothers and sisters, parents and friends, not a hair of our heads will perish (v. 18) and by our endurance we will gain our lives (v. 19).

Glory

Amid all the dark ruins of the world, we may however look with expectation for the Coming of the Son of Man, in power and great glory (v. 27). The Lord who went through the pain and darkness of Calvary, and was raised in glorious resurrection will make clear his triumph over evil, and the glories of the Kingdom of God established upon earth. Our faith tells us that in the end, the scales will be balanced and weighed; we must look for that Day with hope and trust, that God's plans are for peace and not disaster.

Second Sunday before Advent *Second Sermon* Parables

'Jesus went out of the house and sat beside the sea.' Matthew 13.1–9, 18–23

Seaside Scene

We have a delightful picture presented to us – the scene, a peaceful seaside; and Jesus, like any hard-working person, is glad to take a brief breather (all too brief as it turns out) sitting beside the sea, alone, in peace and quiet. That peace and quiet does not however last long; word gets round rapidly amongst the folk of the area, and – firstly in twos and threes – then by dozens, and eventually by twenties and thirties, they come – so that the whole foreshore is packed. Those at the back cannot hear; so Jesus is taken aboard a small boat and rowed a little way out, able to be heard now by most if not all.

What is Jesus saying?

He has launched out into a series of short stories, each with a message. All are set in scenes that his listeners will know and recognize – the farmer sowing his seed, hoping for a good harvest even from difficult ground; another farmer obsessed by the sudden invasion of weeds; the smart farmer sowing tiny mustard seed, knowing that given time he will get a big tree which will attract plenty of good fat birds; and the farmer's wife, busily working the leaven into her flour, to give hefty loaves for hungry countrymen.

What does he mean?

The disciples want the parable of the sower explained to them. What is the point? they have not understood Jesus' story. He explains: If the message of the gospel is given to someone who doesn't understand it, and makes no attempt to have it explained, the devil will sweep it away very soon, leaving the soul bare and desolate. Another person will receive the message of the Gospel joyfully, but soon their enthusiasm fades; and if the gospel comes into conflict with the demands of his work, and his position is threatened, he will drop it all. Then there is the person deeply involved in the fashionable world, making money and having fun – the gospel is a dead loss and is dropped. Lastly, is the person who takes the Gospel message to heart and mind, studies the words of Jesus, and with every effort, spreads the message amongst those he or she meets with, mixes with, knows something of their needs and problems, and can bring the words of Christ to their minds and hearts. Here indeed is the fruitful believer.

The Sunday next before Advent 22 November 1998 Christ the King

'God the Father has delivered us from the dominion of darkness, and transferred us to the Kingdom of his beloved Son, in whom we have redemption, the forgiveness of sins.' (Colossians 1.13,14), and 'One of the criminals who were hanged ... said to him, "Jesus, remember me when you come in your kingly power." And Jesus said to him, "Truly, I say to you, today you will be with me in Paradise."' Luke 23.42

Jesus our King!

We must not think of Christ merely as a historical figure, who once lived upon earth and assumed a position of teaching and authority, and who left behind him a group of friends who taught what he taught, preached his message, and – inspired by his example – spread the Good News.

Not so! For us, in the here and now, Jesus is the risen, living Christ, the Saviour, our living Lord. Yes, he died upon the cross, but 'he is risen and is still with us!' Our King and Lord, who led into Paradise that dying thief who recognized, in the agony and terror of death upon the cruel cross, the power of Christ.

Christ takes precedence of all, as St Paul says. Christ is at the head of humanity; he is indeed its King. And he knows and loves his subjects; he is our Lord.

Mediator

Christ our King is also, Christ our Mediator. Through his glorified humanity, we can come to God. 'The glory you have given to me, I have given to them', he said to his Father in his great High-Priestly prayer at the Last Supper. As Christ won humanity for himself by his death and resurrection, now he draws us close to himself through the liturgy of the Church. So it is that we are brought to the Throne of Grace, and to join in the heavenly worship; remember 'through Jesus Christ our Lord' is the ending of the liturgical prayers of the Church.

All we ask, and all we receive, and all we need, is through Jesus Christ our Lord.

The Heavenly Kingdom

'We await a Saviour', writes St Paul. And so, at the great hour of the Final Day, the majesty and greatness of Christ the King will shine forth – the majesty of him to whom 'All power is given in heaven and on earth'. Christ's triumph will be complete. He who went through the darkness and agony of Calvary, to his glorious Resurrection, will manifest his victory over evil and death by the complete coming of his Kingdom, that heavenly commonwealth which now we glimpse, but then will truly see in all its wondrous glory.

> *'Jesus my King, I thee adore;*
> *O make me love thee more and more.'*

Sunday next before Advent *Second Sermon* Are you the King?

'Pilate entered the praetorium again and called Jesus, and said to him, "Are you the King of the Jews?" (John 18.33) Jesus answered, "My kingdom is not of this world; if my kingship were of this world, my servants would fight, that I might not be handed over; but my kingship is not from the world".' (John 18.36)

The origin of the King (1 Samuel 8.4–20)

The prophet Samuel was most unhappy at the pressures to have a King over the people of Israel, and did all he could to dissuade them. He warned them of the cruelties and greed of kings – especially in those early days, when the king seized power more by his own physical strength and the brutalities of his soldiers. The young men would be forced into the army; the young women to the palace to be servants. All the cream of harvest and fruits, flocks and herds, would be taken for the royal use. Worst of all seemed to be the rejection of the Lord God as King, after his care and concern, even from the days of the Captivity in Egypt. However, from all this and through disappointments and failures, eventually, the prophets said, 'God would raise up a true king and shape a righteous kingdom' (e.g. Jeremiah 23.5).

The New King

This king would appear like a new, green shoot springing from a stump of a tree that had been cut down, but in whose roots true life still surged. The Child of Bethlehem came indeed like a new, weak shoot springing from the stock of the tree. That shoot grew, and is still growing.

Christ came from human stock, though in essence divine; he came into this world by human birth. Consequently he is one of us. As a descendant of David, he was born a king, an ideal ruler, summing up in himself the ideals of Jewish kingship. He is a Messiah who saves; he truly delivers us, and he truly reigns in our hearts – Christ the King and Saviour in one.

The King of the Jews (John 18.33–37)

In the Gospels we do not find Jesus as king – not robed in majesty, but a bruised and handcuffed figure. 'Are you the King of the Jews?' asked Pilate. 'My kingship is not of this world', says Jesus.

'So you are a king?' says Pilate. Jesus replies, 'You say that I am a king . . . I have come into the world to bear witness to the truth. Everyone who is of the truth hears my voice.'

Our King
Christ our King reigns from a cross, a brutal instrument of death made for criminals. He is reigning over 'Skull Hill', a place of death, outside the city. The poor, the outcast and rejected – these are his subjects. Proclaiming his kingdom and his majesty, over his head is pinned a parchment, reading 'Jesus of Nazareth, King of the Jews'.

The Kingdom is ours if we give our hearts to Jesus. 'Fear not, little flock, for it is your Father's pleasure to give you the kingdom' (Luke 12,32).

Sermons for Holy Days, Saints' Days and Special Occasions
1997

Monday 1 December
St Andrew the Apostle (tr. from Nov. 30)
Called

'Faith comes from what is heard, and what is heard comes by the preaching of Christ.' Romans 10.17

Ready Obedience
Andrew was one of four fishermen who were called by Jesus from their work, to be his helpers, apostles as we know them – that is, from the Greek – a messenger, or, one sent. St Andrew's ready obedience, and ability to bring people to Jesus, makes him a symbol of the missionary down the ages. So, on this day and, in particular, on the Eve – the day before – we remember and pray for, and give thanks for, the missionary work of the Church.

A missionary work which is not by any means confined to overseas, but embraces many causes and societies, and individual efforts, in many directions at home and abroad – all with the one and the same great aim – that of bringing Jesus and the Good News of the Gospel to the world.

Christian Duty

Not all of us can be missionaries in the exact sense in which we use that word, but all Christians are called to show Andrew's 'ready obedience' and without delay help to spread the Gospel; even in the small but important circles of our own ordinary humdrum daily life.

No need to be 'goody-goody' nor a 'bible-thumper', nor to follow the example of some sects whose persistence and sometimes almost threatening style, can defeat their own ends. Instead, let our example be of concern and love, sympathy and care – first steps in bringing others to the faith we know and love.

Abroad

The same will be true in situations abroad, where official Christian missionary work is forbidden or restricted. Those who work in overseas firms and organizations, those with skills in electronics, machinery, agriculture, building and planning, the doctors and nurses – these have a great and increasing part to play in the missionary work of today, since they can go where no cleric or professed evangelist would be allowed. By their example, their love and concern, they can sow the seeds of a desire to know more about this Christianity, the force that motivates its believers, and Jesus who came two thousand years ago to save the world and its peoples.

Changing Hearts

So much of the conflict, the wars, the hatred and divisions in the world today are due to a lack of love, an ignorance of the Christian ethic at its widest and simplest, and instead of self-seeking, the urge to grab, the lust for power, often cruel and brutal. Remember that is was Christian influence that redeemed our own country in the Dark Ages from tribal wars and savagery; this redemption needs to be applied widely or increasing intolerance and brutality will permanently ruin 'civilization'.

Saturday 6 December *St Nicholas of Myra* 'Santa Claus'

'Let the children come to me, and do not hinder them; for to such belongs the kingdom of God.' Luke 18.16

In St Nicholas, we have the origin of the figure of 'Father Christmas' or 'Santa Claus' so well known at the Christmas season. Red jacket or cloak, white beard, red hood and white fur – how the children love to cuddle up to him and hear what presents they are going to get! It seems a long step from his origin as a bishop; he was much adopted as patron of sailors and ships, which is why so many churches in seaside towns have him as their saint – about 400 churches in England alone are dedicated to him. His miracles are many, ranging from quieting the fury of the sea and saving the lives of innumerable storm-tossed sailors, to reviving three boys who had been killed and pickled, and providing dowries for three impoverished girls who would otherwise have been forced into lives of sin – from which transaction the pawnbrokers have adopted their sign of the three golden balls. Helper of children, Nicholas is said to have died in AD 326 and been buried at Myra, then translated later to Bari in Italy. On the Continent, St Nicholas rides a horse on Christmas Eve and gives away presents to good children, while his servant whips those who have been naughty!

Monday 8 December   *The Conception of Our Lady*   Hail Mary

'We know that in everything God works for good with those who love him, who are called according to his purpose; for those whom he foreknew he also predestined.' Romans 8.28,29

Chosen

The doctrine that the Blessed Virgin Mary was preserved from any stain of original sin was widely accepted from early days, in both East and West. It does not mean that Mary was conceived without the sexual union of her parents; rather, it is perhaps most simply stated as the belief that Mary received, at the moment when her soul was infused into her body, the graces that Christians normally receive in Baptism. Since 1854 (the date of the definition by the Roman Church of the Immaculate Conception) Orthodox theologians have generally rejected the doctrine; before then, many of them accepted it in some form. The Anglican Bishop Ken (1637–1711) taught it in his stanza:

The Holy Ghost his temple in her built,
Cleansed from congenial, kept from mortal guilt;
And from the moment that her blood was fired
Into her heart celestial love inspired.

St Thomas Aquinas, writing *c.* 1272, says that although the Church of Rome does not keep the feast, some other Churches do, and therefore the celebration is not to be entirely reprobated!

Friday 26 December *St Stephen the First Martyr* Rejection

'His own people received him not.' *John 1.12*

Rejection

Christ came to his own people, but they did not all rise up to welcome him; far from it – in the end he was rejected, tortured, killed. It is fitting therefore that the joy of Christmas over the birth of the Saviour, should be followed at once by the note of sorrow and rejection, to remind us of what has happened and will happen, to faithful disciples of the Lord.

Our Martyrs

In our own way, we remember with sorrow Archbishop Janani Luwum of Uganda; the Archbishop of San Salvador, Oscar Romero; the Kikuyu martyr Andrew Kaguru; great men like Martin Luther King – all murdered for the Christian Faith – to say nothing of an unnumbered throng of equally brave but not humanly known followers, who have also suffered martyrdom in our own time.

From them rises up a constant cry, 'Lord, how long?' George Bernard Shaw put into the mouth of St Joan of Arc, in his famous play, these bitter words – 'O God that madest this beautiful earth, when will it be ready to receive thy saints? How long, Lord, how long?'

Repentance

The gospel reading is a reminder that what happened to Stephen – and to a long line of martyrs that have followed him – was forecast by our Lord. But the gospel also sets before us Christ's warning of the consequences of refusing to break with the past, by the only possible way – the way of repentance, of submission to the will of God.

Jerusalem was indeed destroyed, and the Temple ruined and left desolate; the Lord's words came bitterly true. Let us see to it that this warning does not come too late for ourselves.

The fine Collect for today leads us to pray for constancy in suffering, and comes from the pen of Bishop John Cosin with the stamp of suffering upon it. Cosin knew what it was to suffer for the truth's sake; exiled for almost twenty years in poverty for his loyalty to the Church and to the faith as he had received it. And even in our day we need the grace of constancy and the strength to stand by the truth.

Saturday 27 December *St John, Apostle and Evangelist* **The Disciple Jesus Loved**

'This is the disciple who is bearing witness to these things, and who has written these things; and we know that his testimony is true.' John 21.24

The Inner Circle

John the apostle and evangelist, with his brother James, were sons of Zebedee, a prosperous fisherman – or rather, head of a fishing firm which operated on the Sea of Galilee. John was one of the small group – the 'inner circle' – of disciples privileged to be with their Master during some of the most important moments of the earthly life of Jesus.

John and James appear at first as young firebrands – 'Sons of Thunder' – Jesus nicknamed them, appropriately enough. They were the disciples who wanted to call down fire from heaven upon the village that refused to give hospitality to the Lord and his apostles; and they pushed themselves forward in asking to be given chief places in the coming Kingdom. But John developed, and we know him best as the Apostle of Love; he grew into a stature of great spirit and deep devotion and love. He was one of 'the Chosen Three' who were closest to the Lord; he saw the glory of the Transfiguration, he was close beside Jesus at the Last Supper – close enough to whisper in his ear; he was close to Jesus in the Garden of Gethsemane; he stood close to the Cross with the holy Mother Mary and Mary Magdalene. Later, he was at the empty tomb, and after Peter had entered, John went in 'and saw and believed' – the first of Christ's followers to begin to understand the mighty act of God in the Resurrection.

The Witness
John's witness to Christ is obviously proportioned to his nearer and closer observation. His Gospel abounds in small details (the 'green grass' that the crowds sit down on at the Feeding of the Five Thousand; the Samaritan woman and her water jug) which suggest a careful eye-witness. Above all, John's voice is the persistent proclaimer of the Divinity of Jesus, whether he is writing his letters of encouragement or warning, or telling of heavenly visions (presuming that he either wrote the Apocalypse, or that it is a reflection of his mind) or writing his Gospel.

By tradition John is said to have become bishop of Ephesus, from where he wrote his epistles (and perhaps Revelation) and cared for Mary, Christ's mother, until she died. He then retired to Patmos, a little island, where he ended his days.

Monday 29 December *The Holy Innocents* (tr. from Dec. 28) **Innocent Suffering**
'The Kingdom of God belongs to such as these.' St Mark 10.14

Bitter Grief
Into the midst of the joys and delights of the festival of Christmas, the great feast of Christian happiness, comes the scream of bitter grief. 'A voice was heard in Ramah, lamentation and bitter weeping; Rachel weeping for her children because they were not.' And this is no poetical fancy; it is savage, deadly truth which pierces deep into the hearts of the mothers – and fathers – who have lost their precious little ones.

When the Lord of Heaven and earth is born a Babe in Bethlehem, there – within just a few days – is this bitter contrast to peace and love – the streets of his birthplace run with the blood of children.

Today
But this is the same dreadful scene that we watch in horror and disgust, day by day, on our TV screens, and see in our newspapers – dreadfully wounded children, still alive – only just; and the bodies of their playmates, torn and shattered, in the streets and market places of Bosnia and Serbia, of Ruanda and the Sudan. Victims of politics and power-stretching as cruel and brutal as anything known in the Bible or history. The promise of Spring all unfulfilled, the cold hand of death, like a sharp frost, has killed the blossom before the fruit was formed, cut down the tender plant that was made to grow strong and fair. And we cannot see a child, broken like a shattered toy, without seeing too, at least in our mind's eye, the broken-hearted mother. A grief so deep that words cannot be found – only the scream of agony. Think too, today on this day which sanctifies all childhood, of the children who suffer now, not dying almost painlessly, but by the slow agonizing torture of weakness and starvation, in so many places helpless and hopeless.

Christ
But then, at this Christmas-tide lift your hearts to Christ, and think what his birth did to change the world. In his love and in his name, hands are stretched out to succour the afflicted in desperate situations, all over the world. It is little enough that can be done, in view of the needs – but it is a contrast with the first Christmas. We forget too easily what Christianity has really done for the world. Think of the recklessness about child-life which we find in classical literature; the practice of child-murder in savage races; or the callousness to suffering which we can still see in non-Christian countries. Yes, there are many exceptions, but it was a new thing in the world when Christ told us to cherish children because 'of such is the kingdom of heaven'.

Monday 29 December *St Thomas Becket, Archbishop of Canterbury and Martyr* **The Sword's Point**

'I will raise up for myself a faithful priest, who shall do according to what is in my heart and in my mind, says the Lord.' 1 Samuel 2.35

A Changed Man

Thomas Becket was born in London in 1118; his mother has been thought to have been an Arab, a Saracen, but this is disputed. Undoubtedly a brilliant scholar, and a remarkably strong-willed and intelligent man, he made the Church his career. He rose rapidly; the King, Henry II, made him Lord Chancellor in 1155; and as a bosom friend of the monarch, his future seemed assured. Vigorous, hot-tempered, fond of hunting, popular, magnificent, he was advanced to Canterbury in 1162 with the world at his feet.

As archbishop, however, Thomas abandoned all luxury; in his own words 'from being a proud, vain man, patron of play-actors, follower of hounds' he became 'a shepherd of souls'. He also opposed all encroachments of the King on the rights of the Church and the liberties of the clergy. For seven years the disputes went on, becoming more difficult and violent; he went into exile but returned to England on December 1st 1170. King Henry, enraged, let fall imprudent words before his knights 'Will no one rid me of this pestilent priest!'

Murder in the Cathedral

Four knights rode to Canterbury, and in the evening of December 29th murdered the archbishop in a side chapel of his cathedral. It was in defence of the Church, and its ideals and jurisdiction, that he died; his last words were 'I die willingly for the Name of Jesus, and in defence of his Church.' The ordinary people treated him as a martyr at once; he was formally canonized three years later by the Pope (1173).

His shrine made Canterbury one of the most important and famous cities in Christendom, and to it came people of all ranks and qualities, the sick and the sad, the rich and the poor; kings, nobility and peasants. The shrine was stripped of its valuable ornaments, and the relics removed and burnt, under Henry VIII. The stained glass – or most of it – showing the miracles that took place at the Shrine, remain to our own time; a modern version of the Shrine, commissioned from Sir Ninian Comper, was never built but devotion to St Thomas had grown again and is now centred on the 'Altar of the Sword's Point' marking the spot where St Thomas was martyred.

1998
Thursday 1 January *The Naming and Circumcision of Jesus* **Obedience**
'Obedience to the Law' – Collect

Sacrifice and the Law
Circumcision is an ancient custom not only with the Jews but with other races also; the scholars claim that it began with the ancient Egyptians and was adopted by the early Hebrews, as indeed the Bible seems to say (see Joshua 5).

What did it originally mean? Was it a puberty rite, to show that a boy had become a man? Or did it have sacrificial overtones, going back to the obligatory sacrifice of the first-born? Whatever its origins, circumcision had become a regular and important part of Hebrew religious ritual, and Jesus, like any other Jewish boy, was made 'obedient to the Law'. After his example, then, we ought to be completely self-consecrated to God's service – mind, spirit and body. Worldliness and the carnal-bodily-lusts are not to claim mastery over us. In these days of 'soft-porn', on sale in every paper-shop, with video 'nasties' and so on, we should take these warnings seriously.

The Name of Jesus
There is only one way out – to rely upon Christ, to call upon the Name of Jesus. In our baptism, we promised to 'faithfully bear his Name' – that Name which means quite simply, 'Saviour'.

It was in the Name of Jesus, that Peter performed the first miracle after Pentecost; and in the Name of Jesus millions of people today go about their work and live their lives, continually sending up small 'arrow prayers' – 'Lord Jesus, help me' – 'Jesus, be to me a Saviour' – 'Jesus mercy'.

In the Name of Jesus we too can 'in all ways obey his blessed will'.

Monday 19 January   *The Confession of St Peter* (tr. from Dec. 18)   **The Rock**

'Jesus asked his disciples "Who do you say that I am?" Simon Peter replied, "You are the Christ, the Son of the Living God!"' Matthew 16.15,16

The Shout!
That great exultant shout came when the other disciples seemed hesitant, tense, fearful even, at the question Jesus put to them – it flummoxed them. Were they afraid to commit themselves? Were they still so uncertain as to the true identity of the One who had led them, instructed them, lived with them, day by day, for so long? Whatever the reason, they were tongue-tied; it was left to Peter – enthusiastic, eager, always ready to leap ahead where 'the angels fear to tread!' The man Jesus himself called 'Blessed' at one moment, and then a few seconds later described him as 'Satan' to his very face – this was no ordinary individual.

Weaknesses
It is easy, all too easy, to identify the weaknesses which led Peter astray; overconfident in his own judgement; over-hasty in making decisions, and in acting on them; over-eager for popularity and success. Not bad qualities in themselves, but how easily they can lead into error and sin at critical times.

Why then did Jesus choose Peter to be an apostle, and how did he come to be the leader of the band?

In the first place, Peter was always ready to acknowledge his mistakes, to make amends and start afresh. In the second place, Peter was the one to see further than the rest; Peter was the first to acknowledge Jesus as Messiah. Thirdly, Peter was deeply stirred by the teaching and personality of Jesus; he showed a vast love and deep devotion to Jesus. Thirdly, there is the easy readiness of Peter to admit past errors and sins – remember his broken-hearted sorrow at his betrayal of the Lord; and his plain recognition of his mistaken opposition to the admission of Gentiles. But above all, remember his eagerness in love and devotion to his Saviour.

Twin Pillars
Peter with Paul form the twin pillars of the Church of God; both sealed their commitment to Christ with their blood – and on their blood and on their faith these twin pillars were set up, on the foundation stone, Jesus Christ himself.

Sunday 25 January   *(Epiphany 3 1998)*
Conversion of St Paul   **The Light**
'Suddenly there came a light from heaven all around him. He fell to the ground and heard a voice saying, "Saul, Saul, why are you persecuting me?"' Acts 9.4

The Persecutor
We hardly ever expect God to actually work any great change in us, do we? We go on, in our small steady way, day by day, Sunday by Sunday.

Perhaps in Lent we may make a small effort to improve our Christian standards; we may make a periodic account of our doings and try to tot up, to see in what way we are progressing – or perhaps falling away. Our expectations are not very high are they? And yet, if we look at St Paul, we see what God can do.

We may not be exactly saints; but he was the great persecutor of the Church of God, breathing out threats and slaughter. We may not do much good; he was the chief of evil-doers, 'thinking within himself that he ought to do many things contrary to the Name of Jesus of Nazareth.'

The Conversion
But God bestowed his grace upon him – forced his grace upon him, we might well say – struck him down in the open road, blinded him that he might the better see. The prince of persecutors became a principal apostle.

Paul himself says, that he obtained mercy in order 'that, in him,

Christ Jesus might show forth all his sufferings, for an example to those who would thereafter believe.'

And Us?
Let us take heart then. For if God can work so great a miracle in Paul, maybe he may yet work a much smaller one in us. Let us pray that God may take us and use us, transform us if needs be, and make us into instruments for his great love and power.

Thursday 19 March   *St Joseph of Nazareth*   Trust
'When Joseph woke from sleep he did as the angel commanded him.' Matt. 1.24

A Blow to Pride
Joseph occupies a rather ambivalent position in our thinking about the great story of Redemption. He seems to exist only to give his name to the pregnant Mary, to act as supposed husband and supposed father. Mary appears on her own at the wedding breakfast at Cana; no mention of Joseph being there.

Did he die quite soon, as tradition has it? Was he an old man? we do not know. He appears as the spouse of Mary; he guides and guards the mother and child through the Flight into Egypt, and the early years at Nazareth, quietly and humbly.

It says a great deal for his love of Mary and his trust in God that he accepted the situation and played his part in it.

Our Trust
How many of us, we may well wonder, would have accepted a similar situation? The demands of love and faith can be great. Did Jesus ever feel that the long quiet years with Joseph and Mary in Nazareth were a waste of time? Like Joseph, Christ accepted the situation and lived humbly and usefully through it.

Humility

Christ came to teach us that the only way back to God is by obedience, rooted in humility. And so, as St Paul tells us, he who was God came to us in human form, accepting an obedience which in the end, brought him to death.

Isn't Christ always telling us that he came to do his Father's will, not his own? And he asks us to make that our prayer too, in our daily use of the Lord's own prayer: 'Your will be done, on earth as it is in heaven.' Trust, and be obedient.

Wednesday 25 March *The Annunciation of Our Lord* God's Will

'Behold I am the handmaid of the Lord; let it be to me according to your word.' Luke 1.38

A Big Splash

Today, if we want to get on, to get somewhere in the world, to achieve name and fame, we know we have to make a big splash.

Publicity – acting big, thinking big. Get in with the right people, get yourself talked about. Appear on the box; get noticed in the gossip columns, share a radio or TV programme with well-known names. Make a splash and get carried along on the wave of success. That's the way of the world, is it not? Now look today at God's way.

The Task

The task God set himself was the freedom of the human race from the bondage of sin, and the leading into a new and higher life. This he aimed to do not by the use of divine force, but by the conquest of human hearts by love. 'God so loved the world that he gave his only-begotten Son.'

And that Son laid aside his power and majesty, and became one of us.

The Time

The known civilized world was ruled by one State, the Roman Empire, then at the height of prestige and prosperity, with an unrivalled system of law and order, communications never

equalled until today, and a language known in every corner. Christ
came among us, as St Paul puts it, 'when the time had fully come'.

The Mother
Humanly speaking, would we not choose a member of the imperial
family, perhaps, with all advantages of wealth and position, at
Rome, the centre of the world. No, the mother chosen was a Jewish
girl of sixteen, unknown outside her native town – 'the Virgin's
name was Mary' is all we know about her.

And God even asked her consent; his messenger came not with
a command, but with a request which Mary did not understand.
'She was greatly troubled at this saying.' She asked questions. But
it was Mary's 'Yes' that set in train our world's redemption.

'Hail, full of grace, the Lord is with you!'

Thursday 23 April   *George, Martyr, Patron of England*   **Strong in the Lord**

St George is included in a list of saints published in AD 495 by
Pope Gelasius, 'whose names are justly reverenced among men,
but whose acts are known only to God'. His veneration was
centred at Lydda in Palestine; now known as Lod, near Tel Aviv.
Tradition has it that George was a Tribune in the Imperial Guard,
was converted to the Christian Faith, and suffered in the persecution of Diocletian. St George became popular in England
through the Crusades. King Richard and his English soldiers
invoked St George when suffering badly at Antioch; victory followed, and St George became the inspiration of the English in
particular, and the returning Crusaders established his popularity
in this country.

He was named as the national Patron by Edward III, who established the Order of the Garter under George's protection in 1348.
So, an Eastern martyr became England's patron saint. The ideals
associated with St George – chivalry, honour, fair play and courage
– still retain their value for many, and we could do much worse
than uphold and strengthen them in our time.

Saturday 25 April   *St Mark the Evangelist*   A Happy Ending

'We are to be children no longer, tossed by the waves and whirled about by every fresh gust of teaching.' Ephesians 4.14

A False Start

Mark the Evangelist is usually identified with Mark, cousin of Barnabas, who accompanied Barnabas and Paul on their missionary journey to Cyprus; but who, to Paul's indignation, deserted them at Perga in Pamphylia and went back to Jerusalem. Nor was this the end, for 'there arose a sharp contention, so that they separated from each other' later on in Antioch, between Paul and Barnabas. The latter went to Cyprus and took Mark with him. However, after some years, Mark regained the friendship of Paul; we read of him attending the Apostle in his Roman imprisonment, praised as a 'comfort' and a 'fellow worker' (Col. 4.11). So all was well.

The Gospel

Not only was Mark connected with St Paul, but also with St Peter. In the first letter of Peter is a reference to 'Mark, my son . . .' (v. 13). Tradition connects Mark closely with Peter, and tells us that his gospel is largely based on the reminiscences of Peter; and there is a good deal of material about Peter in Mark's gospel, so that he may well be described as 'The interpreter of Peter'. Interestingly enough, 'the young man who fled away naked' at the arrest of Jesus (Mark 14.51–52) is usually interpreted as Mark himself. He lived in Jerusalem with his mother, at whose 'safe house' the Last Supper was prepared; Mark may well have waited at table, and known Jesus and the disciples from previous visits.

Like Mark, let us not be 'put off' permanently by our failures, but rise up from them, take up our task again, ask for grace to be renewed with fresh vigour and in good heart.

Friday 1 May   *SS Philip and James, Apostles*
Follow Me

'Jesus found Philip and said to him, "Follow me." Philip was from Bethsaida, the city of Andrew and Peter.' John 1.44.

Apostles

The word 'apostle' means 'one sent', a messenger; and Christ's commission comes to mind: 'Go into all the world, and preach the gospel to every creature.'

Only St John gives us any details about Philip; it seems likely that his interest in the new Teacher had been aroused by Andrew and Peter. The call of Jesus would not be to a heart unprepared; much thought and prayer must have preceded the final decision. Philip was present at the feeding of the five thousand (John 6.5–14) when he answered Jesus' enquiry about buying enough bread, with 'Two hundred denarii would not buy enough for each to have a little'. And it is Philip who is associated by 'certain Greeks' at the Passover celebrations, who wanted to 'see Jesus'. Being himself a Galilean, they may have known him and thought him more liberal than a stricter Jew.

James is known as 'James the Less' to distinguish him from 'James the son of Zebedee' and 'James the brother of the Lord'. He may be the 'James the Younger' who stood with Mary and other women at the Crucifixion (Mark 15.40).

Martyrs

We do not know whether either or both were martyred; traditionally James was killed at Jerusalem and Philip at Hierapolis in Asia Minor. The two saints appear in the calendar today together, due to the historical accident of a church in Rome being dedicated on this day in the 6th c., and claiming to possess relics of both.

Thursday 14 May   *St Matthias the Apostle* (BCP Feb. 24)   Chosen

'You have not chosen me; I have chosen you, says the Lord.' John 15.16
'Let another take over his charge.' Acts 1.20

Responsibility

Following the Ascension of the Lord, and before the Day of Pentecost, the disciples with Mary and others (Acts 1.14) met together in prayer for nine days; Peter took the opportunity to remind them that the defection and death of Judas had left them with a vacancy, and that this should be filled with 'one of the men who had accompanied us, during all the time that the Lord Jesus went in and out amongst us – one of these men must become with us a witness to His resurrection' (Acts 1.21–22). Two men were nominated – Joseph called Barsabbas, surnamed Justus, and Matthias. After prayer, the disciples cast lots, and the lot fell upon Matthias, who was then enrolled with the eleven.

Nothing further is told of Matthias after his selection. By tradition he was eventually arrested and finally beheaded (with an axe, hence his emblem in art). Matthias seems an example to us of a faithful companion, promoted to a position of trust and giving good service, even if his actions and service are unheralded and indeed unknown.

Monday 1 June *The Visit of the Blessed Virgin Mary to Elizabeth* (tr. from May 31) **Rejoice!**

'In those days Mary arose and went with haste into the hill country, to a city of Judah and she entered the house of Zechariah and greeted Elizabeth.' Luke 1.39

Supernatural

In both women, their respective conceptions are supernatural and miraculous. Elizabeth is an old woman; Mary is a virgin. The destiny of the children? Elizabeth's child is to be the herald of the Messiah; Mary's child is to be the Son of God.

The Magnificat

In her wonderful son, Mary declares the sheer givenness of the grace of God. It needs to be received, received by faith, with humility and a hunger for God's will to be done. Her song ends with her memory of the father of the faithful, Abraham, who believed God even in time of great stress 'and it was reckoned to him for righteousness'.

Receptiveness

What distinguishes Mary from any other woman is the receptiveness of her faith. So, however we may venerate Mary we see and know that all is the gift of God. Those who are mighty and rich in their own estimation, are put down and sent away. Mary who believed is blessed; she who magnified the Lord is magnified herself.

The Orthodox Icon, where the Mother of God seems to fill the picture, monumental and majestic – yet, if you look more closely, you see that she is pointing to the Babe in her lap; and it is that Babe who gives us his blessing.

Thursday 11 June *(Thursday after Trinity Sunday, Thanksgiving for the Holy Communion)* Corpus Christi

'Do this as a memorial of me.' 1 Cor. 11.24

Joy

Our eucharists should always be joyful, even on occasions which we would count as sad. The Church celebrates the sacrifice of Christ with joy and not with sorrow, with thanksgiving not with regret or tears.

It is true that Maundy Thursday is so under the shadow of the Cross, that our full joy cannot be displayed; hence today is traditionally chosen as the occasion for a further and unclouded festival. Thursday is the day on which Christ instituted his supper; Corpus Christi is the first free Thursday after the great pageant of the re-enacting of the events of the life, death, and triumph of the Lord is completed in the Church's Calendar.

Sacrifice

That sacrifice was the purpose of God's sending his Son into this world, to us; how can we be sorrowful at the achievement of so great a task, so wonderful a work? There can be no room for regret nor sorrow – for if there is one thing that our Creator certainly desired, it was that Sacrifice that makes our salvation possible.

A Feast
With what then, do we celebrate that wonder – by a representation; and our representation is a feast, is joyful, is a wedding, is a drinking of wine together, is a coming together of friends, is a re-union! We make merry with a bridegroom because he has obtained what he desired; we rejoice with the Divine Son because he has his desire also. He desired to unite his Church with himself, and in dying he has accomplished that. It is the overflowing of the bridegroom's pleasure that enlivens the guests – and so it is that the Church rejoices in the overflowing of the joy of God.

The Sacrament
This sacrament is not something special and apart from our religion, our faith. Really it *is* just our religion, sacramentally enacted. In it we find all and everything that Christ himself is; and Christ should be everything and all, to every Christian. In particular, Christ is the supreme bond between us, we who are his followers and his friends.

Everyone who communicates at this eucharist – or any eucharist – eating the Bread, drinking the Wine – is bound to his or her neighbour by this – the same Christ who lives in one, lives in the other. Our care for our fellow Christians should be as real, as careful, as our care for Christ; and that love and spirit in us which does the caring – that is also Christ.

Christ in All
Christ in each of us cares for Christ in all. The same bond unites us with those who are gone before, our departed friends and loved ones; and with the great figures of the Saints who now rejoice in the full light of Paradise. At the eucharistic feast we are joined together, in one communion and fellowship.

Friday 12 June *St Barnabas the Apostle* (tr. from June 11) **Openhearted**
'A good man, full of the Holy Spirit and faith.' Acts 11.24

An Apostle

The title 'Apostle' in the New Testament is not confined strictly to the Twelve, or to those, who like Matthias, had walked with the Lord on his missionary journeys. In several passages we find St Barnabas referred to as 'An Apostle; and of course, St Paul is another and greater example, who was never one of the Twelve.

Barnabas was a well-to-do Levite farmer from the isle of Cyprus; he gladly disposed of his possessions in favour of the infant Church. This generous action may have been the inspiration of that Early Christian Communism, so much favoured by St Luke, which was practised for some considerable time by the followers of Christ's Way (see Acts 4.32).

A Leader

No doubt the Apostles in Jerusalem were somewhat disconcerted to receive news that Greeks as well as Jews, were joining the Church in large numbers; and so they sent a trusted and reliable person – Barnabas – to go and find out just what was going on, and report back (Acts 11.19–24).

Barnabas may well have shared some of the misgivings of the Twelve, but on seeing the joy and faith of the new converts, he put away all his doubts and, we are told, 'was glad, and exhorted them all to remain faithful'.

Preacher and Teacher

Barnabas may be overshadowed by his companion, Paul, but there is no doubt that he played a prominent part in the missionary work of the Church, and was a great teacher and preacher.

He was not only generous materially – he was large-hearted, ready to believe the best of others. He persuaded the suspicious Apostles to accept the new converts in Antioch, and it was Barnabas who got them to accept Paul. Again, it was Barnabas who gave the backsliding young Mark another chance, which enabled him eventually to return to the companionship and favour of Paul.

His Secret

Barnabas' secret is no secret – 'He was full of the Holy Spirit and faith'; he must have been one of those who bubble over with enthusiasm and love. What need there is today for a warm-hearted, open and accepting attitude for us Christians; ready always to see the best rather than the worst in others, and with a generous readiness to give, and give again.

Wednesday 24 June   *Birth of St John Baptist*
The Fore-Runner
'A voice cries, "In the wilderness prepare the way of the Lord." Isaiah 40.3

The Birth
Although St John has a prominent place in all the gospels, only Luke gives an account of his birth. He was the son of elderly parents, Zechariah the priest and Elizabeth, and was related to Jesus on his mother's side.

His father was struck speechless, because he doubted the vision foretelling John's birth. When his speech was restored, Zechariah uttered the fine canticle of praise we know as the 'Benedictus', used at Morning Prayer in the Prayer-Book Office. The name 'John', incidentally, as chosen by John's father, is 'God's Gift'.

In the Desert
A very serious follower of the Hebrew Faith, John took to living in the wilderness the life of an ascetic. He preached strongly and even fiercely on repentance, and the need for the People of God to prepare for the Great Event – the Coming of the Messiah and the Kingdom of God. He baptized his followers as a sign of repentance and new life; Jesus himself was baptized by John in the River Jordan (Matthew 3.11–17).

His Life and Death
John had many followers, some of whom became disciples of Jesus; but because of his denunciation of the sins of Herod, especially Herod's incestuous marriage, John brought vicious revenge upon himself through Herodias (Herod's new wife) and was thrown into prison. From prison, John sent messengers to Christ, asking for answers to queries about the future, and who Christ was; but in the meantime Herodias plotted with her daughter Salome, the dancer; and Herod was led to make a foolish promise, which

however he felt he had to keep. Thus the queen managed to arrange for the violent death of John, who had become her hated enemy.

Monday 29 June   *SS Peter & Paul the Apostles*
The Twin Pillars
'The two anointed ones.' Zechariah 4.14

Tradition and Change
From early days the two great apostles, St Peter and St Paul, were always commemorated together as being the 'Twin Pillars' or the 'Two Founders' of the Church of God on earth. At the Reformation in England, this double dedication was changed, and in the beautiful first English Prayer Book, today's date was assigned only to St Peter. Why this was done is not clear; possibly Cranmer felt that in some way the double festival gave an authority to Rome that otherwise it would not have had; or maybe he thought there was something unscriptural in the title.

No one ever thought that the two saints were martyred on the same day, surely; it was the love and devotion of the Early Christians that put the 'Two Pillars' on the same festival, seeing how they balanced and complemented each other. So there is a great deal to be said, for returning to primitive practice, as the new Lectionary allows; coming into ecumenical custom is in itself a good idea.

Peter
In the New Testament, Peter is represented in various roles – the fisherman, whose new mission under Christ is to 'catch men' in the net of the Church. Peter is the prophet, who penetrated to the true identity of Christ – 'You are the Son of God!' and proclaims his faith. Peter is also the shepherd, whose task is to guide and tend the sheep, the People of God; to protect them and to love and cherish them. Peter is also the repentant sinner who denied his Master at his moment of most need – but was restored to favour after the Resurrection.

Paul

And so is Paul, let us not forget – Paul the repentant sinner, the one who most bitterly persecuted the infant Church of God, until there came that fateful vision from heaven above of the Lord Jesus, that turned around – converted – this powerful learned and energetic figure.

Paul has left his stamp upon the Church, and upon Christian theology, through his letters to the infant churches scattered round Asia Minor. He instructs, warns, orders, implores, begs with tears, threatens with severity, opens his heart. He takes the first giant steps into the mysteries of our Redemption – many have followed, but Paul was the first.

And it was Paul who was the first to take Christianity beyond the bounds of the Hebrew people, and see the beginnings of the world-wide vision of all nations united in Christ.

Characters indeed

Very different in character and in personality as well as in backgrounds and in approaches – it is yet to these two different and differing personalities. (Paul even, we find – on one occasion at least attacked and contradicted Peter (Galatians 2) that we owe the enormous living and vital growth of the Church in the early days.)

Friday 3 July   *St Thomas the Apostle*   Courage

'Thomas, called the Twin, said to his fellow disciples, "Let us also go, that we may die with him".' John 11.16

Gloom

The situation was gloomy in the extreme. A huge and black shadow hung over the small band of the disciples. The authorities had begun to show their hand – there had been this clash between the blind man healed by Christ, and the Pharisees. In his blunt forthright way, this fellow had stood up for Christ – 'Why, here is a marvel! You do not know where he comes from, and yet he opened my eyes . . . If this man were not from God, he could do nothing!' Furious, the Pharisees reply, '*You* were born in utter sin, and would you instruct *us*?' and cast him out – as we would say, excommunicated him (John 9.24–34).

Then followed the bitter words of reproach from Jesus in the 'Parable of the Good Shepherd' (John 10.7–18). Words of condemnation that would have pierced to the heart some – at least – of those who heard him. But others 'took up stones to stone him' (10.31). But Jesus 'escaped from their hands', and went away across the Jordan, and there remained.

Courage

Jesus now proposes to go and call upon Mary and Martha, having heard of their brother Lazarus's sickness and death. Only two miles from Jerusalem! Right into the jaws of the lion, we might say. Asking for trouble! Thunderstruck, hesitant, scared, the disciples keep a shocked silence. It is Thomas who shows courage and speaking up boldly, says: 'Let us go also! that we may die with him!'

Does it seem strange that it is this same courageous man, bold to risk his life with that of his Master, who refused to accept the stories the others told him, about the extraordinary events after the Passion? The coming of Christ, alive after the cruel crucifixion – alive and with them again!

Practicalities

Thomas was a practical man. Dangers he could see and understand had no effect upon him – but he had to see and understand. Imagination, vision, and the ability to take the leap of faith – this was not in his make-up. Yes, he doubted; but once he had seen, touched, spoken to the Lord – all was crystal clear.

God knows – what we forget – that the road to faith may lie through doubt. Thomas doubted; but to him it was given, once he had seen, spoken to, touched his Lord – all was crystal clear. 'My Lord – and my God!'

When we have doubts, let Thomas be our example; he was faithful indeed to the truth once he knew it; and he did not evade his Lord's call – his courage was shown again, on his long missionary journey to India, and to martyrdom there. Let us hold to what we know to be true; then the Master will as surely as ever come and stand among us and say, 'Peace be with you!'

Wednesday 22 July *St Mary Magdalene* The Beloved

The Gospel according to Luke records 'Jesus went through cities and villages, preaching and bringing the good news of the Kingdom of God And the Twelve were with him, and also some women who had been healed of evil spirits and infirmities: Mary called Magdalene, from whom seven demons had gone out.' Luke 8.1–2

In the Early Light

Mary had come to the tomb very early; St Luke tells us the reason – it was to complete the sad rites of preparation for burial, the washing and anointing of the body with oils and sweet spices. These actions could not be carried out by any pious Jew on the eve of the Sabbath nor on the Sabbath itself. So, it was early on the Sunday morning that Mary arrived. We are told that as soon as she saw the stone had been moved, she ran and went to Peter and John. They came back with her, went into the tomb, and found it – empty.

Who was it?

The idea of a resurrection seems not to have entered their heads; presumably they all assumed that someone – the authorities? – robbers? – had come and taken away the body. The two men returned to their homes; perhaps they thought the best policy was to keep quiet for the moment, until it was clear who *had* taken away the corpse. But Mary could not keep away.

In tears she returns, and hoping against hope, peers again into the tomb. There are two men there! Did she think they were police, or guards? At least they seem friendly, and listen to her grief. She has lost her Lord! Anguish at this final blow fills her heart.

Loss

We can all find something answering to this loss, in our small ways. If we look back we can see clearly why we have lost Jesus – that is, the joyful realization of his love and presence, the great experience of the Christian religion.

This is what sin always does; it blinds our spiritual sight, so that we cannot see God. Mary turns in her distress to another figure standing nearby; she thinks he must be the gardener. We too cannot see: or recognize God, even if he is close beside us, if our eyes are blinded – not by tears of love, as were Mary's, but by the effects of sin. What were our prayers like this morning? What time and trouble do we give to our Bible reading? How often do we come to Communion, properly prepared and truly looking for our lost Lord? Can either business or pleasure justify us in neglecting our Saviour? Do we put our Saviour first: 'Seek ye first the kingdom of God . . .'

Mary was there first. Like Mary, let us be early at the meeting place; let us put our appointment with Jesus before all else; and then indeed we may hear his voice saying in his clear and lovely accents, our own name; and we will recognize our Lord.

Saturday 25 July *St James the Apostle* **The Witness**

'About this time King Herod attacked certain members of the Church. He beheaded James the brother of John.' Acts 12.2

Martyr

The original Greek word from which our word 'martyr' comes, means simply 'witness'. The early Christians used the title 'martyr' about the apostles, for they had been with Christ throughout his ministry, they were familiar with his teaching and his works, his death and his resurrection. They were indeed 'witnesses', as St Peter puts it, 'We were eyewitnesses of his majesty . . . we were with him on the holy mount' (2 Peter 1.16–18) or St John, 'the life was made manifest, and we saw it, and testify to it, and proclaim to you eternal life' (1 John 1.2).

Later, in times of persecution and terror, the word 'martyr' came to be applied to those who had been persecuted for the faith, and to those who had openly proclaimed or admitted their belief in Jesus, and so were 'witnesses' to him. Finally, 'martyr' came to be confined to those who were actually put to death for their faith.

Witness

James, therefore, was a martyr in both senses, for he was one of the apostles and had been with Jesus all through the Lord's ministry on earth; and he was also one of those killed for the faith, as we read in Acts. Indeed, after Stephen, James was the next to give his life for Christ.

Down the ages and up to today, how many faithful men and women have suffered the same or similar fates. 'The blood of the martyrs is the seed of the Church' wrote Tertullian the historian away in AD 220.

Thursday 6 August *The Transfiguration of Our Lord* **Light and Glory**

'As he was praying, the appearance of his countenance was altered, and his raiment became dazzling white.' Luke 9.29

Mystery

There is always a sense of mystery when God reveals himself to human beings. The Old Testament story of Moses and the Burning Bush – blazing but not burnt up; and from that bright light comes the voice of God. Elijah found God, not in a dazzling light, nor in a roaring wind, nor in an earthquake; but in the still small voice. It was these two great figures from the past, to whom God had appeared and spoken, that the disciples saw in the new light of Christ, talking with him. But the disciples were terrified, bewildered, frightened out of their wits. In his confusion, Peter seems to be thinking of the Feast of Tabernacles, the Jewish festival when all the people go out and sleep under the sky, protected only by branches of trees – a memory and reproduction of the time in the Wilderness, which eventually led them to their salvation, the Promised Land.

There is so much about God that is mysterious, and we do not understand; it is good for us to have a sense of mystery in our churches. Not everything in our services, any more than in our religion, should be wide open and immediately accessible; some things we have to approach step by step, passing through one veil after another until we come to the light. Here, the Greek and Russian churches have an advantage over ours – the screens and the doors which are closed give something of the feel of the spiritual approach to God.

Maybe one day we will understand it all, but that is a long way off; and in the meantime we must put our trust in the God who created us for his own marvellous purposes, and all the universe as well.

Saturday 15 August *The Blessed Virgin Mary* Incarnation
'Blessed is she who believed.' Luke 1.45

The Word made Flesh
It is impossible for the mere mortal mind, to understand more than the smallest part of what the Incarnation means. The joining of human and divine in Christ; omnipotence with the weakness of a child, the Creator of the world with a mere creature, the timeless with our mortality.

Mary's Flesh
Yet this is what 'incarnation' involves, and it was Mary whose flesh took the strange and impossible burden of God. God, who is pure spirit, took on flesh. The Second Person of the Holy Trinity made himself small, a child in Mary's womb, in order that he might grow up amid 'all things made by him', and experience their pressures amid the stresses and strains of living a human life among humans.

The Bible
If we go back into the ages of prophecy, and the remote records of myth and folklore, we can find there intimations and predictions of how this intimacy, this Incarnation, was to be achieved.

'A virgin will conceive and bring forth a son' – 'A flower will spring from the root of Jesus' – 'Unto us a child is born, unto us a son is given.'

In the New Testament we can read how it was that at Bethlehem the child was born, and at Nazareth the young shoot grew and flowered. We can understand how a mother's love followed her Son through his life, in good times and in bad, to the last bitter days of pain and death, when 'there stood by the Cross of Jesus, his mother'. Every manifestation of his work, many of his words,

216

his way of life – all these were treasured by his Mother, who from earliest days 'kept all these things in her heart'.

United in Eternity

Such a union of love and hope and trust could not be broken by death. As Jesus threw aside the bonds of the grave, and again greeted and touched and fed and guided into new life, his rejoicing disciples, so also with his beloved Mother. And that reunion once made, persisted and was never broken again, we can surely have no doubt also.

With the angel, we may say, 'Hail, highly favoured, the Lord is with you'. And with Elizabeth, we may add, 'Blessed are you among women, and blessed is the fruit of your womb'.

Monday 24 August *St Bartholomew the Apostle* **Called to Proclaim**

'I am among you as one who serves.' Luke 22.27

Identity

The Church has identified Bartholomew with Nathanael; his name may be really 'Son of Tolmai' and the scholars would say that the apostle's real name would be 'Nathanael Bar-Tolmai' rather like 'Simon Bar-Jonah' (Matthew 16,17).

Nathanael is never mentioned in the first three gospels, and Bartholomew is never mentioned in the gospel of St John. It was Philip who brought Nathanael to Christ (John 1.45) and in three of the lists of the apostles, Philip is coupled with Bartholomew, which would be very natural if he and Nathanael were the same.

In the Collect for the day, we ask God who gave 'grace truly to believe and to preach your Word' to Bartholomew, and that the Church may 'love that word which he believed, and may faithfully preach and receive the same' Bishop Cosin added 'and receive' – perhaps he was thinking of the different functions of the clergy (to preach) and the laity (to receive) – but we must recognize that the *whole* Church is called to the proclamation of the Gospel.

We may preach as effectively by our lives, as any sermonizer may; and if we have not ourselves received the truth of the Gospel, our preaching – whether by word or deed – will be ineffective.

Monday 14 September *Holy Cross Day* **The Rood**

'Far be it for me to glory except in the cross of our Lord Jesus Christ.'
Gal. 6.14

Ancient Custom

Today's festival was called 'Rood Mass' by our forefathers; it commemorates the erection by the Empress Helena of a great basilica, on the site of the Empty Tomb, to contain the relic of the Cross which she had discovered amid the ruins of the Holy City. This basilica was consecrated on September 13th AD 335; and on the next day, being Sunday, the precious relic was exposed from a lofty place within the building. The custom was continued annually, and the festival has since been observed on this day, both in East and West, as an occasion for glorying in the Cross.

When St Paul tells us that he glories in the Cross, he is of course, using symbolic language. He 'glories in the Cross' because it sums up, in a most touching symbol, the essence of the Christian Gospel.

Love of God

First, it speaks to us of the wonderful love of God. It is not always easy to believe in the love of God; at times it may be hard indeed. We need no proof of God's power – 'the heavens declare the glory of God'; we need no proof of God's wisdom; it is displayed in the miracle of life, in the constancy of nature, in the petals of every wayside flower. But that God is Love – that needs proof. The watchword of Nature, it has been said, is not peace, but war. There is enough evidence in nature and human experience to stagger the strongest faith in the love of God – except for one thing, the Cross of Christ. Here is the everlasting proof of the love of God.

The Cross

The fact that God was in Christ reconciling the world to himself, answers the deepest and most fundamental need in universal human experience. It is the Cross, and the Cross alone, which throughout the ages of Christian history has brought peace and comfort to the hearts of sinners, and given them the power to conquer their sins and to rise to a higher and nobler life.

G.D.R.

Monday 21 September *St Matthew, Apostle and Evangelist* **'Follow Me'**

'Jesus saw a man called Matthew, sitting at the tax-office; and he said to him, "Follow me".' Matthew 9.9

Matthew
The disciple Matthew in the gospel reading is, most probably, to be identified with the 'Levi' mentioned in Mark and Luke. In St Matthew's own account, we are told that he was seated in the custom-house when Jesus called him. Mark and Luke also note that Levi was a tax-collector, and in all three accounts Jesus is criticized by his opponents for eating at the same table with tax collectors and other persons of disrepute.

Tax Collectors
Who were these tax collectors (or 'publicans' as earlier versions have it)? They were collaborators with the Roman Imperial State, extortioners who took money from their own people, often by threats, menaces and the methods of the Mafia. They paid over what the State demanded and kept the surplus to line their pockets. Tax collecting was farmed out, in other words, and those who took on the dirty business may have ended up wealthy, but were hated and despised.

Yet Jesus noted that it was the publican rather than the Pharisee who offered in the Temple acceptable prayer. 'Lord be merciful to me a sinner'; and there are frequent favourable references to publicans in the sayings of Jesus as recorded in St Matthew's Gospel.

The Gospel
It brings out the aspect of the ministry of Jesus which the Pharisees found most shocking – Jesus invites into the intimacy of table companionship not only 'sinners' – so called by the Pharisees, as

those who did not keep the strict Law – but also the double-damned tax collectors.

In the teaching of Jesus, the Pharisees are represented by the Elder Brother, to whom the Father – sincerely – says, 'Son, you are always with me and all that I have is yours' (Luke 15.31). They have received genuine righteousness from God, but have turned it against him in the form of *self*-righteousness, plus contempt of others.

Those Outside

The primary mission of Jesus in the Gospels is to those who are *outside* the scope of God's action – or rather, those who have been made to *feel* they are outside his love.

A Church which is 'established', like the Church of England, should always keep reminding itself of this, and beware of equating Christianity with respectability; of condemning sin only when it also offends against convention, and limiting its loving care to those who are clean and tidy, obedient and well-mannered.

'Christ Jesus came into the world to save sinners' – let us make sure that this 'Comfortable Word' may enter into the hearts of our parish.

Tuesday 29 September *St Michael and All Angels* The Company of Heaven

'You shall see heaven wide open, and God's angels ascending and descending upon the Son of Man.' John 1.51

'Angels and Archangels'

'With angels and archangels, and with all the company of heaven . . .' Familiar words, that carry us along in the mainstream of the Church's worship.

But, do they correspond to any reality in which we can today believe? The existence of a realm of purely spiritual beings is taken for granted in the New Testament. Every writer mentions Satan, the rebel against God, and most mention lesser evil spirits – demons and so on. All refer directly or by implication, to 'angels', the 'unfallen spirits, instruments of God's providence, and on hand to help us human beings from time to time, to avoid the toils of sin or to take the *right* course and not the *wrong*.

Spirits
If we believe in the existence of the invisible God, Creator Spirit, there seems no logical difficulty in believing in the existence of invisible created spirits. The word 'angel' is the Greek for 'a messenger'. Messengers from God can be visible or invisible, and may assume human or even non-human forms. Christians have always felt themselves to be attended by helpful spirits – swift, powerful and enlightening.

Art
Angels are often depicted in art, in our churches, as statues or in stained glass, in human form, usually with wings to signify their swiftness, perhaps with swords to signify their power, and wearing dazzling raiment to signify their ability to enlighten. Unfortunately, this type of pictorial representation – and especially the rather sexless, effeminate creatures too often shown, leads many to dismiss 'angels' as either a kind of adult fairy tale or as simply mythical.

This would be a great loss, and a more realistic attitude needs to be taught.

Our Angels
We should not be afraid of frankly acknowledging the foolishness of so many attempts to render angels in graphic form, floating in white robes or in medieval armour, in illustrated bibles and prayer books, in paintings and in drawings. But at the same time, we should be ready to look for the 'angels' in our daily lives, whether as other human beings, or the voices we may hear over the radio, the pictures we see on TV, the words of a book we read – all can be messengers of God's truth and enlightenment. They can also be warnings – and the role of 'warner' is another that is traditionally given to the angels.

Sunday 18 October   *St Luke the Apostle and Evangelist*   **The Physician**

'Luke has written of all that Jesus did and taught from the beginning.'
Acts 1.1

Physician, Writer, Gentile, Travelling Companion ...
Most of our Gospel readings this year, under the new system, have been from St Luke. What do we know about him, the author of two great books – his 'Gospel' and his 'Acts of the Apostles' – really two volumes on the life of Jesus and the Church he founded. It is a little startling to realize that the writer who contributed most to our New Testament was a Gentile, with a pagan, non-Jewish background, with a knowledge of our own wider world. A man of cultured, orderly, meticulous mind (Luke 1.1–4) and also a medical man, a physician if not exactly a 'doctor' in our sense. His conversion to the Faith probably came from some experience like that of the Ethiopian eunuch; a foreigner, yet returning from Jerusalem, reading the Old Testament, puzzled at some things in Judaism, wonderfully prepared for further illumination, welcoming baptism with joy.

And what a life he had as a Christian! Companion of St Paul, encountering the newborn Church in all its variety, gladness, spiritual joy, gifts of the Spirit, fellowship – all this shines through his writings. He met men and women speaking as those who knew, from within, the truth of God, the love of Christ, and the joy of redemption.

All in all, Luke's message concerning evil and personal salvation is a hopeful gospel for individuals. But Luke sees, in the Christian movement he had met, much more than this. He saw a motive and a power making for moral reform, he saw the forgiveness of sins, and renewal of the sinner; he saw healing and consolation for the sick, in body and mind. He saw a new era for women, with fairness, dignity, tenderness and opportunity, in Christ; he saw for men conversion from the power of riches, dishonesty and avarice, with the true use of wealth through generous righteousness. Luke offers us a rich portrait of the Founder of the Church he knew and rejoiced in; the Saviour of individuals and of society, the Son of God offering to others the limitless grace of the Father.

Wednesday 28 October *SS Simon and Jude, the Apostles* Unity in Faith

'If you love me, keep my commandments.' John 14,15

Simon

Simon is numbered among the Twelve in the gospels (e.g. Matthew 10.4) and in Acts 1.13, but nothing further is recorded about him. His name is a commonly chosen one, but he is distinguished by the adjective 'Canaanite' or 'Zealot', to indicate that he had been a member of a violent militant sect who bitterly opposed the Roman overlords. Judas Iscariot was another disciple who had been associated with a violent group – the 'Siccari' or 'Knife-men' – assassins like the IRA in our time.

What a tribute to our Lord's power and personality, that he could include in his band of followers, both ardent nationalists and a collaborator like Matthew. We can think that they were joined together in unity of spirit, as Christ linked them to himself – and as bound to him, so they bound themselves to each other.

Jude

He is the 'Judas, not Iscariot' of John 14.22 and is elsewhere called 'Labbaeus' or 'Thaddeus'; the brother of James the Less and son of Mary, wife of Cleopas. Jude is a specialized patron saint – appeal to him in cases of 'last minute' or 'lost causes'; and he enjoyed a great vogue in the personal columns of *The Times* and *Daily Telegraph*. His speciality comes from a phrase in the Epistle of Jude – 'Some saved, as by snatching them out of the fire! . . .'

Unity

The lesson of Simon and Jude for us is simple – all difficulties and differences, all confusions, mean little in the sight of God. To him the causes that divide us humans from one another are far less important than what unites us; too small to be really considered even. Unity together as human beings, unity of faith in Christ, unity of love and hope – these far outweigh petty words and problems, and divisions of language, beliefs and ideals.

Lord, help us to see that 'unity of spirit' that already exists for humanity, and to sweep away the clutter of man-made obstacles, so that we may realize our human unity and our human need of each other, together in our love and worship of God our heavenly Father and Jesus Christ his only Son.

Sunday 1 November *All Saints' Day* **The Saints of God**

'I heard the noise of a great multitude, crying "Alleluia! The Lord our God has entered into his kingdom. Happy are those who are called to the supper of the Lamb!"' Rev. 19.6,9 (ASB Postcommunion Sentence)

Saints
Today, this glorious festival we rejoice in celebrating, is the festival of *all* saints. Today we are to think about, remember, rejoice with, not only those great and noble heroes and heroines of the Faith, but also just as much those in that innumerable company of the faithful ones, most of whom are not known to us by name nor by time. But remember this – if they are not known to us, their names are entered in the Book of Life, and they share in the joys of heaven just as completely and just as wonderfully as the most noble and most radiant of the heavenly throng.

Grace
We believe that our God gives power to face and overcome trials; the saints confirm our belief by their examples. We know that a belief in the unseen Power that directs and rules the world, that is, our God – Creator and Maker of this vast universe just as truly as he is creator and maker of this little space-ship Earth which we know as our home – that belief truly gives men and women power to face trial and pain and hatred, and to overcome these things, even death itself. The saints show that their faith in God and his Christ can make them conquerors over all the cruelty and trials that this life can produce. So, if we are inclined to despond over failures, or to be depressed over our continued trials, this great Festival says to us: 'These people have won the victory in the end; they have won the crown of life, and so can you!'

Power

In that innumerable company of the faithful, we can find instances of those who are like ourselves in our own individual trials and difficulties and pains. They come very close to our own lives and to our own experiences. It may well be that under trial they become despondent, looked back in dread, and peered forward through the mists to a future they feared. How often have we done the same! Yet, in the end they conquered in the battle. Our Lord took them, just as they were, with all their frailties and weaknesses – and gave them strength, sincerity and hope. Through their weakness they were made strong. All Saints' Day says to us, 'Why should it be impossible for you to do the same?'

Our Place

It is more than probable that we will never become great saints in the eyes of the world. Yet, the weakest of us may be granted a place in that great multitude which cannot be numbered, by putting ourselves in the hands of the power of the Divine Saviour and living our lives in his might and under his direction and care. How do we become Saints? We have only to be what God wants us to be, and to do what God wants us to do; to forget ourselves and never to forget God. We need perfect simplicity towards ourselves; perfect contentment with all that comes our way; perfect peace of mind in utter self-forgetfulness. This becomes easier the more we realize the greatness, and goodness, and all-ness of God.

O Lord, in every age you reveal yourself
to the childlike and lowly of heart,
and from every race you write names in your book of life:
Give us the simplicity and faith of your saints,
that loving you above all things, we may become what
you would have us be, and do what you would have us do.
So may we be numbered with your Saints,
and enter with them into eternal joy and glory,
through Jesus Christ our Saviour. Amen.

All Saints' Day *Second Sermon* **Following the Lord**

'If any man would come after me, let him deny himself and take up his cross daily and follow me.' Luke 9.23

'Who do you say that I am?'

Peter's confession, or recognition, of Jesus as God's Anointed – 'The Christ of God' is not be divulged, made public, since Jesus – the Son of Man – is destined to suffer, be rejected by his own people, be killed – but on the third day raised. This must have been extremely depressing for the little band, but their sorrow must have been lifted up, first by the Lord's description of the path that any follower can take, through pain and death but to life again, saved by the living power of the Lord. Jesus then makes the parallel between the clever man who gains the whole world, but in the process ruins himself, and is lost; and the follower who denies his association with the Lord, and is himself denied when the same Lord returns in glory – 'the glory of the Father and the holy angels'. The last verse (27) is referring to the vision of the Transfiguration which will be witnessed by Peter, John and James after 'about eight days' (v. 28) and is in fact a glimpse of the heavenly glory of the incarnate Lord.

Everyday Life

All Saints' Day is a reminder to us, not only of the great names and heroic deeds of Scripture and of Church history, but of the countless ordinary men and women of long ago and today, whose lives have borne witness for God. A great deal had to die in these men and women, so that they could serve God as faithfully as they did. Their selfish wishes, their pride, the sinful side of their nature, and much else, would have prevented them giving themselves to God, so they let these things die. Here is a death that should take place in us also; and from this death, God will open up to us a new and wonderful life. Here indeed is a fulfilment of Our Lord's saying, which we have just heard: 'Whoever would save his life will lose it; and whoever loses his life – gives up the sinful side – will save it.'

God our Father,
  give us the will each day
  to live in life eternal.
  Let our citizenship be in heaven
  with your blessed and beloved,
  the whole company of the redeemed;
  and with countless angels,
  praising, worshipping and adoring him
  who sits upon the throne for ever and ever.
  Amen.

(Patterns for Worship 52.19)

Monday 2 November *Commemoration of All Souls* **'The Faithful Departed'**

'God will wipe away every tear from their eyes, and death shall be no more; neither shall there be mourning nor crying nor pain any more, for the former things have passed away.' Rev. 21.4

All Souls

The autumn brings with it All Saints' Day, when we give thanks to God for the outstanding Christians who throughout the ages have inspired us; and then All Souls' Day, when we remember those we see no longer but whose memory we cherish – our relatives and our friends who are now at rest.

Some people argue about whether we should pray for the departed, and whether there is any purpose in so doing. Let us have no worries nor misgivings; if there is life after death – and surely we who are here now, are convinced that there is – then those who have entered into that new life will not be idle, and surely one thing they will be doing is to pray.

Prayer

If we take our faith seriously, then we should indeed feel the supporting prayers of many people who are no longer with us, but are alive in Christ. In a familiar church or some other place where we knew each other, we may indeed feel the strength and love that flows from the prayers of the faithful departed.

And if *they* pray for *us*, what more natural than that *we* should pray for *them*?

We recognize the fact that they are closer to God now; but the final judgement, the ultimate joining together of Earth and Heaven, so the Bible teaches, still lies in the future. So all of us, this side and the other side of the future, need praying for.

Disrepute

The idea of praying for the dead fell into disrepute at the time of the Reformation, because people had the idea that the more masses that could be said for the soul of a dead person, the better off he or she would be – but this was a sad abuse, and part of a system that had become corrupt and in need of cleansing, along with the thinking that was behind it.

Too Drastic

But to sweep everything away was too drastic. And discouraging or even forbidding prayer for the departed has not worked; the terrible losses of life in the First World War broke down such restrictions, and a more reasonable and truly Christian doctrine has gradually taken over.

Nor is this thinking confined to Anglicans or Roman Catholics. Here are some fine words by the Quaker, William Penn, founder of Pennsylvania in America. Three hundred years ago he wrote:

'They that love beyond the world cannot be separated by it. Death cannot kill what never dies; nor can spirits ever be divided that love and live in the same divine principle – the root and record of their friendship. Death is but crossing the worlds as friends do the seas; they live in one another still. But there must needs be present that love which is omnipresent. In that divine glass they see face to face; and their converse is free and pure. This is the comfort of friends, that though they may be said to die, yet their friendship and society are, in the best sense, ever present – because immortal.'

Harvest Thanksgiving   'Let the Earth be Glad'

'The earth and all that is in it, is the Lord's; let the heavens rejoice, and let the earth be glad.' Ps 24,1; 96,11

Harvest Time is here!

How right and good it is, that every year we thank God for his miracle of seed-time and harvest. More than ever, we need to be reminded of his gift of life in food and in the abundance which sustains all our lives. It is so easy to forget, or to take for granted.

And today, in the midst of our abundance, we must not forget those millions of our fellow human beings who go hungry in this world, through no fault of their own, through human error, political manipulation, bad harvests, through the horrors and brutality of war, or fearful natural disasters.

It seems almost a crime to be living in such a rich country as ours, where no one need go hungry; perhaps our remembrance of those in need will help to put what we think are our own important problems – no so-and-so in the grocers, only this and that, can't see any special what-ever-they-may-be in the stores – into a better perspective.

Greed

We humans are an acquisitive lot, rarely satisfied; and generally speaking the more we have the more we want. So today is the festival of things we need – and that is not the same (by a long chalk) – as the things we would like to have. Our Lord Jesus Christ taught us to pray 'Give us this day our daily bread'. Bread for today, and leave tomorrow for God. Remember in the wilderness how the Children of Israel were given the manna? Collect just enough, they were told, for this day, one day at a time; take more and the sweet flakes went rotten and useless.

What we need – and what we want

The point of all this is, not to suggest that we should be prodigal or reckless, but to draw the distinction between what we really need, and the greediness which is truly unhealthy.

Our daily bread – if there happens to be some jam to go with it, so much the better; but it is for what we really *need* that we are bidden to pray. Keep that in mind today.

Perception

Lastly, here is a different outlook:

A boy aged sixteen, living in a simple country village, several hundred years ago, wrote this piece of verse:

'Wide fields of graine along a vallie spread,
The show'rs of raine mature the swelling vine;
I see the Lorde is multiplying Breade,
I see Him turning Water into Wine . . .'

May we have that kind of perception in our own time and place, here and now, for God's miracles do not end with our Harvest Home. Continually, he works further miracles in our hearts and minds, turning our thoughts towards the needs of others, giving us the inspiration to do all we can to help, leading us to a wider and more true religious concern with the world of suffering, of despair, of poverty, of sorrow and lack of hope. Lord, what we do is little enough, but take it – and as you took the bread and the fishes, feed the multitude. Be thankful for God's bounty to us; praise him for his goodness, and above all, make us mindful of the needs of others.

Remembrance Sunday   'Remembering'

'If God is on our side, who is against us? He did not spare his own Son, but gave him up for us all.' Romans 8.32

(see also p. 182)

Shall we forget?

We hear the same questions again this year: 'Why bother with Remembrance Sunday? – It means nothing to the young – aren't old wars, old hatreds, best forgotten?'

We cannot forget, but we can fail to remember. Our modern age was born on the Somme, and we live with the consequences of great wars in a world still without peace. The neglect of Remembrance-tide is more than a failure in gratitude and sympathy for the dead and the bereaved, though it is at least that.

It is, above all, a refusal to face our own world as it is, and ourselves as we are now. Such a denial of the recent past which has for good or ill, shaped our present, is an impoverishment of the human spirit, and a form of faithlessness.

Contradictions
A new generation of Christians must learn to cope with the complex of emotions that honest remembrance brings. We have to take account not only of the horror of war, but of the courage it reveals in ordinary men and women; not only the despair but the patient resolve; not only the degradation but the flowering of every human virtue in adversity; not only the hatred, but the love.

War brings into focus all the contradictions of human life.

So, in remembrance we may find grounds for hope, in the very conditions of hopelessness.

The Heart of Hope
Remembering is at the heart of hope. For God in the hopelessness of a fallen world, set up the Cross, and set it up in No-Man's-Land; of all places a place of violence, undeserved suffering, pain and grief, and of courage and integrity in utter weakness. He set up in hopelessness, the very place where hope is to be found. There is no other.

It is no sign of security and safety, for these are not to be found in our world. But, it is a sign of hope, even if all security and safety are absent. The Crucified reveals the nature of the Presence of our God, in this world which is ours also.

If Christianity survives it will be in part, at least, because of the lonely Figure dying in agony upon the Cross; crying out in agony to the Father whom he believes to have forsaken him, remains before us ceaselessly interrogating men and women . . . concerning the significance of his supreme hour.

Our Response
Our response to that profound questioning of our lives, our meanings, our world, can only come out of honest remembrance, honest recognition. It must come out of seeing the world which wars have created, in horror and pain; and by seeking the God who has identified himself with the very hopelessness and the dereliction. 'Never such innocence again.'

INDEX OF TEXTS

INDEX OF SUBJECTS

Authors quoted: Julian of Norwich . . . p. 53 Bertrand Russell . . . p. 25 Teilhard de Chardin . . . p. 113 Werner Pelz . . . p. 172 Oscar Wilde . . . p. 145

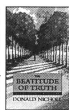

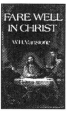

THE CHURCH UNION

THE CHURCH UNION was founded in 1859 and grew out of the Oxford Movement in the Church of England. Today it continues to proclaim the glory of the catholic faith and to promote that faith through its work of education, evangelisation and publishing. Its aim is to support and encourage all people, lay and ordained, in their Christian ministry. FAITH HOUSE exists as a focus and centre for this work, having a bookshop, meeting rooms and full time staff available to serve both individuals and organisations. A 'phone call or letter will bring you a pack explaining the work of the CHURCH UNION in more detail together with a complimentary copy of the quarterly journal "THE CHURCH OBSERVER".

THE CHURCH UNION AND FAITH HOUSE BOOKSHOP
7 Tufton Street, Westminster
London SW1P 3QN

Telephone 0171-222 6952   Fax 0171-976 7180

Nearest Underground: St James's Park

FAITH HOUSE BOOKSHOP

FOR . . . all books for parish or individual use, ordered for you if not in stock

FOR . . . confirmation, Advent and Lent courses and all parish stationery and registers

FOR . . . candles, wafers, incense and charcoal

FOR . . . crosses, crucifixes, ikons, rosaries etc.

FOR . . . cards and certificates for all occasions

We will always try to give helpful and informed advice if you have a question, or offer assistance if you do not know exactly what you want.

We operate a world-wide mail-order service and accept all major credit/debit cards

Open: 9.30am – 5.00pm Mon – Fri (10.00am opening on Thursday)

The Book of Common Prayer

contains some of the most majestic and beautiful prose into the English language. Over the centuries it has been the repository of doctrine from which Anglican beliefs could be learned. A devotional power-house, the Book of Common Prayer is a deeply valued means of communication with our Maker.

The Prayer Book Society

★ seeks to defend and uphold that doctrine and to promote the worship enshrined in the Book of Common Prayer

★ does NOT propagate Prayer Book fundamentalism but believes a modest amount of flexibility in usage is both sensible and to be desired

The Prayer Book Society aims

★ to encourage the use of the Book of Common Prayer for the training of Ordinands and Confirmands

★ to spread knowledge of the Book of Common Prayer and the doctrine contained therein

★ to encourage use of the Book of Common Prayer for public worship.

ARE YOU A REGULAR READER OF THE SOCIETY'S TWO MAGAZINES?

**ISSUES OF *"FAITH AND HERITAGE"* ALTERNATE WITH
*"FAITH AND WORSHIP"***

Please support
THE PRAYER BOOK SOCIETY

write now to:

**PBS OFFICE, ST JAMES GARLICKHYTHE
GARLICK HILL, LONDON EC4V 2AL**

CHRISTIANS AWARE

Dedicated to work for justice and peace.
Peace is born of Love.
Love is born of Understanding.
Understanding is born of Listening......

An international and ecumenical movement.
Its main aim is to develop multi cultural understanding
and friendship locally, nationally and internationally, in
a spirit of sharing. Thus, new energy is generated for
action towards human development and wholeness,
through conferences, work-camps, international
exchanges and local community work. There are no
experts. We are continually reminded of the advice of
Ronald Wynne who has worked for many years in
Botswana: *"Do not try to teach anyone anything until
you have learnt something from them."* Christians
Aware recognises the importance of openness,
adaptability and faith in the future.

....Christians Aware Listens

Christians Aware
10 Springfield Road, Leicester, LE2 3BD
Tel. 0116 270 9931 Fax. 0116 270 3288
Company N. 2417029   *Charity No. 328322*

chrstawa

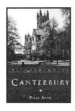
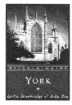